A Daybook for May in Yellow Springs, Ohio

A Memoir in Nature

and a Handbook for the Month,
Being a Personal Narrative and Synthesis of Common
Events in Nature between 1981 and 2020
in Southwestern Ohio, with Applications
for the Lower Midwest and Middle Atlantic Region,
Containing Weather Guidelines
and a Variety of Natural Calendars,
Reflections by the Author
and Seasonal Quotations
from Ancient and Modern Writers

By

Bill Felker

Bill Felker

A Daybook for the Year in Yellow Springs, Ohio
Volume 5: May

Cover from a watercolor by Libby Rudolf

Copyright 2020 by Bill Felker

Published by the Green Thrush Press
Box 431, Yellow Springs, Ohio

Printed in the United States of America

All rights reserved, including the right to reproduce this book or portions thereof in any form whatsoever.

ISBN-13: 978-1986502733

ISBN-10: 1986502732

For Judy

with love

*For Judy
Bill*

Bill Felker

A Daybook for May

No one suspects the days to be gods.

Ralph Waldo Emerson

Bill Felker

Introduction

Here are no stories told you of what is to be seen at the other end of the world, but of things at home, in your own Native Countrey, at your own doors, easily examinable with little travel, less cost, and very little hazard. This book doth not shew you a Telescope, but a Mirror, it goes not about to put a delightful cheat upon you, with objects at a great distance, but shews you yourselves.

Joshua Childrey, 1660

The memoir gathers together meteorological commentary, extensive notes about common events in nature, syntheses of these events and astronomical information based on my years of writing almanacs. Although I have organized my memoir on a scaffolding of back-yard natural history and observation, I am not a naturalist and have had no training in the natural sciences. All of what is contained in the *Daybook* is the result of my search for myself and for home.

This particular aspect of my search began in 1972 with the gift of a barometer. My wife, Jeanie, gave the instrument to me when I was succumbing to graduate school stress in Knoxville, Tennessee, and it became not only an escape from intense academic work, but the first step on the road to a different kind of awareness about the world.

From the start, I was never content just to watch the barometric needle; I had to record its movement, then graph it. I was fascinated by the alchemy of the charts that turned rain and Sun into visible patterns, symbols like notes on a sheet of music, or words on a page.

From my graphs of barometric pressure, I discovered that the number of cold fronts each month is more or less consistent, and that the Earth breathes at an average rate of about once every three to five days in the winter, and once each six to eight days at the peak of summer.

A short apprenticeship told me when important changes would occur and what kind of weather would take place on most any day.

That information was expressed in the language of odds and percentages, and it was surprisingly accurate. Taking into consideration the consistency of certain patterns in the past, I could make fairly successful predictions about the likelihood of the repetition of such paradigms in the future. As Yeats says, the seasons "have their fixed returns," and I found points all along the course of the year which appeared to be fixed moments for change. The pulse of the world was steadier than I had ever imagined.

My graphs also allowed me to see the special properties of each season. August's barometric configurations, for example, are slow and gentle like low, rolling hills. Heat waves show up as plateaus. Thunderstorms are sharp, shallow troughs in the gentle waves of the atmospheric landscape. Autumn arrives like the sudden appearance of a pyramid on a broad plain. By the end of September, the fronts are stronger; the high-pressure peaks become taller; the lows are deeper, with almost every valley bringing rain. By December, the systems loom on the horizon of the graph like a range of mountains with violent extremes of altitude, sometimes snowcapped, almost always imposing and sliced by canyons of wind.

From watching the weather, it was an easy step to watching wildflowers. Identifying plants, I saw that flowers were natural allies of my graphs, and that they were parallel measures of the seasons and the passage of time. I kept a list of when each wildflower blossomed and saw how each one consistently opened around a specific day, and that even though a cold year could set blooming back up to two weeks, and unusual warmth accelerate it, average dates were quite useful in establishing sequence of bloom that always showed me where I was in the progress of the year.

In the summer of 1978, Jeanie and I took the family to Yellow Springs, Ohio, a small town just beyond the eastern edge of the Dayton suburbs. We bought a house and planned to stay. I began to write a nature almanac for the local newspaper. To my weather and wildflower notes I added daily sunrise and sunset times, moonrise and moonset, average and record temperatures, comments on foliage changes, bird migration dates, farm and gardening cycles and the rotation of the stars. The more I learned around Yellow Springs, the more I found applicable to the world beyond the village limits. The microclimate in which I immersed myself gradually became a key to the extended environment; the part unlocked the whole. My Yellow Springs gnomon that measured the movement of the Sun also measured my relationship to every other place on Earth.

My occasional trips turned into exercises in the measurement of variations in the landscape. When I drove 500 miles northwest, I not only entered a different space, but often a separate season, and I could mark the differences in degrees of flowers, insects, trees, and the development of the field crops. The most exciting trips were taken south in March; I could travel from Early Spring into Middle Spring and finally into Late Spring and summer along the Gulf Coast.

My engagement with the natural world, which began as an escape from academia, finally turned into a way of getting private bearings and of finding what I loved and believed. It was a process of spiritual as well as physical reorientation. In that way, all the historical statements in this collection of notes are the fruit of a strong desire to define where I am and what happens around me.

The Daybook Format

The format of my notes in this daybook owes more than a little to the almanacs I wrote for the *Yellow Springs News* between 1984 and 2018. The use of quotations, daily statistics, the weather outlooks, the seasonal calendar, and the daybook journal were and still are part of my regular routine of collecting and organizing impressions about the place in which I live.

Setting: The principal habitat described here is that of Glen Helen, a preserve of woods and glades that lies on the eastern border of the village of Yellow Springs in southwestern Ohio. At its northern edge, the Glen joins with John Bryan State Park to form a corridor about ten miles long and half a mile wide along the Little Miami River. The north section of the Glen Helen and John Bryan complex is hilly and heavily wooded and is the best location for spring wildflowers. The southern portion, "South Glen" as it is usually called, is a combination of open fields, wetlands, and wooded flatlands. Here I found many flowers and grasses of summer and fall. Together, the two Glens and John Bryan State Park provide a remarkable cross section of the fauna and flora of the eastern United States.

Other habitats in the daybook journal include my yard with its several small gardens; the village of Yellow Springs itself, a town of about 4,000 at the far eastern border of the Dayton suburbs and the Caesar Creek Reservoir twenty miles south of Yellow Springs. My trips away from that environment were principally northeast to Chicago, Madison, Wisconsin and northern Minnesota, east to Washington and New York, southeast to the Carolinas and Florida, southwest to Arkansas, Louisiana and Texas, and occasionally through the Southwest to California and the Northwest, two excursions to Belize in Central America, several to Italy.

Quotations: The passages from ancient and modern writers (and sometimes from my alter egos) which accompany each day's notations are lessons from my readings, as well as from distant seminary and university training, here put to work in service of the reconstruction of my sense of time and space. They are a collection of reminders, hopes, and promises for me that I find implicit in the seasons. They have become a kind of a cosmological scrapbook for me and the philosophical underpinning of this narrative.

Astronomical Data: The *Daybook* includes approximate dates for astronomical events, such as star positions, meteor showers, solstice, equinox, perihelion (the Sun's position closest to Earth), and aphelion (the Sun's position farthest from Earth).

I have included the sunrise and sunset for Yellow Springs as a general guide to the progression of the year in this location, but those statistics also reflect trends that are world-wide, if more rapid in some places and slower in others.

Even though the day's length is almost never exactly the same from one town to the next, a minute lost or gained in Yellow Springs is often a minute lost or gained elsewhere, and the Yellow Springs numbers can be used as a simple way of watching the lengthening or shortening of the days, and, therefore, of watching the turn of the planet. For those who wish to keep track of the Sun themselves in their own location, abundant sources are now available for this information in local and national media.

Average Temperatures: Average temperatures in Yellow

Springs are also part of each day's entry. Since the rise and fall of temperatures in other parts of the North America, even though they may start from colder or warmer readings, keep pace with the temperatures here, the highs and lows in Yellow Springs are, like solar statistics, helpful indicators of the steady progress of the year throughout most of the states along the 40th Parallel (except in the mountains). The daybook journal entries can be cross-referenced with the list of monthly average temperatures between 1981 and 2018 in order to compare the daily inventories with the month's weather in a given year.

Weather: My daily, weekly and monthly weather summaries have been distilled from over thirty years of observations. They are descriptions of the local weather history I have kept in order to track the gradual change in temperature, precipitation and cloud cover through the year. I have also used them in order to try to identify particular characteristics of each day. They are not meant to be predictions.

Although my interest in the Yellow Springs microclimate at first seemed too narrow to be of use to those who lived outside the area, I began to modify it to meet the needs of a number of regional and national farm publications for which I started writing in the mid 1980s. And so, while the summaries are based on my records in southwestern Ohio, they can be and have been used, with interpretation and interpolation, throughout the Midwest , the Middle Atlantic states and the East.

The Natural Calendar: In this section, I note the progress of foliage and floral changes, farm and garden practices, migration times for common birds and peak periods of insect activity. Some of these notes are second-hand; I am a sky watcher, but not an astronomer, and I rely on the government's astronomical data and a few other references for much of my information about the stars and the Sun. I am also a complete amateur at bird watching, and most of the migration dates used in the seasonal calendar come from published sources. And even though I keep close track of the farm year, the percentages listed for planting and harvesting are interpretations of averages supplied by the state's weekly crop reports.

At the beginning of each spring and summer month, I have included a floating calendar of blooming dates which lists approximate flowering times for many plants, shrubs and trees in an average Ohio Valley season. The floating chronology describes the relationship between events more than exact dates of these occurrences.

Although the flora of the eastern and central United States is hardly limited to the species mentioned here, the flowers listed are common enough to provide easily recognized landmarks for gauging the advance of the year. I found, for example, that a record of my drives south during March and April complemented the floating calendar and allowed me to see the approximate differences between Yellow Springs and other locations. I also learned that April in the Lower Midwest is more like March in the Southeast and more like May in the Upper Midwest. The Natural Calendar summaries, then, provide guidelines for moveable feasts that shift not only according to fixed geographical regions but also according to the weather in any particular year.

Daybook Entries: The journal entries in the daybook section provide the raw material from which I wrote the Natural Calendar digests. They offer a record that anyone with a few guidebooks could make, and they include just a small number of the natural markers that anyone might discover.

When I began to take notes about the world around me, I found that there were few descriptions of actual events in nature available for southwestern Ohio. There was no roadmap for the course of the year. My daily observations, as narrow and incomplete as they were, were especially significant to me since I had found no other narrative of the days, no other depiction of what was actually occurring around me. In time, the world came into focus with each particle I named. I saw concretely that time and space were the sum of their parts.

As my notes for each day accumulated, I could see the wide variation of events that occurred from year to year; at the same time, I saw a unity in this syncopation from which I could identify numerous sub-seasons and with which I could understand better the kind of habitat in which I was living and, consequently, myself. When I paged through the journal entries for each day, I was drawn back to the space in which they were made. I browsed and imagined, returned to the journey.

Companions: Many friends, acquaintances and family members have contributed their observations to the daybook, and their participation has taught me that my private seasons are also community seasons, and that all of our experiences together help to lay the foundation for a rich, local consciousness.

Bill Felker

The Month of May
May Averages: 1981 through 2020
Normal May Average Temperature: 61.6

Year	Average
1981	57.3
1982	67.9
1983	56.7
1984	57.2
1985	62.8
1986	63.8
1987	66.4
1988	63.5
1989	58.8
1990	58.5
1991	69.3
1992	60.5
1993	62.0
1994	58.6
1995	60.4
1996	60.0
1997	55.8
1998	66.0
1999	63.7
2000	64.6
2001	63.5
2002	58.6
2003	60.0
2004	65.6
2005	57.3
2006	59.7
2007	65.6
2008	58.4
2009	62.6
2010	64.3
2011	62.5
2012	68.3
2013	61.0
2014	64.4
2015	68.0
2016	61.1
2017	61.6
2018	70.3
2019	65.3
2020	60.7

Bill Felker

May 1
The 121st Day of the Year

Now the bright Morning-star, day's harbinger,
Comes dancing from the east, and leads with her
The flowering May, who from her green lap throws
The yellow Cowslip, and the pale Primrose.

John Milton

Sunrise/set: 5:36/7:29
Day's Length: 13 hours 53 minutes
Average High/Low: 68/47
Average Temperature: 57
Record High: 88 – 1951
Record Low: 26 – 1963

Weather

Rain falls one May 1 out of three in my record, and odds are about the same for completely overcast conditions. Highs are in the 50s fifteen percent of the time, in the 60s fifty-five percent, in the 70s twenty-five percent, 80s five percent. Frost comes once or twice in a decade.

The Weather in the Week Ahead

This quarter of May brings highs above 60 on 75 percent of the afternoons, and warm 70s or 80s a little more than half the years. May 2 is typically the coldest day of the period, bringing cool 50s on 35 percent of the afternoons, and a 20 percent chance of 70s or 80s. Frost strikes only 10 to 15 percent of the mornings and is most likely after the first high pressure system of the month passes through around the 2nd of the month, and after the second system arrives near the 7th.

Each day of the period carries at least a 30 to 35 percent chance of a shower, but some of those days have a much better chance of sun than others. The 6th has an unusual 90 percent chance of clear to partly cloudy skies, making it historically one of only a handful of such days in the year. The 8th through the 10th are not all that far behind, each having an 80 to 85 percent chance of sun.

The May Outlook

Normal temperatures continue to rise at the rate of one degree every three days this month. Average highs move from the upper 60s on May 1 to the upper 70s by the beginning of June. Lows climb from the middle 40s to the middle 50s.

The day's length grows by 53 minutes in a Yellow Springs May, gains 25 minutes in sunrise time, 28 minutes at sunset. For all of that, the rate of the day's expansion slows by 19 minutes from April's frantic pace.

Distribution of high temperatures is normally five days in the 80s, fifteen days in the 70s, seven days in the 60s, and four days in the 50s.

The warmest May days, those with the best chance (40 percent or better chance of a day above 80 degrees) are the 11th through the 14th, the 16th, the 20th through the 22nd, the 25th, and the 31st. The coldest days in May, those with at least a 40 percent chance of highs below 70 degrees, are the 1st through the 8th, the 12th, 13th, and 15th.

In an average year, May is the second wettest month of the Yellow Springs year. Rainfall is ordinarily greatest as strawberries begin to set fruit toward the end of the month, thus the name, "Strawberry Rains."

The cloudiest days in May, those with less than a 45 percent chance of sun, are the 5th, 12th, 25th, 26th, and 29th. The wettest May days, those with at least a 45 percent chance of precipitation, are the 12th, 18th, 19th, 22nd, 25th, 26th, 27th, and, wettest of all with a 70 percent chance of rain: the 29th.

The driest days in May, those with no more than a 30 percent chance of rain, are the 3rd, 6th, 7th, 11th, 13th and 15th. The May days with a better than an 85 percent chance of sunny or partly cloudy skies, are the 6th, 8th, 10th, 11th, 14th, 16th, 17th, 23rd, and 27th.

Springcount to Summercount: Twenty-three major spring cold fronts cross the nation between the middle of February and the last week of May. Three passed through in February, seven in March, six in April, six more spring fronts in May. The final weather system of this month often is the first front of Early Summer. Fronts will reach the Midwest around the following dates; they will come through about two days earlier in the West, a day or two later in the East.

May 2: The first three days of May are often marked by a "Lilac Winter" high-pressure system that chills one of the most fragrant times of the year. During this brief season, frost comes about ten percent of the time in the North, but usually stays away in the South. Temperatures warm significantly as the front moves away, and chilly afternoons in the 40s and 50s are relatively uncommon as the May 7 front approaches.

May 7: With the arrival of the second major high pressure system of the month, there is a slight possibility of a return of Lilac Winter, and frost is frequent on May 8. The period of May 8 through 14 historically brings more storms to the nation than any other period except the days between May 17 and 24.

May 12: The day before this front arrives often has the warmest weather history of the month, bringing 80s more often than any other day until June. But the arrival of the front can bring flurries and storms. This is also one of the last frost-bearing fronts to move across the nation. Although gardens in the North are not immune to a freeze throughout the entire month of May, the greatest danger of loss from low temperatures recedes quickly as this high moves out over the Atlantic. Sometimes the weather stagnates between the May 12 front and the May 20 front, creating conditions favorable for a heat wave across the South.

May 15: This front and the next two are often followed by the "Strawberry Rains," the wettest time of May in the lower Midwest and the Mid Atlantic states. May 15 is a good target date for having fields planted in order to avoid a serious delay in seeding. Spring rains and humidity can increase the risk of internal parasites and foot problems in livestock. Chances of frost are extremely low just before and two days after this front arrives.

May 20: The days surrounding this front are some of the most turbulent of May, often marked by rain, tornadoes and high winds. The May 20 system also brings the threat of frost to the northern tier of states, but it typically spares tomatoes and eggplant below the 40th Parallel.

May 24: This is usually the last frost-bearing front to Wisconsin and Minnesota gardens, and the days following its arrival are unseasonably cold one year out of three. Even though more than half of May 25ths and 26ths along the 40th Parallel are in the 70s or 80s, a full 40 percent are not, giving them the most potential for chilly conditions since the May 15. Chances of totally overcast conditions rise all the way to 50 percent. As the sixth high-pressure system of the month moves off to the east, the likelihood for cold temperatures quickly decreases.

May 29: Rain is often heavy as the final front of May approaches. When this high moves away, however, it usually leaves sunny, dry conditions. Along and below the 40th Parallel, summer heat typically begins several days later. Heat stress can slow the rate of gain in livestock. Protection from the weather, plenty of water and adequate feed and supplements may help to reduce weight loss.

Key to the Nation's Weather In May

The typical May temperature at average elevations along the 40th Parallel, the average of the high of 72 and the low of 54, is 63 degrees. Using the following chart based on weather statistics from around the country, one can calculate approximate temperatures in other locations close to the cities listed.

For example, with the base of 63 you can estimate normal temperatures in Minneapolis by subtracting 5 degrees from the base average. Or add 7 degrees to find out the likely conditions in Atlanta during the month.

Fairbanks	-16
Cheyenne	-13
Portland	-9
Minneapolis	-5
Chicago	-5
Des Moines	-2
AVERAGE ALONG THE 40th PARALLEL:	**63**
Washington D.C.	+2
St. Louis	+3
Louisville	+3
Little Rock	+7
Atlanta	+7

New Orleans +13
Miami +15

A Floating Sequence
For the Blooming of Shrubs, Trees, Wildflowers and Perennials

The following list is based on my personal observations in southwestern Ohio over a period of 30 years. The dates are approximate, but I have tried to show a relatively true sequence of first blossoming times during an average spring. Although the dates on all flower calendars are somewhat arbitrary (and may vary by up to 60 days between the Canadian border and the South), a "floating calendar" can be used throughout the country by adjusting the sequence to fit the climate and the particular year.

Many of the events mentioned in this May *Daybook* occur up to a month earlier in the South and up to a month later in the North. For example, if May apples bloom in your woodlot on April 5 instead of May 5, subsequent blooming dates will follow more or less in the order given, but on different dates. Since microclimates, as well as precipitation, temperature, soil quality and the day's length, determine blooming times, personal records can refine and reorder sequences to reflect local conditions.

April 13	Wisteria (*Wisteria frutescens*)
	Bellwort (*Uvularia*)
	Hawthorn (*Crataegus monogyna*)
	Cressleaf Groundsel or Butterweed *(Packera globella)*
April 14	Large-flowered Trillium (*Trillium grandiflorum*)
	Winter Cress (*Barbarea vulgaris*)
	Jacob's Ladder (*Polemonium caeruleum*)
April 15:	Redbud (*Cercis canadensis*)
	Mid-Season Tulip (*tulipa*)
	Trout Lily (*Erythronium americanum*)
April 16:	Domestic Strawberry *(Fragaria ananassa)*
	White Violet (*Viola canadensis*)
April 17:	Buttercup (*Ranunculus acris*)
	Money Plant (*Epipremnum aureum*)
	Thyme-Leafed Speedwell (*Veronica serpyllifolia*)

April 19: Dogwood (*Cornus*)
          Watercress (*Nasturtium officinale*)
April 20: Lilac (*Syringa*)
          Raspberry (*Rubus idaeus*)
          Ragwort (*Jacobaea vulgaris*)
April 21: Snowball Viburnum (*Viburnum macrocephalum*)
          Azalea (*Rhododendron indicum*)
          Early Meadow Rue (*Thalictrum dioicum*)
          Columbine (*Aquilegia vulga*ris)
April 22: Bridal Wreath Spirea (*Spirea prunifolia*)
          Late-Season Tulips and Daffodils
April 23: Wild Geranium (*Geranium maculatum*)
          Miterwort (*Mitella*)
          Wild Phlox (*Phlox divaricate*)
          Celandine (*Stylophorum diphyllum*)
April 24: Clematis (*Clematis x jackmanii*)
          Wood Hyacinth (*Hyacinthoides non-scripta*)
          Garlic Mustard (*Alliaria petiolata*)
April 25: Jack-in-the-Pulpit (*Arisaema triphyllum*)
          Wild Ginger (*Asarum caudatum*)
          Bugle (*Adjuga reptans*)
April 26: Meadow Parsnip (*Haspium trifoliatum Gray*)
          Wood Betony (*Stachys officinali*s)
          Honeysuckle (*Lonicera tatarica L.*)
          Buckeye (*Aesculus glabra*)
          Red Horse-Chestnut (*Aesculus* × *carnea*)
          Nodding Trillium (*Trillium cernuum*)
          Star of Bethlehem (*Ornithogalum narbonense*)
April 27: Early-Season Iris (*Iridaceae*)
          Thyme (*Thymus vulgaris)*
          Horseradish (Armoracia rusticana)
          Common Fleabane (*Erigeron philadelphicus*)
April 28: Osage Orange (*maclura pomifera)*
          Lily-of-the-Valley (*Convallaria majalis*)
          Roundleaf Ragwort *(Senecio obovatus*)
April 29: Wild Cherry (*Prunus avium)*
          Spring Cress (*Cardamine bulbosa*)
April 30: Sweet William (*Dianthus barbatus*)
          Korean Lilac (*Syringa meyeri*)

A Daybook for May

May 1:	Catchweed (*Galium aparine*)
	Larkspur (*Delphinium carolinianum*)
	Silver Olive (*Elaeagnus angustifolia*)
	Sweet Gum (*Liquidambar styraciflua*)
	Comfrey (*Symphytum officinale)*
	Spring Sedum (*Sedum ternatum*)
May 2:	Poppy (*Papaver somniferum*)
	English Daisy (*Bellis perennis*)
May 3:	White Mulberry (*Morus alba*)
	Mountain Maple (*Acer spicatum*)
May 4:	Black Locust (*Robinia pseudoacacia*)
	Honey Locust (*Gleditsi triacanthos*)
	Black Walnut (*Juglans nigra*)
	Oaks (*Quercus*)
	Wood Sorrel (*Oxalis acetosella*)
May 5:	Painted Daisy (*Pyrethrum roseum*)
	Golden Alexander (*Zizia aurea*)
	May Apple (*Podophyllum peltatum)*
	Hawthorn (*Crataegus monogyna*)
May 6:	Rhododendron (*Rhododendron*)
	Columbine (*Aquilegia*)
	Sweet Cicely (*Myrrhis odorata*)
	Robin's Fleabane (*Erigeron pulchellus*)
	English Plantain (*Plantago lanceol*ata)
May 8:	Mock Orange (*Philadelphus coronaries*)
	Sweet William (*Dianthus barbatus*)
	Shooting Star (*Dodecatheon)*
May 9:	Chives (*Allium schoenoprasum)*
	Catmint (*Nepeta*)
	Waterleaf (*Talinum fruticosum*)
	Wild Raspberry (*Rubus idaeus*)
May 10:	Sweet Rocket /Dame's Rocket
	(*Hesperis matronalis*)
	Dwarf Larkspur (*Delphinium tricorne*)
	Tulip Tree (*Liriodendro*)
	Yellowwood (*Cladrastis kentukea*)
	Snow-on-the-Mountain (*Euphorbia marginata*)
May 11:	Peonies (*Paeonia*)
	Elms (*Ulmus*)

	Chamomile (*Matricaria chamomilla*)
May 12:	Clustered Snakeroot (*Sanicula gregaria*)
	White Clover (*Trifolium repens*)
	Meadow Goat's Beard (*Tragopogon dubius*)
	Red Clover (*Trifolium pretense)*
May 13:	Common Plantain (*Plantago major*)
	Black Medic (*Medicago lupulina*)
	Wild Multiflora Rose (*Rosa multiflora*)
	Blue Flag (*Iris versicolor*)
	Wild Daisy (*Bellis perennis*)
	Common Bedstraw *(Galium asprellum)*
May 14:	Wild Mallow (*Malva sylvestris*)
	Spiderwort (*Tradescantia*)
	Scabiosa (*Scabiosa*)
	Lupine (*Lupines*)
	Geum (*Geum abendsonne)*
	Baneberry *(Actaea)*
	Fire Pink (*Silene virginica*)
May 15:	Common Orange Day Lily (*Hemerocallis fulva*)
	Stella d'Oro Lily (*Hemerocallis 'Stella de Oro'*)
May 16:	Yucca (*Yucca filamentosa*)
	Blue Flax (*Linum lewisii*)
	Foxglove (*Digitalis purpurea*)
	Blackberry (*Rubus villosus*)
May 17:	Achillea (*Achillea millefolium*)
	Swamp Iris (*Iris*)
	Wild Grape (*Vitis vinifera*)
	Cow Vetch (*Vicia villosa*)
May 18:	Lamb's Ear (*Stachys byzantine*)
	Kousa Dogwood (*Cornus kousa*)
	Yellow Sweet Clover (*Melilotus officinalis*)
May 19:	Climbing Rose (*Rosa setigera*)
	Tea Rose (*Rosoideae rosa*)
	Fringe Tree (*Chionanthus*)
May 20:	Blue-Eyed Grass (*Sisyrinchium angustifolium*)
	Corn Salad (*Valerianella locusta*)
May 21:	Catalpa *(Catalpa speciosa)*
	Pink Spirea (*Spiraea japonica*)
	Wild Parsnip (*Pastinaca sativa*)

May 22:   Privet (*Ligustrum*)
            River Willow (*Salix myrtilloides*)
            Smooth Solomon's Seal (*Polygonatum biflorum*)
May 23:   Astilbe (*Astilbe arendsii*)
            Panicled Dogwood (*Cornus racemosa*)
            Poison Hemlock (*Coniu maculatum*)
            Angelica (*Angelica*)
            Birdsfoot Trefoil (*Lobus corniculatus*)
            Sundrops Primrose (*Oenothera fruticosa*)
May 24:   Japanese Honeysuckle (*Lonicera japonica*)
            Motherwort (*Leonurus cardiac*)
            Multiflora Rose (*Rosa multifora*)
May 25:   Tree of Heaven (*Ailanthus altissima*)
            Yarrow (*Achillea millefolium*)
            Curly Dock (*Rumex crispus*)
May 26:   Poison Ivy (*Toxicosdendron radicans*)
            White Campion (*Silene latifolia*)
            Common Cinquefoil (*Potentilla simplex*)
May 27:   Cottonwood (*Aigeiros*)
            Honewort (*Cryptotaenia canadensis*)
            Japanese Pond Iris (*Iris versicolor*)
May 28:   Elderberry (*Sambucus*)
            Lesser Stitchwort (*Stellaria graminea*)
May 29:   Lychnis (*Lychnis coronaria*)
            Cow Parsnip (*Heracleum*)
May 30:   Canadian Thistle (*Cirsium arvense*)
May 31:   Coreopsis (*Coreopsis lanceolata*)
            Chicory (*Cichorium intybus*)
            Daisy Fleabane (*Erigeron annus*)
June 1:   Rugosa Rose (*Rosa rugosa*)
            Floribunda Rose (*Floribunda*)
            Delphinium (*Delphinium*)
            Moth Mullein (*Verbascum blattaria*)
June 2:   Feverfew (*Tanacetum parthenium*)
            Heliopsis (*Heliopsis helianthoides*)
            Quickweed (*Galinsoga parviflora*)
June 3:   Swamp Valerian (*Valeriana ulginosa*)
            Moneywort (*Lysimachia nummularia*)

	Rape brassica (*Napus*)
June 4:	Campanula (*Campanula rapunculus*)
	Wild Garlic (*Allium ursinum*)
	Scarlet Pimpernel (*Anagallis arvensis*)
	Nodding Thistle (*Carduus nutans*)
	Common "Ditch" Lily" (*Hemerocallis fulva*)
June 5:	Bindweed (*Convolvulus arvensis*)
	Crown Vetch (*Securigera varia*)
	Smartweed (*Polygonum hydropiper*)
June 6:	Pickerel Plant (*Pontederia cordata*)
	Balloon Flower (*Platycodon grandiflorus*)
	Deptford Pink (*Sianthus armeria*)
June 7:	Oakleaf Hydrangea (*Hydrangea quercifolia*)
	Indian Hemp (*Apocynum cannabinum*)
	Virginia Creeper (*Parthenocissus quinquefolia*)
June 8:	Purple Coneflower (*Echinacea purpurea*)
June 9:	Asiatic Lily (*Lilium asiaticum*)
	Carnation (*Dianthus caryophylus*)
	Blueweed (*Echium vulgare L.*)
	Pokeweed (*Phytolacca americana*)
June 10:	Early Season Hostas
	Shasta Daisy (*Leucanthemum maximum*)
	Queen Anne's Lace (*Daucus carota*)
June 11:	Hollyhock (*Alcea rosea*)
	Beardtongue (*Penstemon barbatus*)
June 12:	Mallow (*Malva sylvestris*)
	Avens (*Geum urbanum*)
June 13:	Tall Meadow Rue (*Thalictrum dasycarpum*)
	Great Mullein (*Verbascum Thapsus*)
June 14:	Leatherflower (*Clematis pitcher*)
	Common Sow Thistle (*Onchus oleraceus*)
	Common Milkweed (*Asclepias syriaca*)
June 15:	Large-Leafed Hostas
	Wild Petunia (*Ruellia humilis*)

May Phenology

When lamb's ear, tea roses, pink spirea or privets are blooming, then frost is likely to stay away until autumn.

When daisies flower by the wayside and white mulberries and

mountain maples bloom, then daddy longlegs hunt in the undergrowth and darners by the water's edge.

When redbud trees are getting seedpods and the first crickets sing in the sun throughout the Ohio Valley, then horseshoe crabs mate along the Carolina and Georgia coastline.

When lilac flowers fade, hawthorn lace bugs and hawthorn leafminers emerge in the hawthorns. Pine needle scale eggs, cooley spruce gall adelgid and Eastern spruce gall adelgid eggs hatch, too.

When poppies bloom, white-throated sparrows, ruby-crowned kinglets, yellow-rumped warblers, magnolia warblers, tanagers, grosbeaks, and orioles migrate through the East.

When tulips are in full bloom in the North, the best of the spring wildflowers have all disappeared in the Southwest. But prickly pear cacti are still flowering in the desert.

When mock orange reaches full flower, black vine weevils and greater peach tree borers appear. Then come the rhododendron borers and the dogwood borers!

When the great spring dandelion bloom reaches into the Northeast, pelicans and trumpeter swans will be laying eggs near Yellowstone Lake, and gosling will be hatching almost everywhere.

When multiflora roses come into flower, then the bronze birch borer emerges and oystershell scale eggs hatch.

And when American holly blooms (about the same time as the multiflora roses), then potato leafhoppers will be hopping in the potatoes.

When hummingbirds arrive at feeders, thrushes, catbirds and scarlet tanagers arrive, too.

When strawberries come into full bloom, then wild cucumber will be sprouting along the rivers.

When summer phlox are two-feet tall, catbirds call in the bushes.

When apple blossoms fall, then rare, medicinal golden seal blooms in the woods.

When mayflies swarm by the water, spitbugs make their spittle shelters in the parsnips, and the first cut of hay is underway.

When chives bloom in the garden, then crappie fishing peaks in the shallows.

When flower clusters of the sweet-gum tree fall, then the first strawberry could be red.

When azaleas lose their petals, morel season is about over for the year, and swallowtail butterflies come looking for flowers.

When flea beetles feed in the vegetable garden, cedar waxwings migrate north, and fiddler crabs emerge from their tunnels in the estuaries of the South.

When the first brown "June" bug appears at porch lights, then young fireflies glow in the night grass.

When the last locust flowers fall to the ground, then mulberries ripen. In the wetlands, wild iris are in bloom.

When cottonwood cotton floats in the wind, then deer give birth, and pollen from grasses will be reaching its peak. Panicled dogwood is budding, and grackles feed their pesky young.

When blackberries have set fruit across the South, then sunflowers are in full bloom in southern California, and spring wheat and oats are just about all planted in the North.

When nettles are waist high, then cutworms roam the garden.

When Canadian thistles start to bud, frost usually stays away from peppers, cantaloupes and cucumbers. But armyworms and corn borers wander in the fields.

When the first Canadian thistle blooms, the corn should be at least eight inches tall.

When spring crickets sing, leafhoppers visit the garden and snapping turtles lay their eggs in the sand.

When the first elderberries bloom, bean leaf beetles and alfalfa weevils assault the field and garden.

Frostwatch

Between May 1 and June 1, only a few mornings of light frost occur in Ohio. Chances of freezing temperatures after the dates listed below are:

May 1:	45 percent
May 5:	35 percent
May 10:	25 percent
May 15:	15 percent
May 20:	10 percent
May 25:	5 percent
May 31:	2 percent

Estimated May Pollen Count
On a scale of 0 to 700 grains per cubic meter: Pollen from flowering trees usually peaks about May 10, but trees continue to be the major source of pollen in the air until grass pollen replaces it in the third week of the month.

May 1: 400   May 5: 540   May 10: 500   May 15: 300
May 20: 250   May 25: 160   May 31: 100

Estimated May Mold Count
On a scale of 0 to 7,000 grains per cubic meter:
May 1: 2600   May 5: 3000   May 10: 2000   May 15: 1100
May 20: 250   May 25: 150   May 31: 100

Natural Calendar
One of the ones that Midas touched,
Who failed to touch us all,
Was that confiding prodigal,
The blissful oriole.

Emily Dickinson

The first week of May (or the first week of Late Spring) brings Daddy Longlegs Season to the undergrowth and Petal-Fall Season throughout town. Darner Season commences along the waterways. Dandelion Blooming Season ends throughout the Lower Midwest as Ruby Throated Hummingbird Season and Baltimore Oriole Season begin at feeders there. All along the 40th Parallel, Bellwort Season, Golden Seal Season, Golden Alexander Season and Solomon's Seal Season mark the woods. Scarlet Pimpernel Season appears in the lawn. Sweet Gum Flowering Season, White Mulberry Flowering Season, Black Walnut Flowering Season and Oak Flowering Season spread through the high canopy. In the garden, it's Poppy Season, Columbine Season and Rhododendron Season.

Prospectus
From this space in the year, you can travel to the whole panoply of early, middle and late spring. For just a few days, all of those seasons lie out totally accessible to anyone who will go to

see them.

As May begins, the Ohio Valley lies between the first stirring of color in northern Minnesota and the leafing of all the trees along the Gulf of Mexico. If you travel to the Canadian border now, you will find the first cottonwoods budding there, the first crocus, the first daffodil and tulip foliage pushing out of the ground. It is still the second or third week of March in Miami Valley time.

Gaining on spring at the rate of approximately one day for every thirty miles south, you will the see the grass showing color near St. Cloud, Minnesota. By Minneapolis, it's the first of April in our time: A few tulips are in bloom, and forsythia is out. Daffodils are blooming. Maples flower, and willows glow.

Into Wisconsin, down to Madison, the tree line comes alive with golds and pale greens, and dandelions appear in the lawns and fields. Through Chicago and northern Indiana, the intensity of coloration grows with each mile, all the winter branches filling in. Past the Ohio River, late May's clover time comes into flower, first the white, then pink, then the tall sweet clovers into South Carolina. The canopy closes in and loses its early brilliance by the time you pass into southern Georgia. In Mobile, Alabama, the leaves are full size. Mulleins and thistles and lilies are open, and you know for sure you've seen all of spring.

Daybook

1981: Most maple leaves are fully developed now.

1982: Lilacs, apple trees in bloom, full crab apples.

1983: As garlic mustard blooms, the forest floor leaves middle spring behind. The low April plants disappear under the tall *Cruciferae.*

1986: Buckeyes flower.

1987: Most maple leaves have formed, many trees dropping new seeds. Redbuds and crab apples are almost done, many dogwoods in full bloom. Locusts leafing, high canopy greening in browns, yellows and greens. I saw a snake hunting in the river at sundown.

Buds on black raspberries and honeysuckles, mock orange, mulberries. Rhubarb full grown. Buckeyes full bloom, daisies begin to open. Sweet rockets budding for a week now. Garlic mustard full bloom. Mountain maple full bloom.

1988: Middle Prairie is purple with purple deadnettle, gold with knee high winter cress, bright green with clover and pennycress, yellow with faded leaves of spring beauties and shepherd's purse, full of white and yellow cabbage butterflies. In the woods, the paths are covered with violets. On the ridge, dandelions are still thick, and they spread as far as I can see. Mint paces the daisy fleabane, four inches tall. Wild cucumber sprouts now have three regular leaves. Bouncing bets are two inches. Sycamore leaves not quite an inch, elms half an inch long. Shepherd's purse almost all to seed. Shrill chant of toads from the river banks.

1989: First major dandelion seeding throughout the county. Elm leaves an inch-and-a-half long.

1990: First wild geranium and first sweet rockets bloom. Ranunculus at home full bloom.

1991: Cascades and Covered Bridge in Glen Helen: Wild geranium, spring cress, sedum, swamp buttercup, buckeyes, ragwort, garlic mustard, violets, phlox, spiderwort, Jacob's ladder all full bloom.

1993: Buds forming on the chives. First dwarf iris blooms. A few cherry petals fall slowly in the warm breeze. The latest apple trees (including the back yard apple) open their first buds. First lilacs in the yard, other bushes some full bloom, some still starting. First bud on the small yarrows. Three dahlia bulbs have sprouted, leaves an inch or so long. Spring beauties and dandelions hold at full bloom. Honeysuckles have first buds. The golden green of April persists, pastures, rolling hills glowing.

1994: Hyacinths have all faded now, gone by the end of April.

1995: The first chives opened in the garden today. Ginkgoes at school maybe an inch wide. Ash, locusts and sugar gum are starting to come out.

1996: Landmarks in this coldest of my springs so far in Yellow Springs: The latest of the daffodils, the smaller ones, are still full bloom, the others gone. Quince still red, forsythia maybe a fourth still in flower. All the maples in the yard are blooming. Major leafing has begun of box elders, and the north brush line of the yard is filling in now, almost obscuring the street. The small, short tulips which bloomed maybe five days ago at the southwest garden are still open, the tall mid-season tulips are holding too, reds and yellows. Bleeding heart is in full bloom. Cherry tree is in full bloom, doing well in the cool rains. A few pear flowers are left downtown, the apples are just coming out, started maybe two to three days ago. Across the area, flooding is widespread, the water deep into Glen Helen. Yesterday there was standing water all over the yard. And snow flurries!

1998: Purple deadnettle yellows by the roses. Huge bud heads on the chives with horseradish well into bloom. Columbine, bleeding heart, wild geraniums, money plant, dead nettle: full flower. Sweet rockets early blossoming along the south wall. Oaks leafing. Full dogwoods now, late lilacs, some rich, some decaying. Wood hyacinths full. The landscape is only a few days from where I was in Montgomery, Alabama on March 23.

1999: Locusts and Osage barely starting, white mulberry leaves maybe half an inch. Daisies and pyrethrums budding, pink quince full bloom.

2000: Pink quince in full bloom. White lilacs underway. Dorothy reported seeing cecropia moths mating a week ago.

2001: Wisteria blooms at the front porch for the first time ever, two pale violet clusters. Beside them bright pink azaleas. Wood hyacinths coming out in the south garden. White lilacs dying back. redbuds turn to leaves. Into Ross County, the mountains are green, the brightness intense across the countryside. Bridal wreath and snowball viburnum through the foothills. End of the great dandelion bloom throughout southern Ohio. Locust and ash are leafing at my Wilberforce parking lot, and the ginkgo by my window. Rose of Sharon along the borders of the yard. Corn and soybean fields cultivated to a fine powdery, velvety surface.

2002: Yellow Springs into South Carolina with John: Box turtle seen along the road below Chillicothe. Dogwood and apples in bloom in West Virginia, wisteria in Charleston, then we regress to pre-Yellow Springs conditions in the mountains. Descending through Virginia: tulip tree and poison hemlock in flower at the North Carolina border (suddenly putting me at the fourth week of Yellow Springs May). Poppies, daisies, sweet rockets, wild cherry seen in northern and central North Carolina, well into the lower Piedmont. Approaching Charlotte: Yellow swallowtail sighted, blackberries in bloom, stella d'oro lilies seen, Japanese honeysuckle blossoming, full Early Summer. Red daylilies below Columbia. Near the Santee Reservoir not far from Charleston, South Carolina, the wheat is at June 20th height for Yellow Springs, almost ready to cut. We've traveled 600 miles today and about six weeks.

2003: A wren is nesting in the shed. At about 5:20 a.m., after the cardinals and doves and the jay have started, a new birdsong, a steady "chip" call of a female cardinal.

2004: A red admiral butterfly explored the hyacinths opening along the west wall this afternoon. Casey's red-flowering buckeye blooms about this time.

2005: First star of Bethlehem opened today. Termites swarmed in the greenhouse. Lily-of-the-valley is budded.

2006: Bridal wreath is starting to open along High Street. Redbuds are fading, leaves increasing. Wild geraniums are in full bloom behind Mrs. Timberlake's house. Cherry petals have almost all fallen. Apples weaken in the alley. The last periwinkles disappear into their foliage. Serviceberry trees have small green berries on Dayton Street; across the street from them, blue iris are opening. The pair of starlings continues to attack the shiny chimney. Jeanie made the first rhubarb pie yesterday, the rhubarb stalks so long and thick, the best year ever.

2007: Mrs. Timberlake's wild geraniums are in full bloom this morning, and her yellow buttercups are coming in beside them. More celandine is blooming in the yard, more lilacs opening. The purple magnolia that had all its flowers burned in the frost three weeks ago is blossoming again. Wisteria and bittersweet finally leafing, fleabane and sweet Cicely open along the north side of the yard.

2008: Mrs. Timberlake's wild geraniums are in full bloom (no buttercups). A few grackles cluck in the alley, cardinals call in the distance this morning. No red-bellied woodpecker heard. The alley willow is completely leafed out, red mulberry leaves the size of a squirrel's ear. A few sweet rockets have buds now, and sweet Williams approach the budding stage. The first star of Bethlehem opened today and the first late, small, red tulip.

2009: The Indian hyacinths opened yesterday, and our first geranium. The one red tulip near the shed came in maybe a week ago, is now fading. The circle garden of hyacinths, deadnettle and violets is coming into its own now. The first tall allium are opening just a little. Transplanting of resurrection lilies, ferns and small hostas done between showers. Twine attached to poles for the peas to climb. Black walnut leaves have come out now, honeysuckle buds and mock orange buds turning white, ready to start. About 3:00 this afternoon, we heard the cry of an American toad in the pond, the first time we have had a toad calling here in years.

2011: Black walnut flowers falling to the street in front of the Lawsons' house. Nesting grackles loud in the alley, robins, sparrows and cardinals all around me. Virginia creeper leaves have emerged, some an inch or so in length, still red. Mrs. Timberlake's geraniums are in full bloom. Six elephant ears planted in the east garden, five dahlias along the north garden wall. The first Indian hyacinths opened in the warm, cloudy afternoon.

    From Madison, Wisconsin, Maggie writes: "April was a good, if chilly month. I think the blue scylla and the daffodils have appreciated the cool weather, as the latter still look perky (having been around since the 12th or so) and the former finally fading (having been blooming since at least the 5th). And tulips are about to bloom or have just bloomed (depending on the tulip!). Fosythia are at their prettiest, and everything else is budding. Truly, this spring season is an eye popper!"

2012: Soft morning, rain overnight, the air heavy with the scent of honeysuckle, mock orange (which just opened) and locust blossoms, robins singing by 4:40 (at least) : one sparrow fledgling begging for food at the feeders as Jeanie and I watched around 7:15. The whole countryside in full middle-May flower. Around the yard, the red azalea - pummeled by the rain but still radiant, sweet rockets, earliest roses, geraniums, lily-of-the-valley, sweet Cicely, tall alliums, buttercup, garlic mustard, late hyacinths, lamium. Large-budded peonies and chives, buds on the privets. The trellis wisteria and our two trumpet creepers have started to leaf out. Crows, cardinals, grackles, sparrows, robins, red-bellied woodpecker calling. In the neighborhood, the great maple seed drop is over. Tulip trees flower along Limestone Street. Liz's allium, geraniums and forget-me-nots bloom beside her viburnum and orange poppies. A few houses from us on High Street, Mateo's weigela is in full flower, ours fully budded.

2013: I was waiting for the robins this morning. They started just a few minutes before 4:00. The sky was so clear, the Summer Triangle overhead. A screech owl called in the back yard, from the same location as the owls have through the years, at 4:20, but the robins dominated the chorus until 4:45 when cardinals, song sparrows and doves came in within a minute or two of one another. I didn't notice house sparrows chirping until 5:20. As I walked with Bella in the light of the high third-quarter moon, I could see black walnut flowers fallen to the sidewalk.

The day became the warmest so far this year, cloudless and intense. The wisteria came into bloom and the first wood hyacinths. The red crab apple tree is in full flower and the red azalea buds are soft and tender, ready to open any minute.

At Ellis Pond: toads singing, the dandelion bloom holding through the fields. Early buds have formed on the tulip trees, the oaks are flowering: sawtooth, scarlet, shingle and red with catkins, chinquapins and pin oaks holding back. Sugar maple leaves are a third to half size, pecans leafing.

Field pennycress in full bloom by the creek that flows into the fields across the road. In all of this I hold on to a sense of specificity; I mean the need to stop spring at this one place, to name and hold it here, to collect around me this exact grace, to understand its impermanence, but in a seizure of denial to allow myself to be only here, my senses counting without sequence: full, embracing, entranced.

2016: After a week of rain, the weeds and flowers totally lush, a warm day between cold waves. Jonatha wrote at 1:03 p.m. "I just saw a pair of Baltimore Orioles at my feeder. Beautiful!" Across the street, Lil's maple and Mrs. Timberlake's maple are both filling in quickly; the Danielson's maple between them is still in flower. Working in the garden this afternoon, I saw a red admiral near the monarda. Columbines and the first poppies are open downtown.

2017: Santiago, Spain: On the way into the city, Tat and I saw locusts in full flower, At the hotel, small frogs in the two ponds here, late blossoming of golden water iris, small pink dogwood flowers quite late, large red spirea shrub well budded, white water lilies in early bloom. Through the city, only annuals were blooming along the streets, pansies set out by the fountains.

2018: After the coldest April in memory, pear petals are just staring to drift to the streets. Apples and violets and dandelions are still early. At midmorning, I watched a rose-breasted grosbeak at the backyard feeder. The sighting joined several through the years in early May. Jane said that someone had told her they saw a hummingbird yesterday. Then Jill told me that her student, Peter, had seen two male and two female rose-breasted grosbeaks in the morning.

2019: In a warm and sunny morning, Baltimore Orioles sang in the back trees, "tee-tee-tee-tidlee," orange breasts bright. Leslie heard her first this morning, too. The National Oceanic and

Atmospheric Administration just reported that the last 12 months have been the wettest in history for the continental United States, over six inches above average.

2020: Catbird seen in the north honeysuckle hedge, sings off and on through the afternoon. At Gerard's old property, lily of the valley buds are fully formed, as are sweet Cicely buds and common fleabane buds in the back yard. Star of Bethlehem blossoms are showing up all around the dug-up annual garden area. At the arboretum, sawtooth oaks have catkins. From Goshen, Indiana, Judy reports that forsythias are leafing but that the pear trees are still in full flower.

And so we see in Plants and all of Nature the Word of God. Like any Scripture, Earth's Matter is subject to our Doubt. But to the one who listens closely to its Cadence, it reveals the sweet hidden Truth.

Reginald Johnson

Bill Felker

May 2nd
The 122nd Day of the Year

By Goddes fay, by Goddes fay!
It is the month, the jolly month,
It is the jolly month of May.

Francis Thompson

Sunrise/set: 5:34/7:30
Day's Length: 13 hours 56 minutes
Average High/Low: 68/47
Average Temperature: 57
Record High: 87 – 1901
Record Low: 31 – 1961

Weather

High temperatures are in the 80s ten percent of all May 2nds, the 70s forty-five percent. Some years, a brief "Lilac Winter" strikes at this time of the month, and cooler 60s come 20 percent of the time, 50s twenty-five percent. Chances of rain are 30 percent; the sky is mostly clear better than two-thirds of all the years. Although a cool front is due today, frost this morning is rare.

Natural Calendar

You watch the afternoons of spring across the river,
and you know that nothing only is or happens once,
and that our hearts spin like the earth around the sun.

bf

Under the closing canopy, phlox and ragwort are purple and gold. May apples are flowering. Wild ginger, meadow rue, bellwort, bluettes, Jack-in-the pulpit, nodding trillium, larkspur and thyme-leafed speedwell are still blossoming. Wood betony flowers along the path above the stepping stones in the North Glen. White spring cress blooms along South Glen paths. Thyme and horseradish open in the garden. Lily-of-the-valley and star of Bethlehem push out from their buds. Red horse chestnut trees and buckeye trees and Osage orange come in. Sticky catchweed replaces chickweed. Korean lilacs fill in for the fading standard varieties. Oak and elm leaves are at least half size. Some maples are fully leafed, others just starting, some dropping seeds. The high tree line is completely alive all across the county, either with new glowing foliage or with orange buds or golden flowers.

The Stars

Arcturus still hangs a little to the east of the center of the sky at 10:00 p.m., but as that star shifts west, it pulls the chances of a freeze with it. When Arcturus is well into the west at bedtime, frost is usually gone until the autumn. Before dawn, Cygnus, the Northern Cross, is overhead in the Milky Way. Below Cygnus, Delphinus, the Dolphin, swims toward Aquila, the Eagle. In the far west, Hercules follows the Corona Borealis into the horizon. The Great Square fills the east while the Pleiades and Taurus appear on the edge of the tree line.

Daybook

1982: South Glen still has swamp buttercups, toothwort, toad trillium, trillium grandiflorum, wild phlox. Wild geranium is budding. In town, the smallest daffodils are still in bloom, all the rest are gone.

1983: First wood sorrel in bloom at Wilberforce. Early meadow rue and blue cohosh at South Glen. Lily-of-the-valley ready.

1985: Chicory is a foot tall in places.

1987: High oaks flowering and leafing now, rhubarb and horseradish in bloom. Very first honeysuckles open, one Osage branch is starting to leaf.

1988: Major shift in the color of the land, dandelions going to seed everywhere. Chubs are swarming in the clear water just below the bridge on Grinnell. First mayfly seen today. All but a few forsythia flowers have fallen.

1992: At Caesar Creek: Dogwoods and redbuds still full bloom. At least a dozen carp seen swimming back and forth, two caught. Catfish not at their holes yet. In town, cherry and apple done. Lilacs continuing to flower. Small *Thalia* narcissus and large daffodils in the east garden hold. Star of Bethlehem are open. Hosta leaves eight to ten inches, clematis and azalea with buds. Garlic mustard full bloom, rockets, daisies, pyrethrum budding, ranunculus full bloom since the end of April, forget-me-nots are in late full bloom.

1993: Diana Matthews calls: Craig saw a hummingbird today. Checking my notes, I see May 3 is the average date for their arrival.

1998: This morning, early robin chorus heard at 4:15, but I have not found the earliest point yet. Some of the lilacs are rusting now. The first iris (white) seen in Xenia this morning. The redbud trees are leafing more and more, their purple blossoms dropping to the street. In the pond, the ninth water lily leaf has come to the top. The pickerel plant is eight inches high. The watercress planted last week has adapted well, starting to bud, the purple loosestrife continues to spread. The azaleas are in full blossom, and the rhododendrons are just starting to show color.

Now driving the countryside, I can see the full retreat of the dandelions, and when I walk through the wet grass, my boots get covered with seeds. In the pond, the toad tadpoles have eaten almost all the algae which overwintered. They have grown some, developed more speckles, but their bodies do not seem to have changed dramatically since last weekend. Their habits are different, though. Instead of clustering at the west end of the pool, they have chosen the east end, richer in algae. And they seem more aware of my presence, are a little harder to capture for inspection. Even though the tadpoles never interact, they appear to have become more aware of what the others around them are doing; instead of all going their own way, they respond as one to shifts in the cloud cover or to noise.

1999: Lungwort still has blue flowers. Bleeding heart full. The last tulip, red and huge. Tadpoles still tiny, just a few days old. Star of Bethlehem appeared a day or two ago. White hyacinth by the cherry tree garden. Hosta foliage has become decorative in the east garden. By the purple coneflowers, only two foxglove and two monarda seem to have survived the winter. Wild geranium open, and full bloom of the dead nettle in the east garden. Astilbe foliage rising there, adding to the display. In the high canopy, locust and Osage barely starting. Along the south hedge, rose of Sharon just starting to leaf. In the pond, frogs still calling day and night.

2000: Cardinal at 4:43 a.m. this morning. Several sizable patches of blue-purple iris seen today, one in Xenia, the others in Yellow Springs. The first poppies were open across from the playground. In the yard, the honeysuckle has white buds; along the bike path a lot of the plants are open, and cressleaf groundsel has started to bloom beside the full bloom of the winter cress. Wild lettuce almost the size of May skunk cabbage. More sweet rockets coming in. Tadpoles in the pond still small and black; no spots, but they are becoming a little wilder.

2002: South Carolina: hard cold wind and temperatures only in the 50s today. No catfish found.

2003: First cardinal heard at 4:55 a.m., the morning cloudy and about 60 degrees. Blue jay at 5:07, just a minute or so after the doves. Lilacs all rusting. Susi's bridal wreath spirea and our snowball viburnum are open all the way. All redbud and crab apple and tulip color is gone, petals disappearing. Blue and violet wood hyacinths coming in. Sweet rockets just beginning at South Glen, silver olives in full bloom there, water cress full in the stream along Grinnell Road. Sycamores and white mulberry trees are filling in with leaves now. Wild cherry budding.

 From southern Minnesota, John writes: "So it's finally getting around to being spring. The lilacs are about two days away from blooming. I think my irises should be out tomorrow. Grass is finally green. First mowing was a few days ago around here."

2004: The red flowers of the new crabapple tree all fell at once today in the cold and rain of Lilac Winter. Apples and redbuds throughout town are rapidly losing flowers and are leafing out.

2006: Most of the red flowers of the new crabapple tree fell yesterday; it only has its leaves today. Most apple petals gone in the park. The ash and maples there are almost completely leafed out now, and the American beech has finally begun to push out its leaves from its sharp, long buds. The linden and oaks are at least half size, and the small-flowered mock orange is in full bloom.

2007: Wild strawberry flower noticed in the apple-tree garden. Red-bellied woodpecker calls have ceased recently. Most dandelions have gone to seed.

2008: Ferns, the sprouting dahlias, monarda and a few more coleus transplanted. Tadpoles found in a shallow pool at the Fairborn quarry. They were small and tame, and we caught a few to bring back to the pond. At the quarry, some plum trees are in full bloom, scrub cottonwoods with half-size leaves, squirrel-ear-size leaves on the small sycamores. The habitat is so plain: sweet clover, dock, dandelion foliage; cottonwoods, red cedars, stunted honeysuckles (many in bloom).

    At home, the pink quince came in today or yesterday. I missed its first flowers, saw it suddenly all open. Snowball viburnums are in all over town, ours just starting to blossom. Ash leaves well formed, keeping their flower remnants. Black walnut flower clusters, the dark clumps, have fallen from Nate's tree. Other black walnuts are just starting to leaf. Gold finches continue to feed heavily, grackles, cowbirds and cardinals at the back feeder. Late tulips still hold, the reds, purples and pinks; bluebells and lungwort still bloom. A small frog or toad jumps into the pond whenever I approach.

    Jeffery Goss writes from Springfield, Missouri: "On April 1, the fields were purple with purple deadnettle, and the first butterfly of the season was sighted. Apricot bloomed April 5, redbud April 7, box elder (catkins) April 8, dogwood April 11, sassafras April 15, lilac April 18. In the insect department: first *Microlepidopteran* approximately April 17, first gallnipper April 22, first mosquito April 24."

2009: I built a fire this morning, the first day of Lilac Winter, but the weather warmed in the afternoon. The toad was calling again, and we went to the Brukner Center in Troy, about 40 miles north of Yellow Springs. Bluebells were very late, as they are at home. Marsh marigolds/cowslips were in full bloom, as were the large-flowered trilliums, wild geraniums, bellwort, anemones, aging miterwort, spring beauties and wild phlox. Many Jack-in-the-pulpits seen, most of them completely developed. Campion-like white flower, with five divided petals, opposite, and nearly clasping leaves. Catalpa trees are starting to leaf. In our yard, the late daffodils have finally disappeared, the white and the small multi-flowered ones. Some tulips still hold. Thyme-leafed speedwell has shown up in the lawn.

2011: An afternoon's drive into northern Kentucky this past weekend showed me the Yellow Springs of the next few weeks. In Cincinnati, locusts and honeysuckles were all in bloom. Near Lexington, the high canopy was definitely thickening with luminous leaves, mounds of pale green light emerging from less advanced woodlots. West along the Blue Ridge Parkway, the lush and creamy florescence of wild cherry trees, locusts and honeysuckles dominated the roadsides. Thistles were tall and budded, and off the freeway in small towns, yellow iris, violet iris and red roses marked the dooryards. Dogwoods, hawthorns and tulip trees were losing their petals. When I stopped, I found blue-tailed dragonflies hunting in the river. Deadnettle and chickweed were yellowing, all gone to seed. Poison ivy was starting to cover the forest floor. Black swallowtail butterflies and sulphurs had joined the blues, the red admirals and the white cabbage butterflies.

2012: At home, the first chives opened and two of our iris, one gold, one purple, bloomed overnight, and the late wisteria has started to flower. Rhododendrons opening in front of Don's house. Grackles seem quieter these days, still come to the feeders, but are less talkative. The red-bellied woodpecker still calls. Another sparrow fledgling being fed in the butterfly bush. First hummingbird seen, then the hummingbird feeder put out in the circle garden. The cottonwood tree near the park has clusters of buds, but is not blooming yet. A red admiral seen late afternoon. High in the 80s today: no Lilac Winter this year!

2013: Xenia Avenue is rich in dogwoods and redbuds and crab apples today. Driving past Janet's house, I noticed her front yard covered with golden ragwort, plants tall and in full bloom. Along the freeway, silver olives are all open. Later, I went to the alley to check on Mrs. Timberlake's geraniums, but her garden had been replaced by a gravel driveway. I have watched her spring flowers so many years, but when the land was paved over last year, I didn't pay attention to the loss. At home, the pink quince bloomed overnight, and the viburnum is opening. The peak of the dandelions has just passed, today maybe the cusp, tomorrow the slide to seeding. The sugar maple along Dayton Street is blossoming and forming small seeds, so many other maples shedding flower husks. Several front-yard gardens toward downtown have full-blooming forget-me-nots.

2014: Greg's Lily-of-the-valley has buds, the spirea on High Street has buds, and iris on Limestone and in the yard are also budded. Apples at the park are in full bloom still, all the pears leafed. Peggy's geraniums are coming in, and mine are budded. Dandelions are still full, but the seeding has just begun. In the alley, the white, six-petaled hyacinths are in full bloom. Annie's decorative grasses, cut back in early spring, are growing now, reach about a foot high. Audrey and Grant Hackett wrote this evening: "My husband and I put our hummingbird feeder up yesterday (May 1) and today (May 2) witnessed one...two...three visits by a male ruby-throated hummingbird! So thrilling to have the hummers back. We live on Pleasant and Park on the north side of Yellow Springs."

2015: Morning run, sun rising out of gold and gray-blue at the east end of Union Street, into the chorus of cardinals and robins (one pair exploding, tussling in a lawn along Stafford Street) last petals of forsythia and pears, crows at 5:20, red-bellied woodpecker at 5:40. As I planted zinnias and tithonias in the north garden, two white star of Bethlehem buds opened wide. Pie cherry flowers more than half fallen at Don's. The first red admiral butterfly flirted with bamboo near the south wall. Peter Hayes reported the first hummingbird at his feeder today.

2016: Yesterday morning, Ed Oxley dropped to show me a photo of a Red-Breasted Grosbeak that had visited his property a few days ago. Now this morning, Jonatha writes to report a Grosbeak in her yard. Later in the morning, Peter wrote: "Two Great Egrets across from our house right now." Then Liz sent a note: "A pair of grosbeaks hung out in the yard all afternoon and were so calm...the male let me get very close (10-20 ft.) to take a picture even. He practically posed! When I told my story after meditation this morning, my friend Chris said that he had THREE male grosbeaks in his yard yesterday! A flock taking a little migratory break? Have you ever seen them here?"

2018: From Portland, Oregon, Jeni writes: "You wouldn't believe all the cherry blossoms and how many places have 'pink snow' right now. On the way to work yesterday, a huge pickup truck passed me by and he had lots of pink petals stuck to the front of his truck! It had rained and so they adhered like you'd see on a parade float! Very fun!!"

This afternoon, Jill's lilac produced its first flowers. Along Dayton Street, all the service berry petals are gone, and the decorative pears are leafing. At 8:14 tonight, Rick Donahoe wrote, "Hey Bill, tree toads trilling in our pond tonight. What else is there?" I talked to Robert a little later. He had just gotten back from the Glen, said the toads were singing like crazy.

2019: Crab apple and redbut petalfall surges now, petals all over the sidewalks and roadsides. Standing in the back yard tonight, I listened to the rhythmic calls of the toads far to the west.

2020: A second and then a third red admiral seen this afternoon, and I glimpsed an orange *Polygonia*. Groundsel and winter cress gild the fields west of Ellis, an the wind strips the seeds from the spent dandelions. In the east garden of my house, a few buttercups are opening.

Journal

The first chirps of the waking day birds mark the "point vierge" [the virgin point] of the dawn under a sky as yet without real light, a moment of awe and inexpressible innocence, when the Father in perfect silence opens their eyes.

Thomas Merton

In his journal, the poet Thomas Merton refers to the *virgin point* of the morning, a time just before dawn, when all beauty of the day is still waiting to flower

By this time in May it seems that the *virgin point* of the year is long past. It seems that point must have occurred in earliest spring, just before aconite and snow crocus bloomed, in the days before the cardinals and the doves and the robins sang before sunrise, the days before skunk cabbage bloomed in the swamp, the days before the trillium, the days before the first butterfly

Of course, in our circular universe where beginnings and endings so often spiral together, virgin days are everywhere, even in the middle of May:

the days before the fledgelings appear
the days before the fireflies flicker
the days before the swallowtails arrive under next week's black swallowtail moon
the days before the first strawberry ripens
the days before the first garden peas
the days before the mulberries set sweet fruit
the days before roses bloom
the days before turtles lay their eggs in the warm river banks
the days before the bright orange trumpet creepers flower
the days before the wheat turns to gold
the days before the longest days of the year

Virgin time is not only an outrider of the future but sweetens the events to come. Virgin time compounds the seasons, prolongs them, heightens them, nurture dreaming and fantasy. And that continual space of anticipation links together all of the consummations, so that emptiness is always process towards and from, a perpetual tidal virginity of motion to and away, a virginity in which the constantly evolving present never loses its delight but continually reaches and holds and loosens and tightens, gives up and subsides, joining all the points, making them not alike but one together.

Bill Felker

May 3rd
The 123rd Day of the Year

Rise early now this month of Maye,
And walk the fields that be so gaye.

Buckminster Almanack, May 1598

Sunrise/set: 5:33/7:31
Day's Length: 13 hours 58 minutes
Average High/Low: 68/47
Average Temperature: 57
Record High: 90 – 1899
Record Low: 33 – 1970

Weather

Today is the May day most likely to register a high only in the 50s: forty percent of May 3rds are typically that cold. Another 40 percent are only in the 60s; fifteen percent are in the 70s, five percent in the 80s. Rain comes one day in three, completely overcast conditions four days in ten. Frost strikes ten to fifteen percent of the mornings.

Natural Calendar

Soil temperatures average in the high 50s by today all along the 40th Parallel. The oats crop is typically all sown, and winter wheat is two feet high. A third of the corn, sugar beets, and potatoes has been planted in typical years. Most of the tobacco beds have sprouted. Asparagus peaks at roadside markets. Weevils build up in alfalfa. Bagworms and powdery mildew attack the wheat. The first June bug (brown *Phylophaga*) appears at your screen door.

The last of the region's livestock moves to pasture. Along the freeways, daisies, yellow sweet clover, blue flax, meadow goat's beard, garlic mustard, sweet rockets and parsnips flower. Meadows host white clover and red clover, tall meadow rue, catchweed, sweet rocket, fire pink and angelica. Blackberries, black raspberries, multiflora roses and elderberry bushes bloom in the hedgerows. Mock orange, locusts, wild cherry trees, yellow poplars (tulip trees), Kousa dogwoods and peonies join the early iris, sweet Williams, climbing roses and rhododendrons.

In the deep woods, late Jack-in-the-pulpit, nodding trillium, Solomon's seal, columbine, waterleaf, shooting star, and clustered snakeroot bloom. The leaves of the understory reach full size, and the high canopy starts to fill in above it. Redbuds, crab apples and dogwoods cede to honeysuckles and azaleas and rhododendrons. In most years, the great dandelion bloom has ended in the Lower Midwest and Mid-Atlantic region, still holds in the Northeast and the Upper Midwest.

Daybook

1982: Leaves have started on the rose of Sharon.

1984: This is the best time of the violets, spring beauties and dandelions. Lilac open, pink magnolias still full bloom.

1985: Red clover and black medic are in bloom. New daddy longlegs crouch in the fresh wingstem foliage. Some touch-me-nots have six leaves, some eight. Goat's beard is budding. Violets holding. Wood nettle paces the wood mint, up to two feet high. Geraniums, sedum, tall buttercups, ragwort, Jacob's ladder, water cress, fleabane, spring cress, sweet rocket, catchweed, sweet Cicely all full bloom. Small flowered buttercup coming to the end, its seed burs forming. First green flower on the clustered snake root. Knotweed five feet high. Garlic mustard, late bloom, dominates the woods. Bobwhite calling. First mosquito seen.

1986: First wild strawberry flower noticed today.

1989: Buds well formed on the poppies. Poplar full-leafed now. Tree line a pale green, patchy but predominantly turning. First common fleabane flowers. Knotweed chin high. Hops six to eight feet into the honeysuckles behind the north garden. Horseradish heading up. Sugar maple leaves half size. The white mulberry tree is blooming at the northwest corner of the yard.

1991: Cascades in Glen Helen: Last of the large-flowered trillium in bloom, pink with age, Solomon's plume fresh, full. Some anemone hold. The ground cover belongs completely to Late Spring, garlic mustard towering over the other growth. In town, some iris have been out since the first of May. First orange poppy opened today in the south garden; other yards have many open. Watercress full bloom along Grinnell Road going down towards the river. Horseradish and comfrey early full in the yard.

1993: Brome grass completely formed on the north side of the newspaper office. At school, ginkgo leaves have grown to maybe an inch wide in the past four days. Sweet gum is in flower. Clumps of shepherd's purse have gone to seed. A last magnolia flower holds on the north side of my office building. At home, tulips still full bloom, almost all forsythia flowers fallen, at least half the leafing done. Apple tree full bloom.

1995: The cold spring continues, keeping all the redbuds and dogwoods in middle spring. Tulips are getting old now, but they are also kept in color by the weather. The silver maples have leaves maybe a fourth of their normal size now, and the reds are starting to get their leaves. Quince is still in bloom about town. The late daffodils are still strong in the south garden. Japanese knotweed is almost six feet tall now, dock and burdock lush. Along Grinnell Road, the last of the clump of cowslip flowers weakens, but golden ragwort replaces it. At Grinnell Pond just a little down from the bike path, the woods floor fills in with garlic mustard and violets, middle spring swallowed up. Red columbines hang from the cliffs and rocks.

1998: The Osage are starting to leaf now. Hollyhock stalks are four feet tall. First radishes pulled from the garden yesterday.

2000: To Caesar Creek: Sunny, cool, water and barometer high, northeast wind. Few bites all day; caught one fresh-water drum, silver with a triangular shape. The tree line was greening all along the shore, seemed ahead of the countryside. Bird watching better than fishing: a pair of orioles seen; and my catfish spot had few catfish, but it did have a pair of Prothonotary warblers flying back and forth to their hole in a dead tree. Geese were paired and loud all around me, honking and bobbing and swimming back and forth. Upstream, one pair had three goslings which were the size of my shoe, had been born maybe April 20? Carp were rooting, splashing, frolicking. Flickers and jays and bullfrogs and an occasional toad were calling, swallows swooping. Three yellow tiger swallowtails seen. The river was full of golden winter cress and cressleaf groundsel in full bloom. A buckeye tree still showed flowers at the water's edge. Sycamore leaves: about an inch, elms an inch, cottonwoods and maples maybe half size, Virginia creeper maybe a fourth to a third size.

2001: Ticks and mosquitoes all around at Conrad's estate. Sweet Cicely in full bloom there, along with a large patch of Jack-in-the-pulpit. Very late pink large-flowered trillium. Black snakeroot taking shape. The goose at Conrad's pond had hatched a gosling recently, and wood ducks were nesting. One wild cherry tree was in bloom, another getting ready. At Susi's, the white anemones started to open today.

2003: At 3:45 this morning, only faint twittering from the robins. By four, they were clearly awake. Very first Korean lilac flower opened today. Lily-of-the-valley is still in full bloom on Dayton Street. First purple iris noticed blossoming. Most of the maples, pears, apples, peach trees have filled in around town. Cottonwoods are half green, and the city canopy is close to looking like summer, a rapid and radical transformation in less than a month.

2004: Now all the red tulips under the new red crabapple are disintegrating as the wood hyacinths on the west side of the house reach full bloom.

2005: Lily-of-the-valley is blooming now.

2006: A cardinal sang outside the back door at 5:01 this morning. Some black walnut trees in town are just starting to leaf, pacing the tree of heaven, both varieties still bare among the closing canopy. One black walnut near Casey's, though, is flowering. Silver maples are dropping their giant, winged seedpods. First question mark butterfly of the year seen this afternoon. It came by and landed near me as I was laying bricks for the patio.

2007: First honeysuckle blooms in the alley and in the yard. One violet iris and one sweet rocket seen flowering as I rode back from downtown. Wood hyacinths and lily-of-the-valley full now. The new anemone has blossomed in the apple-tree garden.

2008: Don's pie cherry has set fruit at the same time as the service berries. One purple anemone is open in the apple-tree/circle garden. The first chives are flowering. Silver maples have huge green seed wings, some dropping in the rain. The red maple at the park has reddish seeds. Tomatoes and red onions planted in the north beds. Very first purple hyacinth opened by afternoon. Greg's lily-of-the-valleys are coming in now.

2009: The Korean lilac is starting now in the yard, and the two hawthorn trees at the park are ready to come in. One flower bud is open.

2010: The weekend's rain has made the Korean lilac (in full bloom) lean as though it had been pulled up at its roots. In the alley, bridal wreath, honeysuckles, snowball viburnum, white violets, geraniums in full bloom. White and red mulberry fruit is almost fully formed, but still green and bristly. Multiflora roses budded, box elder trees with seeds. Suddenly early fleabane. In the dooryard garden, the pink azalea continues strong and beautiful. This afternoon, the first skipper flew by the back porch. Locust trees were in bloom all the way to Beavercreek.

2011: Rain and cool continues. Flooding throughout the Ohio and Mississippi valleys. A few alliums open in Liz's front yard.

2012: Close to record heat today, high in the upper 80s. Robins were singing when I went outside this morning at 4:40, and I heard the first cardinal ten minutes later. Honeysuckle, viburnum, Korean lilac and azalea flowers fall heavily now. Knockout roses seen in full bloom throughout Dayton. Fritillary in the circle garden at noon. Locusts and wood hyacinths still strong throughout town and the countryside. Indian hyacinths done for the year, the wood hyacinths starting to discolor. The transition period ahead, past wood hyacinths, should be filled with perennial salvia, blue flags, standard iris, sweet Williams, sweet rocket, clematis, knockout roses, catmint. The phase before that, the phase of the wood hyacinths, includes bleeding hearts, standard lilac, the Korean lilac, and the azalea.

Two fish, Flash (bright gold) and Bubba (white and orange), placed in the water garden, one hardy water lily and ten water hyacinths, too. Dahlias planted south of the porch. From Goshen Indiana, 200 miles northwest of Yellow Springs, Judy writes: "Saw two plants: Dame's rocket and ox-eye daisy that are growing on the banks of our pond out back, along with fading wild ginger and striped white violet, small-flower crowfoot, fringed *Phaecilia*, Solomon's plume, celandine, bristly gooseberry, star of Bethlehem, clustered snakeroot, white spring cress, false rue anemone and common fleabane, along with blue phlox. Just a few large trilliums left there, and a few toad trilliums, but going fast."

2013: First star of Bethlehem opened in the yard, and the trumpet vine is leafing. Liz has two alliums in bloom this morning, her forget-me-nots are very blue, and her poppies have budded. Bridal wreath spirea just starting downtown. From Goshen, Judy reports that the koi in the pond by her condominium are frolicking and splashing around and that goslings have been out for a week or two.

Into the North Glen with Bella: May apples and Solomon's plume with buds, spring beauties and bluebells, the last of the middle spring wildflowers, fresh poison ivy leaves all shiny, leafcup two feet high, nodding trillium, aging pink large-flowered trillium, one last lesser celandine, wild geranium, wood betony, sweet Cicely, Jack-in-the-pulpit, miterwort, meadow rue, bellwort, columbine, sedum, ragwort, small flowered buttercup, catchweed blooming, bloodroot leaves swollen to two or three times the size they were when their blossoms were out. Spicebush leaves were one to two inches long, tinged with red. Skunk cabbage leaves were fully developed, massive, completely covering their wetland.

2014: Poppies budded in the alley. Rose of Sharon, buds having broken a week ago, are slowly leafing, maybe an eighth of an inch.

Bluebells getting floppy. Lilacs late, but still very full around the neighborhood. So many violets in the lawns, many of them very pale lavender. The tallest new bamboo stalk is about eight feet tall. The pink quince has come into full bloom. Lori Young from Springfield sent photos of a family of foxes that shows them nursing and playing between May 3 and 9. The size of the pups would indicate that they were born in early April or late March.

2015: Out at 4:20 this morning to run: robins in early full song when I left, cardinals holding off until 4:40, a wren chattering and Rick's American toads calling when I came down Wright Street at 4:50, doves at 4:55 and a blue jay sharp and strong at 5:00. While I was working at the shop today, Jeanie's Indian hyacinths came into bloom in the circle garden, joining the one white wood hyacinth. The green flowers of the viburnum by the north side of the house are turning white; the azalea buds are fat and red, but they haven't opened yet. The red crab apple flowers still hold above them. More zinnias planted today, no sprouting of previous plantings yet.

2016: Sweet rockets opened on the west side of Jill's outbuilding, probably at the same moment as two of her orange poppies bloomed on the south side. Low white sedum and nodding waterleaf fully open along the bike path.

2017: Arriving in Rome from Barcelona and then riding to Spoleto with Tat to see Neysa and Ivano: locusts seen open along the roadsides (placing the season at about the same point as that of Santiago in Spain), elderberry bushes in flower, hills deep green, hay fields all cut and some hay baled, ginestra blooming. At Neysa's house, small red cyclamen-like flowers scattered among the trees.

2018: Departing for Keuka Lake in western New York with Jill: Allium and Indian hyacinths in the circle garden budded, bamboo sprouts up to three feet. A few poppies and full-blooming forget-me-nots at Liz's house. The tree line is filling with green. The apples are in bloom. In the dooryard garden, the wild geraniums are budding. As we drove north, we travelled parallel to the Great Dandelion Bloom until we reached the long road west in New

York. Then the dandelions slowly thinned, and we left the time of flowering apples and redbuds and entered full daffodil, weeping cherry, star magnolia, pink magnolia, forsythia time and shedding maple time, early April in a normal year and easily three weeks behind the conditions in Yellow Springs.

2019: Pink quince petals starting to fall now. Heavy rain has flooded the porch and the yard – but a few tithonia seeds have survived to sprout, and milkweed stalks are rising now, some four inches. In the south garden area, the bamboo is finally finding its stride, some stalks four feet. One purple allium open, and one Indian hyacinth. One salsify bud at Ellis.

2020: Last night's half inch of rain brought down almost all of Don's wild cherry blossoms, and petalfall is underway for the crab apples. The hyacinths in the circle garden are almost blooming, the state of the year much like that of last year and the year before. Rick reports frogs all over his pond and yard. Christina's pale violet iris are flowering along her south wall. A garden of dark purple sweet rocket is in full bloom near the back entrance to the Catholic cemetery. On the way from our walk, Jill and I saw thyme-leafed speedwell blossoming by the street, and tall blue speedwell in a lawn. Peggy's Korean lilac bushes are still blooming, still very fragrant.

And some of us stayed there forever
With the rambler rose, the lilac,
The blue keen wind.

John Knoepfle

May 4th
The 124th Day of the Year

Come, we'll abroad: and let's obey
The proclamation made for May,
And sin no more, as we have done by staying.
But, my Corinna, come, let's go a-Maying.

Robert Herrick

Sunrise/set: 5:32/7:32
Day's Length: 14 hours
Average High/Low: 69/47
Average Temperature: 58
Record High: 88 – 1902
Record Low: 28 – 1903

Weather

As the first cold front of the month moves into West Virginia and Pennsylvania, high temperatures warm into the 80s twenty percent of the time and into the 70s another 20 percent throughout the Lower Midwest. Sixties occur 45 percent of the days, and highs only reach the 50s on 15 percent of the afternoons. Rain comes one year out of three, and skies are overcast 40 percent of the time. Chances of frost are just five percent.

Natural Calendar

Along the Eastern seaboard, horseshoe crabs are mating, their numbers especially great when the moon is either new or full and the tide is high. Along the 40th Parallel, some touch-me-nots have six leaves, some eight in average years. Knotweed is chin high, hops eight feet. The most precocious poppies have opened. Poplars are well leafed now, and the rest of the tree line is a pale, glowing green. Redbuds get seed pods; scarlet pimpernel opens below them. Clustered snakeroot season starts in the new shade. Eastern wood pewees arrive. Northern spring field crickets have hatched in milder years.

The Shooting Stars
Before dawn, the Eta Aquarid meteor shower brings between ten and 40 shooting stars a minute through Aquarius.

Daybook
1982: Lily-of-the-valley season is just beginning in the middle of hydrangea season. Sedum is blooming, the high canopy filling.

1983: Dogwoods and redbuds in bloom throughout the village. Ragwort and phlox give the lower woods their dominant colors, gold and purple. Three butterflies seen today, one cabbage white, one orange sulphur, one black swallowtail. Rhubarb flowers opening.

1984: Buckeye and dogwood full bloom.

1986: Lily-of-the-valley full bloom. Jack-in-the-pulpits are strong. Oaks appear to open just a little. Hydrangea season. Purple buds on the sweet rockets. They'll bloom this week. First sedum, sweet Cicely, early golden Alexander. Angelica, heavy and succulent, is up to my knees. Thin-leafed coneflowers nine inches, wild petunias four inches. First daisy opens at the south wall. From Grand Lake St. Marys about 100 miles to the north, I received a report that about a third of the goslings are born. They will peak mid May, be all hatched by the first of June.

1987: First sweet rockets open.

1988: Hosta is seven inches, pacing the pokeweed. Ferns unwinding. Cherry flowers falling in the wind, at least half gone. At South Glen, the purple deadnettle is reddening. Penny cress is growing so tall, tall as the winter cress, changing the color of the pasture from its bright, rich, April white and gold to May's green (until the clovers bloom). Redbud still full bloom now, apples and crabs too.

1989: Cherry blossoms almost gone, apples staying near full. Sedum blooming under the high canopy.

1990: End of most flowering fruit trees in town.

1991: First raspberries and locusts bloom. First scorpion fly.

1993: Maggie calls from Madison, Wisconsin: bloodroot gone, bluebells and tulips full, Dutchman's britches full, Jack-in-the-pulpit just out of the ground. Here in Yellow Springs, spring beauties have disappeared, and the blue bellflowers all withered in the last 24 hours. The pyrethrums, geums, astilbe, sweet rocket and daisies have budded, the next tier of flowers ready to replace the last of the daffodils and tulips. Forget-me-nots are at their peak. They are a good transition flower between middle spring and Late Spring. The first two ranunculus opened today. Redbuds and apples still full bloom, apple blossom scent heavy. Pears mostly leafed, many cherries holding. The canopy is half in at Wilberforce, the forest laced with sky and green. Still the luminescent glow of April persists, the violets and pinks and pale greens. Full moon tonight.

1999: Frogs still call. Now bridal wreath is best, and the leaves fill in quickly overhead. Color remains that of bright middle spring, but it is multiplied now by the fattening canopy.

2000: Sweet Cicely in bloom in the south garden.

2001: Orchard grass emerges from its sheaths, so sweet for chewing.

2003: Doves and cardinals both singing at 5:55 a.m. Late tulips still strong in some town gardens.

2005: Redbuds and lilacs hold at full, and most crabapples. The bush crabapples at the triangle park just opened a day or two ago. American beech just starting to leaf. Late tulips hold on very strong in this cool weather. Wood hyacinths open beside them. Pink quince all in bloom, as the red quince flowers fall.

2006: Allium and late red tulips are in full bloom in the yard, allium lush in front of Liz's house on Stafford Street. The bright purple of the redbuds has become dull as the flowers cede to leaves.

2007: Allium buds starting to unfold. Chives buds big and fat (they pace the allium). First pink and violet anemones open as the wood hyacinths reach full bloom. Bridal wreath spirea and snowball viburnum seen for several days around town. Doves mating this morning before dawn, the fourth day in a row that I have seen the ritual. All the redbuds, their flowers killed in early April, are leafing out pretty much on schedule. An indigo bunting visited the backyard bird feeder when Jeanie and I were sitting out about 10:00 a.m., the first time we had seen a bunting here.

2008: A flock of maybe a dozen grackles in Mrs. Timberlake's tree about 10:00 this morning. Iris in the yard well budded; the plants have spread, maybe doubled since last year. Osage trees are barely budded now. Redbuds losing their luster. Red azaleas in the front garden are coming in. The first violet Indian hyacinth opened at about 2:00 this afternoon. Baltimore oriole heard singing in the back trees this afternoon, red-bellied woodpecker on and off. Honeybees humming in the full-blooming pink quince tree by the pond. All of the red quince flowers are gone.

2010: Poppy buds at home, several peony buds cracking, but full bloom of poppies and peonies on Elm Street. Silver olive bushes covered with flowers along the highway south to Xenia. Clematis seen full near downtown. At home under the honeysuckle, the bluebells are almost done. Ranunculus in bloom in front of Don's house, sweet Cicely opening in the alley.

2011: Very first Korean lilac flower. Pink quince full bloom. Our red crabapple blossoms hold well, but petal fall continues at the park. Sweet Cicely barely open. Red quince gone.

2012: Robins very loud from at least 4:30 on this morning. Cardinals once at 5:15, but not prominent at all today. Rhythmic sparrow chanting from 6:00. A hummingbird visited the red feeder today, the first time one has come this close. The first scorpion fly seen in the rose bushes. The second silver-spotted skipper seen in the south garden.

2013: The first pale violet iris seen in bloom at the south side of the house at the corner of Stafford and High. Sweet Cicely is budding in the Phillips Street alley, across from the budding poppies. A brief glimpse of a black swallowtail before I went to work at 10:00. Casey called in the afternoon: He saw the first hummingbird of the year.

2014: In Goshen, Indiana, 200 miles northwest of Yellow Springs, Judy saw "four colors of violets, lavender, yellow ones, carpets of early meadow rue, large-flowered trillium (some just emerging) and toad trillium, spring beauties, one set of Dutchman's britches, some not even blooming." Quite a difference from here in Yellow Springs where the Dutchman's britches were gone a month ago.

2015: Warmth settles across the country. Inventory in the yard: Virginia bluebells and white bleeding heart still full bloom, perennial salvia with small heads, one iris bud, early wild geraniums, the red crab apples full but shedding, red azaleas ready and first one open in the afternoon, Lenten roses full bloom, Peggy's Korean lilac and our pink quince blossoming, garlic mustard and lamium full, common fleabane with first blossoms, some bamboo at eight feet, star of Bethlehem and celandine early full, some Joe Pye sprouts reaching a foot, Endless Summer hydrangea leaves beginning at the base, Liz's first two alliums in bloom, rhubarb half size, Indian hyacinths opening, wood hyacinths starting (so the time of late-spring blue flowers begins), an adult mourning dove with a fledgling (half the size of its guardian) beside it feeding at the feeder, then drinking at the birdbath together. At Antioch, dandelions to seed, apple petals coming down. In Moya's front yard, some of the yellow tulips survive in the middle of her surging weeds. In his yard on the north edge of town, Peter Hayes saw a male and a female Baltimore oriole. The female was carrying nesting material in her beak.

2016: Full dogwoods by the Mills Park Hotel and about town, full snowball viburnum time in the yard and at Don's and more, wisteria flowering at Park Meadows, weigela starting in front of

Mateo's house, my weigela budding, the latest tulips holding in the north garden. Through the countryside, remaining patches of dandelions have gone to seed. Liz reports visits by a female rose-breasted grosbeak from the 2nd through today.

2017: Spoleto, Italy, walking with Tat and Neysa and Ivano in the hills around Campello: Bright orange poppies along the road, climbing roses and rosemary vines full bloom and common, red cyclamens, two varieties of ginestra (but not the thorny kind), winter grain still deep green but heading up well, purple flowers like snapdragons on single hairy stalk with opposite, entire creased leaves, some buttercups, a few iris, a patch of delicate vinca-like plants, four star of Bethlehems. At Fontanelli, vineyards had only a few inches growth, seemed behind those in Galicia a week ago. And no jasmine in bloom.

2019: Petalfall intensifies, petals, pink and white, swept and mounded along the alleys and sidewalks by the yesterday's tide of rain and flooding. Bugleweed (*Adjuga reptans*) is flowering in the lawns. Star of Bethlehem bloomed in the garden overnight. Waiting for Jill in her driveway, I saw two squirrels mating again and again in her silver maple tree. At Ellis, cypress trees have one-inch foliage. The ash grove is just starting to show pale green, but the sugar maple grove is almost completely leafed. On the way to Dayton, several huge gray fields of dandelions gone to seed.

2020: Liz's garden has round purple alliums open, mine still just budded. The first wood hyacinths and Indian hyacinths are starting to open in the circle garden. So much is the same as in years past, especially as in 2015.

Although a life of retreat offers various joys, none, I think, will compare with the time one employs in the study of herbs, or in striving to gain some practical knowledge of nature's domain.

Walafrid-Strabo, Hortulus, 9th Century A.D.

May 5th
The 125th Day of the Year

Wide are the meadows of night,
And daisies are shining there,
Tossing their lovely dews,
Lustrous and fair....

Walter de la Mare

Sunrise/set: 5:31/7:33
Day's Length: 14 hours 2 minutes
Average High/Low: 69/48
Average Temperature: 58
Record High: 90 – 1952
Record Low: 30 – 1907

Weather

May 5 is generally a pleasant day, with a 20 percent chance of a high in the 80s, twenty-five percent of 70s, and 40 percent of 60s, ten percent of 50s, five percent of 40s. Rain falls one year in three; skies are partly to mostly sunny six years in ten; frost occurs ten to 15 percent of the mornings.

Natural Calendar

The season of Late Spring deepens when daddy longlegs begin hunting in the undergrowth and darners are out in the swamps. Cliff swallows migrate as buckeyes and lilacs and garlic mustard come into full bloom. Yellow wood sorrel blossoms in the yard, daisies in the garden, and the first cycle of cabbage white butterflies is often at its peak.

Most dandelions have gone to seed by the time daddy longlegs emerge. Ruby-throated hummingbirds arrive at your feeders then, and golden seal and Solomon's seal come into bloom in the deep woods. There are buds on the black raspberries, mock orange, and mulberries. Sedum opens beside the fading large-flowered trilliums.

The first wave of goslings has emerged from its eggs by this time of the year. The thrush, catbird, and scarlet tanager arrive when wild cucumber sprouts by the rivers and nettles grow past knee high. Oak leaves are the size of a squirrel's ear. Some maples are fully leafed, and some are dropping seeds. All across the country, the high tree line is completely alive either with new glowing foliage or orange buds or golden flowers.

Daybook

1982: The leaf canopy is filling quickly. On the cliffs of the Gorge, columbine is ready to open. Some of middle spring's bluebells, spring beauties, toothwort, and cowslip hold on, but most of the flowers in the woods now belong to Late Spring: Solomon's seal, false Solomon's seal, bellwort, wild phlox, wild geraniums, golden alexander, wood betony, early meadow rue, swamp buttercups, ginger, Jacob's ladder, golden seal (seen for the first time).

1983: Rose of Sharon begins to leaf out, also mock orange. Poppies seen in the village. First fleabane in the yard.

1984: First lily-of-the-valley seen in town

1986: Redbud getting leaves. Scarlet pimpernel just opening below its branches. Clustered snakeroot season starting. First sweet rockets flowering off Grinnell. Larkspur in the middle of its season. Late maples finally leafing. Snowball viburnum full. Dayflower leaves emerged from the ground today.

1987: Grape leaves half size. Hackberry leaves are emerging. The first daisy opened all the way today.

1988: Horseradish flowering. First daisy barely starting to unravel. Osage and rose of Sharon are starting to leaf, oak line still not green. Poplars now fully leafed. Last of the late maples leafing. At Sycamore Hole, two shiners caught, their flanks red, head covered with sharp "horns." Star of Bethlehem bloomed today. Crab apple petals coming down now. Redbud still purple, trillium grandiflorum still full.

1989: Magnificent dominance of garlic mustard in the woods, tall and dense, lush despite last summer's drought; the seeds did better than ever.

1990: Iris have developed buds in the last few days.

1992: Astilbe budding, as well as daisies and pyrethrums. Pink quince full bloom for about three days. Honeysuckle full bloom. First red admiral butterfly seen. Cowslip done for the year.

1993: Ferns have almost reached their full height since the first of the month, and many have opened now, fresh green fronds still curled at the tip. Hosta leaves have unraveled in the east garden. Lupines are budding in the north garden. Most of the cherry petals have fallen. Most of the cowslip is gone. Dayflower foliage is up.

1995: At Jacoby, the fat yellow cowslip is in full bloom among the giant skunk cabbage. Tall white spring cress grows by the brook, golden ragwort beside it, violet wild phlox scattered along the swamp. The slopes are filled with garlic mustard, solid fields of green and white among the still bare trees. Closer to the water, chickweed is tall and spindly, still flowering. A wild cucumber found sprouting near one of the springs. By the road, buckeyes are in full bloom, sweet rockets budding and up to my waist. The first red azalea opened in the east garden this afternoon.

1998: Honeysuckle around the yard is opening now. Full bright yellow cressleaf groundsel throughout the fields. Still full bloom of dogwood and midseason for bridal wreath spirea. First wild strawberries flower in the lawn.

2000: First mock orange flower, first pyrethrum unravels all the way. Full bloom of thyme and horseradish. Red tree peony seen open yesterday. Full blooming hawthorn seen in Dayton, petals falling in the hot breeze. Dogwoods still full, azaleas still full but starting to fade. Flax full bloom, along with the blue and white wood hyacinths and the golden ranunculus. Bamboo has sent up five new shoots, now three feet long. Thirteen leaves on the water lily in the pond. Across the fields, winter cress paling, getting old.

2001: Early full honeysuckle and sweet rocket time along the path. Korean lilac opens at the northwest corner of the house.

2003: A red admiral visited the north garden this morning.

2006: At South Glen, garlic mustard was tall and late, sweet Cicely, ragwort, water cress and wild geraniums full, honeysuckle early full, silver olive full and fragrant, purple waterleaf and sweet rockets starting, May apples fully budded, one fading trillium grandiflorum, one question mark butterfly warming itself on the leaf of a leafcup plant. In the alley, the white lilac has rusted. When I walked Bella again this evening, the purple lilacs were in decline. In the yard, the Korean lilac was opening and the first mock orange had pushed out.

2007: Rachel's ginkgo is just starting to come in (for the second time, thanks to the late freeze). Mateo's Jerusalem artichokes are about a foot tall. The alley willow tree is leafing again, but the foliage is spotty. Some poison ivy leaves fully developed. Blue wood hyacinths continue at their best. Hackberry leaves about a third of their full size. Flax seen north on the highway. Indigo bunting reported by Jayne, most likely in the same migratory group as the one we saw yesterday.

2008: South Glen: Geese still defending their territory. Wood thrush, red-bellied woodpecker and Baltimore oriole heard. Mike also heard several kinds of warblers. The woods has filled with white blooming garlic mustard and white violets. Beneath them, the deep red wild ginger and aging toad trilliums. Touch-me-nots have six to eight leaves. One silver olive bush on the way to the butterfly preserve is full of blossoms. The wild black raspberries are just starting to bud. One blue robin's egg shell found on the path along the river.

In the yard, the late tulips are still very much intact, the lilacs still fragrant. Cressleaf groundsel fully open by the roadside and in the yard. Jeanie and I saw a blue-bodied dragonfly in the circle garden at noon. More coleus planted in the east garden and the bird bath garden, Jerusalem artichokes transplanted to the bedroom window area this evening. Ruby Nicholson called to say that "there was a carpet of white violets" at Tar Hollow in eastern Ohio.

2009: First sweet rocket opened in the yard this morning. Ramps foliage decaying under the mock orange. The first few yellow ranunculus have opened by the east side of the house. Artichokes are up to a foot tall. Late tulips holding. Honeysuckles almost blooming, like the hawthorns in the park. Toad sings about 3:00 p.m. and sang yesterday, too. Robins at sundown, but no grackles then.

2010: Yellow tiger swallowtail in the yard this morning. Standard lilacs disappearing, the Korean lilac still holding full, tulips completely gone. Firefly larva found while working on the foundation for the new shed. Bean leaf beetles have attacked the heliopsis. The cats killed a young bird, probably a sparrow or finch, the first one they have brought home since we started to let them out.

2011: Greg's lily-of-the-valley patch is in early bloom. Rachel's ginkgo leaves are just about full size. A few lilacs are rusting, and bridal wreath is very close to opening, tight white buds straining. Snowball viburnums are open or opening in the yard and into Dayton. The latest tulips hold on in the north garden. One patch of the new red Appledorns is gone, the other still keeping its petals. As I walked Bella this morning before 9:00, song sparrows, house sparrows, robins and cardinals were singing, but no grackles called. In the evening, only robins heard, quieter. When we went to bed, a large black fly kept buzzing around the lamp, a little earlier than last year.

2012: The red-bellied woodpecker continues to call insistently each day. Oakleaf hydrangeas, Annabelle hydrangea, hobble bush hydrangea all are fully budded. White mulberries are completely formed. More knockout roses, spiderworts and sweet rockets come into bloom, bringing color to the side yard gardens. At the south end of High Street, a wild cherry tree is loaded with blossoms.

2013: Walk before dawn with Bella: the sky turquoise and bright pink-orange, the town traffic quiet on this Sunday morning, the doves, cardinals, robins, wrens and song sparrows filling up all the space of the neighborhood. Along Dayton Street in the twilight, I saw what looked like a starling or a robin flapping its wings as though it had been struck by a car and was in its death throes. As I approached, however, death turned to lust as the flopping creature became two mating birds, saw me and chased each other up into the serviceberry in front of Gerard and Helen's house. Late in the morning, the red-bellied woodpecker called; I had been missing him. Petal fall has begun in the park and in the yard, even as the flowers reach their best.

Rick came over around noon, excited to find tiny praying mantises emerging out from their nest-like "ootheca." They were maybe a fourth to three-eights of an inch long and were scrambling out of their winter habitat. He had discovered their sack on the branch of a Bradford pear tree he had cut down, so it is likely, phenologically speaking, that praying mantises typically hatch when pear trees leaf out just after they lose their petals, at the start of Late Spring. And the female laid her eggs five to six months earlier in last year's warm November or December, just before the pear leaves came down.

Later Kathryn called: She had seen two Baltimore Orioles feeding in her maple tree, some of the very first to arrive in southwestern Ohio. All of which puts praying mantis emergence in sync with the arrival of hummingbirds (yesterday's news from Casey) with the arrival of Baltimore orioles and the end of dandelion bloom and the falling of apple petals.

And at Ellis Pond, pawpaw flowers are soft and dark red like wild ginger. Mountain ash has umbels open, the buckeyes and sassafras are in bloom, and the red horse chestnut tree is budded. The sawtooth oak is draped with golden three-inch catkins. And so many of the other trees are leafing, the canopy filling quickly.

2014: In the alley, the bittersweet has leaves almost an inch long. At the edge of the north garden, the tree of heaven has put out nubby branch growth. Also in the north garden, the blue wood hyacinths have started to bloom. At Ellis Pond, late full dandelions, tulip tree leaves about two inches, bur oak and white oak and black oak all with leaves about half an inch to an inch long, scarlet oaks more developed, chestnut oak in flower.

2015: Morning walk into North Glen with Chris: Wild phlox, golden Alexander, wood betony (in full bloom covering an entire hillock), May apples, sweet Cicely, spring beauty, wild ginger, very late trillium grandiflorum, first catchweed, white violets, one nodding trillium, swamp buttercups, small anemone, miterwort, garlic mustard. In the back yard, grackles through the day, and small female house finches, up to four at one time, at the feeder. A female Baltimore oriole came for black sunflower seeds. At John Bryan Park: ragwort common in the woods, thyme-leafed speedwell in the grass, silver olive shrubs full bloom along the roads.

2017: Spoleto, Italy: Walk in the hills toward Campello: Cottonwood cotton piling up in the shallow gutters of the streets, locusts and buckeye-like trees in full bloom. Bladderworts, buttercups, ginestra and sow thistles very common, and a few giant thistles with variegated leaves were budding. Corn was sprouting in the fields, one field of winter grain turning.

2018: Keuka Lake to Ithaca, NY: The hour drive past Seneca Lake into a valley brought full blooming dandelions (and even many to seed) as well as many beds of tulips in the city. From Spoleto, Neysa sends a photo of tiny golden spiders hatching on a sunny green leaf. Tat reports hearing sandhill cranes flying overhead in Madison, Wisconsin.

2019: To Cincinnati with Jill: Sun and mild, the tree line mostly green in many areas. Honeysuckles were opening, cattail foliage was full size, wild cherry trees and silver olive shrubs were in bloom. At Ellis Pond, I found that the wild strawberries had produced their yellow blossoms and that fleabane had grown tall and flowered. In the fields, groundsel is still peaking, and now Canadian thistle foliage is past the top of my boot. At Jill's, her burning bush is in bloom.

2020: Mary Sue sent photos of Baltimore orioles and red-breasted grosbeaks eating oranges at her feeder! Krista announced pawpaws in flower. And from Goshen, Indiana, my sister Judy wrote: "We have goslings! Two plump, fluffy little babies were waddled out by their proud parents this morning. Fewer than usual, but bigger – or else they've been kept hidden a little longer."

Any landscape is composed not only of what lies before our eyes but what lies within our hearts.

D. W. Meinig

May 6th
The 126th Day of the Year

Out of its little hill faithfully rise
the potatoes' dark green leaves,
out of its hill rises the yellow maize-stalk,
the lilacs bloom in the dooryards.

Walt Whitman

Sunrise/set: 5:30/7:34
Day's Length: 14 hours 4 minutes
Average High/Low: 69/48
Average Temperature: 58
Record High: 89 – 1949
Record Low: 31 – 1968

Weather

Suddenly the chances of clear to partly cloudy skies jump from the 55 percent of the last three days all the way to 90 percent. That makes May 6th one of the two sunniest days in May (the 14th is the other day). With all the blue sky, chances of 80s are 15 percent, of 70s forty percent, and of 60s twenty-five percent, leaving only 15 percent for cooler 50s and five percent for 40s.. And from today forward, the chances of a day above 70 degrees are better than 50/50 for the first time since the year began. Thunderstorms often occur with the increasing likelihood of heat. Despite the fact that the skies are rarely totally overcast, showers pass through on this date one year in three.

Natural Calendar

Zeitgebers of this week include the budding of thistles and privet bushes, the reddening of strawberries, the forming of buckeye fruits, the opening of the first peonies, and the full bloom of buckeyes, allium, early yellow roses, meadow goat's beard, sweet rocket, poppies, iris, early mock orange, Korean lilac, red-horse chestnut, wild cherry and locust trees.

Fledgling grackles, sparrows and cardinals are leaving their nests and are begging for food. As mating comes to an end, morning birdsong becomes less insistent. Goslings and ducklings swim the rivers. Lake carp and pond koi are mating. Insects increase in number. The high canopy suddenly fills in. Flowering locust trees join mock orange, honeysuckle and late lilacs to create the most fragrant time of the year throughout the central portion of the United States.

Daybook

1982: First June bug at the front door, 7:35 p.m.

1984: Buds on the honeysuckle and mock orange. Osage and locust just starting. Garlic mustard getting ready to bloom. White and lavender lilacs starting to emerge. Tulips holding. Catalpa leaves coming.

1985: At South Glen, May apples are in full bloom, and the canopy is almost complete. Garlic mustard chest high, late bloom. Blue cohosh is done as well as the meadow rue. It's Early Summer.

1987: As the sweet rockets come in, corn is just sprouting, and the fields of dandelions have gone to seed. Wood sorrel noticed flowering. Sweet Cicely in early bloom. Wood nettle is almost a foot tall. Flies are pesky for the first time. Goslings seen at the river, six babies feeding with two adults on the shore full of grass and violets and garlic mustard. One parent in front, the other behind. At Sycamore Hole, shiner minnows play in the water, full mating time.

1988: First bridal wreath, first snowball, first star of Bethlehem.

1989: Pink quince at southeast corner of the house is in full bloom today. Pale trumpet creeper foliage is out, an inch or two long. Sycamore foliage pacing the white mulberry's.

1990: Half the iris in the yard are budding. Purple deadnettle is yellowing, and dandelions are lanky and old. Only a few red quince remain.

1991: First daisy and pyrethrums unravel in the south garden. In the village, a whole patch of daisies seen. First June bug seen at Wilberforce.

1992: Pears all leafed, canopy closing. Star of Bethlehem and large-flowered anemone full bloom in the south garden.

1993: Virginia creeper leaves have developed to half size in the past week. Ginkgoes and ash a third or more leafed, sweet gum starting to leaf, oaks full bloom, some leafing. Fields of dandelions to seed, other pastures full of bright tall winter cress. In the pussy willow garden, the bugle (*Adjuga reptans*) has opened all at once, and the first lily-of-the-valley is blooming. One fleabane is tall with nodding flower heads. Dwarf iris full bloom in the east garden. First azalea opening. Joel came to school today with the first tick.

1995: At the triangle garden, oak leaves have come out, maybe an inch long. Lindens are filling in now, some leaves an inch long, others two. Petal fall is accelerating, maybe half the petals have come down. Purple lilacs and redbuds still strong. The very first sweet William found at the west end of the north garden. Tulip time is over except for the new appledorns by the mock orange. Blue wood hyacinths have budded and some are open in the south garden. The pink quince has come into full bloom over the past two or three days. The gold buttercups are all the way open, and the red pyrethrums have large buds. Maples fill out quickly. The north, west and east sides of the yard are pretty well filled in with honeysuckle; only the south side is still bare, waiting for the mulberries and the rose of Sharon to come out.

1998: Now the rhododendrons flower and wild cherry comes into full bloom, And poppies throughout town. The tenth leaf of the water lily plant has reached the surface.

1999: Liz calls: morel mushrooms at South Glen, big batch. Today at dusk, long sing-song of a robin. It's summer at Jacoby swamp now, the sweet Cicely has been full for days, the June growth coming up, the nettles and jewelweed through chickweed and catchweed. The east garden is perfect in foliage of hostas and bleeding hearts, ferns and lungworts. Now honeysuckles form a complete shrub barrier around the yard, a barrier that will last through November. Now the red mulberry is leafing, the sweet rockets opening, the iris coming in around town, and the poppies, the late white and violet hyacinths, and the tall cressleaf groundsel.

2000: First dragonfly of the year visited the pond as I cooked hotdogs on the grill.

2001: First red pyrethrum unfolded in the south garden by four o'clock this afternoon. Dutch iris budding in the north garden.

2003: Buds appear on the poppy in the south garden. The very first rhododendron is unraveling. Wild cherry seen in full bloom yesterday along Grinnell Road. The hawthorn at the triangle park is in bloom. Spruce trees there have small one-inch cones. First yellow wood sorrel flower noticed in the strawberry bed. In the north garden, catmint has opened; I can even smell its flowers when I stand away from it.

2005: At South Glen with Mike: Trillium grandiflorum, wild phlox, white and purple violets, spring cress, wild geranium, ragwort, large toad trilliums, buckeyes all in bloom. Chickweed, still in bloom, yellows across the woods floor. Grasses are above my boots now but not high enough to get the calves of my pants legs wet. The far tree line is still mostly brown, even though in town, the maples and pears are almost all leafed out. In the east garden, wild geraniums bloomed a day or two ago. The red azalea is approaching full bloom. In the afternoon, more termites swarmed in the greenhouse.

2006: Bob Parker came to the house the other day. He told me about a pond apple tree, apparently the only one in town, blooming on the north side of Limestone Street. A native of the tropics, this small tree has survived for years in Yellow Springs apparently without ill effects. Its petals resemble those of the pink quince, also in bloom at the beginning of May, and they offer an exotic complement to the end of late-spring fruit tree flowering season.

The center of Late Spring is already closing the canopy over the pond apple. Sycamores, Osage, cottonwoods and oaks are leafing out, and white mulberries and buckeyes blossom. Along the sidewalks, purple iris, orange poppies, sweet William, and florescence of bridal wreath spirea and snowball viburnum have appeared. The delicate Korean lilacs join the fading standard lilac varieties, and bright rhododendrons replace the azaleas.

Serviceberry trees along Dayton Street have small green berries. Daisies unravel, and the bells of the lily-of-the-valley emerge from their green sheaths. Wood hyacinths and star of Bethlehem are at their best.

In Clifton Gorge, columbine is open on the cliffs, and throughout the North Glen, Solomon's seal, false Solomon's seal, bellwort, wild phlox, trillium grandiflorum, wild geraniums, golden Alexander, wood betony, early meadow rue, swamp buttercups, ginger, Jacob's ladder, water cress and golden seal are blooming. White garlic mustard and sweet Cicely still dominate the deep woods of South Glen; violet sweet rockets increase throughout the fields and glades.

2007: First white-spotted skipper seen this morning.

2008: Petal fall accelerating on the crab apples in the park. The first yellow cabbage butterfly seen in the north garden. In the pond, the new tadpoles are still tame, huddled together eating algae. Ranunculus have started to open along the east side of the old house. The very first Korean lilac buds are opening, the first sweet Cicely. Iris seen full bloom in Wilmington this evening. Cowslips still bloom beside the dominant ragwort across from the Covered Bridge. Two blue robin's eggs seen on the sidewalk as we walked downtown. One winged termite caught in the greenhouse at about 11:00 p.m., attracted to the light by Jeanie's chair.

2009: Faint robinsong at 4:00 a.m. Doves come in at 4:55, cardinals at 5:00. No blue jay heard this morning, and the intensity of all the birdsong seems to be gone. Grackles in the alley this morning, but none of the mating excitement. Honeysuckle bushes have finally started to bloom at the same time as sweet Cicely.

From my notes, I can see that 2008 is finally catching up with

2009 – or else this year is slowing down. In Wilmington, the first peonies seen. Silver olive flowers are out. Dwarf larkspur (like the larkspur seen in Troy a few days ago) and white pussytoes on display at the college plant table. This evening, robins and grackles heard as I walked Bella around 7:30. Screech owl in the back lot around 7:15.

2010: Robins, grackles, cardinals and doves loud before dawn. Five blue jays in the yard this morning, the parents screaming and bobbing. A sparrow killed by the cats before breakfast. The first violet iris opened in the yard by 10:00 a.m., the first sweet Williams followed. The deep purple clematis on the trellis and the east fence started to bloom. The Dutch iris are fully budded. Peggy's daisies are opening. The north-side locusts suddenly full.

2011: Robins, cardinals, song sparrows, doves, blue jay – all heard this morning around 9:00. In the alley, huge drooping buds of the poppies, early sweet Cicely. At the circle garden, Indian hyacinths are in full bloom, wood hyacinths coming in. The azalea in the east garden is completely open, and the red crab apple is losing a few petals. Along High Street, bridal wreath spirea is beginning to flower. Robin vespers this evening, and the call of a red-bellied woodpecker. Young raccoons with their mother reported a few days ago. In spite of all the rain of the past two weeks, no mosquitoes seen in the yard.

2012: Another zebra swallowtail this morning. To Fairborn Park: the canopy appears to be complete all around. Cottonwood cotton there in the pond.

2013: Sweet rocket and sweet Williams well budded, quince petals all over the pond, bamboo at least five feet now. Bella and I startled a female mallard in the pine grove at Ellis Pond. She flew off, leaving eleven eggs in her nest.

2014: Liz's alliums have started, five blooms beside her forget-me-nots. Lily-of-the-valley has started to bloom at the Champneys' house. Light petal fall along Dayton Street. Several yards with dandelions all to seed. First star of Bethlehem opened in the north garden; the spring has been so cold that they are about two-weeks late.

2015: A second red admiral, this one resting in the sun on the side of the shed. A turtle seen run over on the road near the wetlands in Beavercreek. Bugle (*Adjuga reptans*) is blossoming, its blue-purple flowers standing straight up in the lawn on the Stafford/Dayton Street corner, dandelions to seed throughout, burning bush starting to flower at Peggy's, first iris open in the yard and along Limestone Street. In the alley, the bluebells are gone (but still good at home), and the bittersweet has buds, half-developed leaves. All about the neighborhood, honeysuckles are budded and should bloom any day, some banks of full azaleas seen.

2016: Rick reported a bald eagle circling above his property at 5:30 this evening.

2018: At Keuka Lake, the weeping willow is yellow green, foliage thin, the space of its branches translucent and allowing the lake and the sunrise to come through. A spindly cherry is flowering, and a couple of lost daffodils and grape hyacinths. At the dock, the birch has leaves half an inch long. Near the house, the silver maple is shedding seeds.

2019: Catchweed, ranunculus and sweet Cicely in flower around the yard. Snowball viburnums all around town, and the white-flowering viburnum Jeanie and I bought in Asheville sa many years ago is filled with blossoms, peaking as the crab apple nearby loses its pink-red petals. At Ellis in the evening, raucous and explosive mating competition of six geese. Leslie reports a scarlet tanager, a catbird, a great-crested flycatcher and a magnolia warbler singing in her yard.

2020: The circle garden gradually reveals its hyacinths now from among the daffodil foliage as peony buds crack a little to show their inner color. In the dooryard garden, the first azalea buds have opened. Three milkweed stalks have risen almost a foot through the weeds in the north garden. Down High Street, Jill and I saw a few early sweet rockets and one Shasta daisy blooming.

Language of flowers….Angry tulips with you darling manflower punish your cactus if you don't please poor forget-me-not how I long violets to dear roses when we soon anemone meet all naughty nightstalk wife Martha's perfume.

James Joyce

May 7th
The 127th Day of the Year

Star-eyed strawberry-breasted
Throstle above her nested
Cluster of bugle blue eggs thin
Forms and warms the life within;
And bird and blossom swell
In sod or sheath or shell.

Gerard Manley Hopkins

Sunrise/set: 5:28/7:35
Day's Length: 14 hours 7 minutes
Average High/Low: 69/48
Average Temperature: 58
Record High: 87 – 1897
Record Low: 28 – 1974

Weather

Mild to warm weather is the rule today: 25 percent of the highs reach the 80s, twenty-five percent are in the 70s, and 40 percent are in the 60s. Only ten percent remain in the cold 50s, and frost arrives just one morning out of ten. Chances of rain remain stable at 30 percent, close to the same percentage as the other days in the first week of May. Although the sun does not usually shine as much as it does on May 6, the 7th has its share of blue skies: 70 percent of the days bring at least a few hours of sunshine.

Natural Calendar

The second major wave of migrating songbirds usually reaches the Lake Erie shore near Toledo. It includes almost all the Ohio species, with dominants being white-throated sparrows, ruby-crowned kinglets, yellow-rumped warblers, magnolia warblers, tanagers, grosbeaks and orioles. Along the coast of the southeastern United States, loggerhead turtles crawl ashore to lay their eggs between now and August.

Daybook

1983: Honeysuckle and lilacs bloom, first lily-of-the-valley and comfrey budding. Skunk cabbage fully developed, each plant's foliage about two feet high, a foot and a half across. Toothwort finally gone, fading completely in the first week of May. Last cowslip at Jacoby.

1985: I heard the first crickets of the year (the Northern Spring Field Cricket) out in the field, past the new spitbugs hanging to the parsnips. First locust in bloom. Buckeyes done, redbuds fully leafed. Some ragwort going to seed. Purple dwarf larkspur discovered. Lizard's tail a foot and a half at the river bank. Dock is seeding. Canadian thistle is heading at Wilberforce.

1986: Cardinals singing by 4:40 a.m. Catalpas and oaks leafing. The upper canopy suddenly begins to thicken. In Dayton, all the trees seem all green, even if thin. Wilberforce: Sweet clover is one to two feet tall now, milkweed a foot. Chamomile is getting petals. First wild mallows (cheeses) bloom.

1987: Wood sorrel, sweet Cicely, first fleabane open. Ichneuman seen at Wilberforce, also first scorpion fly.

1988: First yellow swallowtail. Catchweed blooms, garlic mustard peaks, first large poppy bud, first daisy unravels, first fleabane, first raspberry flower, pink quince and buckeyes full bloom, mulberries leafing and have small berry clusters. New pine growth prominent, paler green against the old dark. Spring completely out of hand now.

1989: Virginia creeper has leafed on the sycamores, its leaves tinged with red. First sweet Cicely blooms. Orchard grass fully formed and blooming. Last cowslip flower seen. Locust leaves two inches at Wilberforce.

1990: Ginkgo leaves half size. The yard two-thirds closed in with honeysuckles. High locusts starting to leaf. Forsythia all leafed out, flowers gone, first clipping done on the front bushes. Tree of heaven has one-inch leaves. Last cherry blossom falls. Rhubarb gone to seed.

1991: New mullein sprouts well established, one-inch long. First clematis half open. Azaleas full bloom. Last days of the redbud, overwhelmed with leaves.

1992: Fields of April's purple deadnettle have turned honey brown. Squirrel, a third of its adult size, comes to the bird feeder. Fox kit, size of a house cat, killed on Grinnell Road.

1993: Janet Hackett reports more Jack-in-the-pulpit than she's ever seen at the Cascades, and the trillium at their late peak, turning pink, shooting star full bloom. At the Covered Bridge, the flowers of middle spring are gone, chickweed is all lanky now. Jacob's ladder full bloom, wild geraniums, some spring beauties, spring cress tall and very prominent. Wood nettle is over a foot high, angelica up to my waist. First daddy longlegs, first clustered snakeroot buds. High canopy closing rapidly. Four-o-clocks have just sprouted at the west wall, iris budding along the north border. Wood hyacinths are the last bulbs blooming in the south garden.

1994: To Cumberland Island, southeastern Georgia: The landscape there is at the end of a Yellow Springs Early Summer, the beginning of Middle Summer. White clover, white sweet clover, yellow and orange daylilies, Mexican hat, wayside goat's beard, moth mullein, purple flowered arrowhead, prickly pear cactus, mimosa trees, and elderberry bushes at the height of their bloom. Horseweed is three feet tall, cattail inflorescence thin and rising through its foliage, beach pennywort is budding, white flower grass is fading.

1996: The cold and wet spring continues. The river has been high for what seems like weeks. The apple and cherry trees are losing their petals, but have held on so late this year. In the woods, buckeye trees are still in flower. Toad trillium and grandiflorum are still open, garlic mustard just starting. Toothworts have gone. Wood nettle is six to ten inches. Some tulips are holding on, some daffodils, too. The first buttercups bloomed in the south garden a few days ago. In the east garden, the azaleas just started to open yesterday, bleeding hearts lush. Crab apples still in full bloom throughout the village, redbuds still open. Dogwoods late, coming in now.

1998: First poppy at home. Twelve leaves now up on the water lily. Flags well headed. Iris in all over town.

1999: At Jacoby, just inside the gate, sweet Cicely and buttercup bloom here and there among the pale green mats of chickweed, the chickweed which is like baby's breath covering the hillsides. Across the stream, a tall stand of ragwort, perfectly deep golden. Here at home, the mock orange and pyrethrum buds are splitting at the same time, flowers starting out.

2000: The first deep purple clematis was open when I came home from work at 7:30 this morning. When I sat by the pond, I saw that the first pale long-bodied spider (*Tetragnatha elongate*) had spun its modest web strands above the pond's waterfall.

2001: Suddenly the locusts are in full bloom everywhere, and the first pale violet iris blossomed in the yard this afternoon.

2002: Returning from Santee Reservoir in South Carolina, returning from summer to spring: Climbing into the Virginia mountains, dogwood found in bloom. Near Charleston, West Virginia, wild cherry and locust, red clover and daisies open. In southeastern Ohio, some blue iris seen, and wheat was about a foot and a half tall. Back in Yellow Springs to azalea time and the end of dandelion season.

2003: One scorpion fly seen in the south garden this afternoon, the first of the year. The first June bug of the year got in the house last night.

2005: A termite inspector came out today, and while we talked he mentioned he had trapped 28 coyotes in Clifton Gorge between December and January last year (at the request of the county). A healthy environment creates so many large predators.

2007: Many coleus planted in the south garden shade today. New, tall *Camassia*/Indian hyacinth opens in the apple-tree garden.

2008: Violet iris seen at Limestone and Stafford, bridal wreath opening (appropriately) at Katie's house as she plans her wedding. One of our iris plants in the north garden has a purple bud. Petals from the pink quince are falling into the pond now; the fall started yesterday. Two days ago in the sun, the flowers were full of honeybees, the sound of their wings soothing, strong. The red crabapple in the east garden is losing petals all at once, the ground rose-pink with its flowers. In the park, almost all the crabs have fallen. The American beech there has suddenly leafed, and the tall beech on Dayton Street is about half leafed. A few white daffodils still bloom in the yard of the house across from Mrs. Timberlake's. Spruce trees show small cones and inch-long pale green growth. In the afternoon, a titmouse sang repeatedly and visited the feeder. Sitting outside at about 8:15 this evening, I heard a steady, rhythmic call in the woods, some kind of wood frog I believe, or possibly a kind of toad.

2009: The toad sang again yesterday evening. This morning, I heard the screech owl in the back woods at 5:45 a.m. The Korean lilac has reached early full bloom, and a bed of violet iris along Limestone Street is completely open. Driving to Maumee Bay State Park on Lake Erie this afternoon, we traveled a week to ten days back into Late Spring. Dandelions were in full bloom again, and we saw many late pear trees and white and pink crab apples. Silver olive shrubs were only budded, cottonwoods two-thirds developed. Red-winged blackbirds were mating throughout the swamps and grasslands. Willows were shedding catkins, sumacs leafing; buckeyes were in bloom, blackberries were budded, iris budded. A white crowned sparrow and yellow warbler identified, and a tree swallow. Baltimore orioles and a great egret seen. Wild black current with yellow flowers (*Ribes americanum*) found.

2010: Male cardinal feeding its baby this morning before dawn. First stella d'oro lily opened overnight, first catchweed flowers and first flowers of the trellis wisteria noticed. Iris full bloom in town.

Standard lilacs collapsing quickly, almost all gone, even the Korean lilacs starting to rust. Petals are falling now from the red azalea in the east garden. White clover and black medic seen, dogwood blossoms suddenly disappearing, mock orange coming in now. Mary and Rick said their koi were starting to mate this week.

2011: To Goshen, Indiana, found April there in late forsythia, mid-season tulips and daffodils, the landscape more luminescent, the trees only beginning to leaf, birches, pears and pink magnolias in late full bloom. Maggie called from Wisconsin, daffodils and tulips there, she said, and bluebells at their best, a few bloodroot still in flower. In Yellow Springs, the dogwood and spirea transition to the center of Late Spring, and the buttercups in the east yard have come into bloom.

2012: Robins and cardinals steady before dawn, robins continuing through the morning. Few grackles at the feeders now, only sporadic. Sparrows far fewer, none of the giant flocking of dozens that occurs in the winter. In the north gardens, more sweet rockets are coming in, filling the spaces between the red roses and the violet iris, catmint and spiderwort. Japanese honeysuckle and wild grapes opening along the street.

2013: Throughout the suburbs and the countryside, dandelions are going to seed all at once, just as the apple blossoms blanch and fall together. Dogwoods, azaleas, wisteria, bridal wreath spirea, lilacs and late pink quince are softening the transition to summer foliage. One of my peony buds is showing color. Spiderwort is budding beside the perennial salvia budding. The very first honeysuckle flower found along the northwest hedge. The red-bellied woodpecker called throughout the afternoon.
    At South Glen, I walked through glades of sweet Cicely and pale, dense chickweed (that spread throughout the forest floor), flanked by golden ragwort and purple wild phlox and wild geraniums, a few spring cress in flower, and garlic mustard. Sweet rockets, waterleaf and black snakeroot were budded, wood nettle coming up through the chickweed, nodding trilliums and large-flowered trilliums all spent, toad trilliums overwhelmed by the new growth, wild ginger still blooming soft and red beside them,

twinleaf leaves grown huge like bloodroot leaves, and showing a long green seedpod. In the woods, where the high canopy was turning green, a red-bellied woodpecker was calling, just like at home. Off near the river, I could hear a toad or a cricket, intermittent.

2014: Red quince, dogwoods, aging redbuds, many crabapples still open, and the first pale violet iris in bloom along Limestone Street. The last tulips are still in flower, and the small white daffodils. The larger of our two small blueberry bushes is blossoming now.

2015: Crows at 5:00 a.m. surrounded by intense birdsong of all kinds. When I was running (gibbous moon clear and high in the southwest), I finally noticed the bridal wreath spirea in full bloom. And all around, the broad-leafed dogwoods. The circle garden: wood and Indian hyacinths and allium reaching full flower. In the dooryard: the red azalea brilliant, the red-pink crab apple petals covering the path from the gate with soft color. The wisteria on the porch's north end has well-developed leaves and one bud, and the trumpet creeper on the porch's south end, and the wisteria on the north trellis are starting to leaf, the wisteria with clusters in bloom. The first male tiger swallowtail flew excitedly through the back trees around noon.

2016: Cloudy and warm. Bushes clipped for the first time. More zinnias planted this morning. At about 1:30 this afternoon, I heard humming in the back yard, went out to find a swarm of honeybees hovering overhead. After a while they moved down and settled on the scraggly old paulownia tree. They were gone by 2:40 p.m. In 2006, a swarm came through on May 29.

    Inventory: Indian hyacinths suddenly gone, allium early full bloom, wood hyacinths still strong, the north-side snowball viburnum full and bright, honeysuckles full, a few last white tulips, full celandine and wild geraniums and lamium and ranunculus, ferns and hostas completely grown and filling in the garden along the north wall of the house, iris throughout town, the yellow bell-flowered bulbs I planted last fall have been in bloom for about a week. First hummingbird seen in the garden.

2018: From Keuka Lake to Yellow Springs: Starting from pear and forsythia and weeping cherry and dandelion bloom, Jill and I drove southwest past mountains faint with blossoms, undergrowth definitely greening, cottonwoods near the steams half leafed and bright, along roadsides that had lost their dormancy since our trip in the middle of April, across the upper arm of Pennsylvania with relatively little change, until we went down past Cleveland toward the heart of Ohio where we saw the first redbud come in about a hundred miles north of Yellow Springs, and then the honeysuckles created a barrier against the highway, the tree lines were no longer the prepubescent golds and oranges of the northern mountains but glowed with fresh April greens (but not the richer May greens). Full dandelion bloom persisted well into the central counties, gray seed heads finally replacing the yellows near Yellow Springs.

2019: The first poppies seen open along Elm Street today, the first iris (golden) on Short Street, the first purple sweet rocket (but I can't remember where). Leslie reports the first cranefly and the first June bug at her screen door. Throughout the village, the most fragrant time of year begins. While the favored generations come to flower and grace lawns and gardens with gentrified beauty, other, less beloved plants carry on their cycles in spite of all the efforts of nativists and exterminators.

In the unplanted fields beyond Ellis Pond, the March and April weeds are all going to seed: shepherd's purse, peppergrass, penny cress, bittercress, dandelions, the small verbena that Jeanie called "blue eyes" and the common chickweed That first wave of the weedy wildflowers bloomed in the very first days of Early Spring alongside of the furrows that had just a year ago been saturated with herbicides. Allowed to flower and seed protected by the heavy rains of April and early May, they will doubtlessly return next year. The more acceptable wildflowers, the spring beauties that lined the path have also disappeared, only the violets holding.

The next generation of rank weeds confidently takes the place of the first. Golden wintercress, garlic mustard, sticky catchweed and cresleaf groundsel, unharmed by the poisons of commercial farming, replace the purple deadnettle that has turned gray and beige in age. Hardy dock grows knee high, hemlock lanky and bushy and branching. Salsify is budding. Basal plantain leaves fill in the bare spaces of the path beside the new prickly thistle stalks. Escaped from domesticated pastures, orchard grass pushes out to fill the waysides. Spitbugs create protective foam on the new parsnip foliage.

I had no inclination to read or to write, but only to spend the hours looking upon the earth's April beauty, so lavishly spread before me here, listening to the field sparrow's song, and smelling the fragrances of the leaves, the musk of the turned soil, the delicate perfume of the pasqueflowers, spending the hours in the sure knowledge that none would ever come again.

August Derleth, *A Countryman's Journal*, April 15

Bill Felker

May 8th
The 128th Day of the Year

In the flowers find a solace,
Fleeting cure for every sadness,
Fragrant physic for your longing,
Certain aid for loneliness.

Celtus

Sunrise/set: 5:27/7:36
Day's Length: 14 hours 9 minutes
Average High/Low: 70/49
Average Temperature: 59
Record High: 89 – 1926
Record Low: 30 – 1947

Weather

Today's high gets above 70 on 60 percent of the years (and a third of those years in the 80s). Mild 60s occur one day in four, and cooler 50s or 40s can be expected fewer than one in five. With the arrival of the second major high-pressure system of the month, there is a possibility of a return of Lilac Winter today and tomorrow, and frost has been recorded in my weather history more often this morning than on any other in May: it strikes 20 percent of all the years. The sun shines 85 percent of the time, making May 8 one of the brighter days of the month. Chances of rain are only one in four, and that makes May 8 one of the two driest days of the month (the 16th is the other prime day for field and garden work).

The Weather in the Week Ahead

An average day in May's second quarter brings rain 25 to 40 percent of the time. The 8th, 11th and the 13th are likely to the driest of the week, the 12th and 14th the wettest. Typical highs almost always reach above 60 degrees after the 10th of May, and they rise to 70 or above at least 60 percent of the afternoons. May 11 is the day with the warmest weather history of the month: a full 50 percent of May 11ths bring temperatures in the 80s, something which doesn't happen again until June 1. Also after May 10, the chances of a killing frost drop below five percent.

Natural Calendar

When apple blossoms fall, then the first sweet rocket, fleabane, sweet Cicely, daisy, fire pink, common plantain, white clover, chamomile, black medic, star of Bethlehem, lily-of-the-valley, sweet William, meadow goat's beard, May apple, and wood sorrel almost always open.

The woods are filled with garlic mustard, green and white among the still bare trees. It's the best time of all for blue forget-me-not, golden ragwort, water cress, wild geranium, miterwort, swamp buttercup, late toad trillium, late trillium grandiflorum, late winter cress, white spring cress and the wild purple phlox.

Mock orange and strawberries come into full bloom when the last crabapple petals are gone. A few early poppies and peonies unravel then. Early iris and lupines are budding. Astilbe and clematis have formed flower heads. Summer hostas are eight to ten inches tall. Ferns, daylilies, comfrey, summer phlox have reached almost two feet. In the parks, the paths are thick with violets.

Mayflies are out along the water. Bullfrogs call. Minnows and chubs are flushed red for their mating season. Flea time begins for pets, a sign that insect activity is nearing the economic threshold on the farm. Spitbugs grow in the shelter of swamp parsnips, announcing that the first cut of hay will soon be underway. The first small groups of monarch butterflies that left Texas in February cross the Ohio River. Flies become pesky in the mild afternoons.

The Stars

Cassiopeia and the Milky Way lie on the northern horizon before midnight. Cygnus rises from the northeast, Ophiuchus from the east, Sagittarius and Libra from the southeast. Centaurus and Corvus are low on the southern horizon, Virgo above them. Hydra snakes across the southwest. Monoceros is setting in the west, Gemini going down due west, Capella and Perseus disappearing into the northwest.

As Leo with its bright Regulus moves off to the west by ten

o'clock at night, the likelihood of frost diminishes sharply, and tender bedding plants, tomatoes and peppers can be set out - as long as you are prepared to protect them on cooler nights. When Leo has moved well into the southwest, and Arcturus is almost in the center of the sky, lanky Hercules behind it, and the Milky Way fills the southeast, then frost should stay away until October.

Daybook

1982: Lily-of-the-valley blooms. Canopy developing quickly, honeysuckle blooming.

1984: Covered Bridge: A few last violet cress, spring beauties. At home, sweet rockets are starting to send up their flower stalks. Sweet Cicely foliage strong, but no buds yet. Jacob's ladder open. Crab apples still in full bloom this Late Spring. Magnolias dropping more petals.

1986: First mock orange flowers.

1988: Catalpa leaves an inch long. No sweet rockets yet. Henbit tall and thick, bright purple, dominant in parts of the yard and taking over from the violets. Several patches of blue iris seen in town. High canopy still not full. Garlic mustard chest high. First June bug gets in the house. At South Glen: honeysuckles, sweet Cicely, catchweed blooming. Purple deadnettle yellows, chickweed patches decaying. Goldenrod six inches high. Dogbane spears like asparagus, eight inches. Carp mating in the stubby lizard's tail along the river bank.

1990: In the yard, just a few tattered tulips left. Lilies are up to a foot and a half high. Forget-me-nots and yellow buttercups are lush. Pyrethrums and daisies about to unravel. A few poppies have big buds. Dogwood still holds full. Tonight, a full moon walk at the Indian Mound: canopy still open enough to follow the path. Fireflies glowing in the flowers. Spitbugs visible on the plants. Columbine, May apple, garlic mustard, sweet rocket, waterleaf in bloom. Some phlox. Swamp full of late, golden winter cress. One white campion identified in the pale moonlight, a few wild geranium, sweet Cicely.

1991: First spider web of the year seen near the comfrey. Dogwoods and lilacs hold on, mock orange early bloom.

1993: First star of Bethlehem opens at the garden gate. Comfrey and horseradish are budding.

1995: At South Glen, the cream-colored six-petaled cohosh is in late bloom. The first catchweed is flowering. Lizard's tail has two to three leaves along the river bank. Last of the bluebells at home.

1998: Four out of our five rhododendrons are opening now. First mock orange here, but others in town well developed. Fourteen leaves on the water lily. Patches of daisies by the roadside.

2000: Azalea petals fall all at once now as two purple rhododendrons, one poppy, three daisies open; mock orange and golden ranunculus are close to full bloom, like iris and poppies throughout town. Thirteen leaves on the water lily in the pond.

2001: A yellow tiger swallowtail crossed the yard this afternoon. At Washington Courthouse, white and red clover, black medic seen. Wheat deep green, close to a foot and a half high. Cressleaf groundsel has replaced winter cress in the uncultivated fields. Sunset observed driving back from school: 8:37 p.m. exactly, versus the 8:36 on my sunrise/sunset tables.

2002: Columbus: Korean lilac is in full bloom, azalea, wisteria, honeysuckle. The courtyard canopy at school is near completion, including the white oaks. All along the 50 miles between Yellow Springs and Columbus and then 30 miles south to Washington Court House, the dandelion heads are white, the end of their great spring bloom. At home, rhubarb is three feet tall.

2003: To Madison, Wisconsin: Locust flower clusters are the landmarks all the way to the Illinois border, the canopy well filled at about the same level as in Yellow Springs. By about 50 miles south of Rockford, Illinois, a little south and west of Chicago, we overtook the spring dandelion bloom. One redbud seen at

Rockford, then full-blooming dandelions into Madison. In the city: more redbuds, full-blooming crab apples, late pink magnolias, early purple and white lilacs, trillium grandiflorum, lungwort, Jack-in-the-pulpit, bleeding hearts, daffodils, tulips, bluebells, violets, a yellow bellwort-like flower, and a few iris (which seem to follow more of a solar cycle than one based on temperature – since they are also starting now in Yellow Springs).

2004: Locusts seen in Dayton full bloom three days ago. Yesterday in the woods, a Baltimore oriole and a great-crested flycatcher seen. In the east garden, sweet rockets are coming in. The first clematis flowers unfolded this morning. Sweet Cicely blossoms in the west garden. Lamb's ear is heading up near the pond. Purple loosestrife transplanted from the pond to the ground, stems about two feet tall. Russian sage sprouts are two to four inches long, butterfly bush and Joe Pye weed to about 15 inches, Most hosta foliage seems summer size. Pink quince flowers are almost all gone. Some of the fresh bamboo stalks have grown up to eight feet.

2005: Bamboo has been leafing for several days now. The red azalea is in full bloom, and the late tulips that have held for weeks. Hackberry just starting as petal fall deepens, most early apples gone (but some late apple trees and shrubs still full), pink quince just starting. Osage orange starting to leaf, is behind the hackberry. White mulberry now expands quickly, pacing the sweet gum, the sycamore, the American beech. Very first Korean lilac flowers open. Wild geraniums in full bloom in the front garden. Iris budded under the peach tree.

2006: American beech leaves, after their deliberate, low start, are well developed now.

2007: First spiderwort opened overnight. Red-bellied woodpecker heard once just before dawn. Anemones continue to bloom in the apple tree garden, highlighting the violet wood hyacinths, the pink-violet dead nettle, the allium and chives (coming in together), and the Indian hyacinths. Poppies seen full in Xenia and along Elm Street. Ramps have all withered. Resurrection lilies have collapsed. Bluebells done under the mock orange. Comfrey completely open.

Star of Bethlehem continues to provide significant blooms to the early May north garden. Mrs. Timberlake's wild geranium garden shows how banks of that flower can create a fine late April and May bed. First tiger swallowtail seen this afternoon.

2008: Honeysuckle is opening along the north garden hedge. Horseradish is suddenly full bloom beside the rhubarb. The red azaleas are still strong, but the standard lilacs are starting to decline in the alley – just as the Korean lilac is coming in beside the porch and the hyacinths are filling the circle garden with violet and pale pink. Song sparrow calls seem to be replacing the cardinal and dove calls. The yard is so green today, the sky gray, light rain, everything glowing with new life. Down Grinnell Road, the white water cress flowers are thick by the spring. Two clumps of sweet rockets, the first seen this year, are in bloom on the way south from Xenia. The tree line along the way to Wilmington is bright and filling in, maybe about the same as Savannah, Georgia, was in the last week of March (six weeks, then, ahead of southwestern Ohio). Corn is up two inches in the fields, winter wheat at least a foot tall, quivering in the wind. Pollen spikes have appeared on the pond iris plants.

2010: To Cincinnati in the morning, gray skies, hard wind and cold: Locusts in bloom the whole way. I made a fire for Jeanie before I left, and we kept it going throughout the day after I got back. In the yard, violet sweet rockets and violet iris provide quiet early May color, and at the southwest corner, the mock orange buds have all opened. I covered the hydrangeas and many of the lilies against frost after supper.

2011: More rain overnight. Robins before dawn, then the red-bellied woodpecker called steadily. Ruby saw the first hummingbirds at her feeder yesterday. Don's cherry has lost its last petal, and a few of his iris have budded. The petals of our red crab apple are almost all down, and the pink quince is starting to shed into the pond. First spicebush swallowtail seen on the Korean lilac.

2012: Starling and cowbird fledglings at the feeder. Robins

peeping steadily throughout the day, probably talking to their young. Along High Street, very early privet blossoms. Locust leaves and many black walnut leaves about half size. Kousa dogwoods full at the park. Meadow goat's beard seen on the way to Fairborn, and budded bull thistles and very tall opening hemlock. Red clover, fields of white clover, lots of yellow sweet clover, some multiflora roses, the last of the garlic mustard, and sweet Cicely all gone. A huge sow thistle blooms downtown across from the health food store. Chives and allium hold. One columbine in bloom near Lawson Place, and a few of Peggy's orange Asiatic lilies have opened. Honeysuckle and wood hyacinth flowers disappearing quickly, oak leaf hydrangea buds increasing quickly. A medium-size camel cricket found in the tub this morning; Jeanie found one in the laundry room last week.

2013: Blueberry bushes are flowering now, allium gaining momentum. The Korean lilac came into bloom overnight, the standard lilacs and wisteria keeping their petals well. A deer surprised in the back woods this morning. The lilies will probably disappear this year when I am gone, just like when we left in 2011. A pair of grackles and the red-bellied woodpecker active around the yard through the day.

    I sent Cathy in Vermont a copy of my description of the great dandelion bloom on Cross-Quarter Day (April 21) here in Yellow Springs. She wrote back:
"I could change your date of April 21 and everything you said would describe what it is like here right now. This is 2-1/2 weeks after Cross Quarter time. Of course, we are further north. I went out delivering with Charles and Andrew this afternoon and the tree blossoms were like a carnival, every kind of pink and bunches of white. The lilacs were even budding out. A few days ago there were forsythia everywhere you looked, and they seemed especially bright."

2014: Along Phillips Street, snowball bushes are almost in full flower, and daisies are leaning across the sidewalk, budding. Joe Pye Weed uncovered in the back garden, overgrown, maybe half a foot tall, spindly. The pink quince is dropping its pale petals, and they cover much of the pond, hiding its silt and algae. On the north side of the house, the apple tree by the gate is still in full bloom, a deep red-pink, and the viburnum has put out all its flowers. First glimpse of a tiger swallowtail as I was eating lunch on the back porch. Ellis Pond at 4:00 this afternoon: toads screaming, water cress leaves deep green, full bloom of its white flowers.

2015: Robins singing when I went outside at 4:00. I heard the first cardinal at 4:20. At John Bryan Park, drifts of dandelions to seed beside large patches of ragwort. Redbuds fading and leafing now, silver olives still full. The first common fleabane and the first ranunculus opened by the pond today. The pink quince on the south side of the house has lost all its petals, as has the red crab apple in the front. The lungwort flowers are finally gone, and its leaves are growing now. Pachysandra has put on fresh growth. The azalea remains full and bright. A male tiger swallowtail seen downtown this afternoon, and the first sweet rocket flowered by the trellis. In the Atlantic, an early hurricane is expected to come ashore in the Carolinas within a couple of days.

2017: Inventory listing on my return from Spain and Italy after an absence of fifty-three days: Mock orange, Korean lilac, Kousa dogwoods, tulip trees, one peony plot, red-flowered "buckeyes," white and pink bleeding hearts, wisteria (some), allium, honeysuckle, garlic mustard, celandine, Jeanie's blueberry bush, poppies, great ragwort, daisies, celandine, sweet Cicely, common fleabane, star of Bethlehem, locusts, late hyacinths, spiderwort, weigelas, the red dooryard azalea (just ready to collapse), east patch of ranunculus (having spread over a number of square yards now, iris, catchweed, ground ivy, lamium, violet clematis, sweet rockets all in full bloom. Budding: peonies, grapes, astilbe, woodland hydrangea. The canopy has not filled in all the way here like it has in Spain and Italy, but the locust flowers perhaps are giving a premature sign of the end of Late Spring.

2018: Inventory on returning from Keuka Lake with Jill after four days away: While I was gone, the red crab apple tree near the dooryard came into full bloom, and hostas in the dooryard garden itself had suddenly risen up over the sprawling snowdrops, and pressed in against the hellebores, which receded before the broad hosta foliage. The buds of the old azalea shrub were just starting to reach out, and the first wild geraniums in that triangle of the garden were open.

Along the east wall of the house, small-leafed celandine was in bloom, and the buttercups were starting. All around the front yard, the forsythia shrubs now provided almost a complete barrier against the street. In the south garden, some bamboo had grown to more than six feet, the gangly lilac shrubs had a few lilacs and the pink quince was in full flower. In the circle garden, the Indian hyacinths were coming in, and the sheaths of the wood hyacinths were pushing up from their basal foliage..

Beside the north side of the house, the ferns, which had been slow to respond to the first warm days, were now spreading out, and the peonies had buds half an inch across. The viburnum was straining to bloom to catch up with the viburnums blossoming around town. The trellis wisteria had a few fat blossom clusters. The buds of Jill's poppies were huge and heavy, ready to open up, and her sweet rockets were fully budded.

2019: To Keuka Lake and a return to Early and Middle Spring: Pink magnolias, weeping cherries, crab apples, late pears, forsythia, daffodils, tulips, dandelions, garlic mustard all in full bloom. A glimpse of a bog of skunk cabbages, leaves well started. Along the freeway, full winter cress, patches of May apples, fresh and shiny. At the lake, the birch tree leaves were the same size as last year, but still holding their catkins. The tree line all across western New York was one of the first week of April in Yellow Springs: pale yellow-greens mixed with yellow-browns and oranges, the tallest trees and those with the most foliage rose like umbrellas through the less advanced understory. From Yellow Springs, Leslie reports gray tree frogs singing.

Sweet daily surprise,
To open my eyes and see the light
and think:
Still I live, I am, endure.

Flavio Herrera

May 9th
The 129th Day of the Year

Then came faire May, the fairest mayde on ground;
Deckt all with dainties of her season's pryde;
And throwing flowers out of her lap around;

Edmund Spenser

Sunrise/set: 5:26/7:37
Day's Length: 14 hours 11 minutes
Average High/Low: 70/49
Average Temperature: 59
Record High: 92 – 1896
Record Low: 27 – 1947

Weather

Chances of highs in the 80s are 20 percent today, and 70s come a full 55 percent of the time. The remaining 25 percent of highs are fairly evenly divided between 60s, 50s, and 40s. Today is the second-last day in May when a high of just 40 degrees has a ten percent chance of occurring. The final day for such odds this spring is May 25. Skies are at least partially blue 80 percent of the time today, but a shower occurs three years in a decade. Chances of frost remain at early May's ten to 15 percent.

The Natural Calendar

Except in years of heavy April and early May rains, the field corn has just come up, warmed by normal high temperatures in the 70s (for the first time since early autumn), and relatively gentle lows in the upper 40s. All the tobacco beds have sprouted below the Ohio River, and tobacco transplanting has begun. Orchard grass is heading. A little alfalfa is budding. Red and white clovers blossom in the pasture.

It is the center of pepper, cantaloupe, and cucumber planting, the quarter mark for soybean seeding. Migrant workers move north to help with setting plants. In the wood lots, Eastern tent caterpillars defoliate the cherry trees. Spittlebugs appear on pine trees, azalea mites on azaleas, cankerworms on elms and maples, lace bugs on the mountain ash.

Daybook

1984: Cherry blossoms mostly gone.

1985: Cascades: I found long tadpoles basking in the sunny water. Parsnips were just starting to bloom. Shooting star past its prime. Full columbine, golden alexander, Solomon's plume. Jack-in-the-pulpit was turning red. Thin-leafed waterleaf just beginning. Sweet Cicely budding.

1986: Water lilies and yellow swamp iris bloom up at Crystal Lake, says Connie. Peonies seen in Dayton.

1988: Today was the first day for sweet rockets.

1990: Wild cherries full bloom. Some corn sprouted, three to four inches high, but rare. Black walnut trees green. Osage and hackberry just opening. Mock orange budding. Only a few red quince hold on. The high canopy is pale green now, oaks leafing, too. First day for comfrey flowers. Star of Bethlehem still full (gone by May 22). Speedwell declines. Greenhouse filled with the rich scent of the mother-in-law's tongue.

1991: Spiderwort opened today. Poppy and iris full bloom all over town.

1992: First sweet rocket opens in the yard.

1993: First sweet Cicely barely opening behind the pink quince in full bloom. First fall-red raspberry flowers. Horseradish budding. Bridal wreath full bloom along Xenia Avenue. Privet buds pace the honeysuckle buds.

1995: In the south garden, the wood hyacinths are coming in now, the whites following the violets. The first sweet rocket opened this afternoon. In the east garden, astilbe has formed flower heads, and the first wild geranium is open. Poison ivy and Virginia creeper

leaves are developed to a fourth of their summer size.
Rose of Sharon has finally begun to leaf. At school, my ash tree has started to get leaves. The foliage of the ginkgoes and sugar gums parallel each other's growth at maybe a fourth of full size. This morning in the heavy rain, all the gum flower clusters fell to the street. At South Glen, it's the absolute peak of garlic mustard, and along Grinnell, the pink honeysuckle is in full bloom, probably started a week ago. All the other honeysuckles are still closed.

1998: Chives opened up today. Rhododendrons have new shoots beside their flowers. Foxglove heading up. Two purple clematis on the east fence. The first daisy and pyrethrum half open.

1999: Daisies are blooming in town, and the first in the south garden here.

2000: Pale violet iris opens in the south garden, maybe a week behind the more precocious plants in town. First chive flower opens all the way. Four clematis flowers on the east fence. This year is ahead of 1999 by one pyrethrum and about four daisies. Then down the path toward Springfield, the afternoon windy and temperatures in the 80s: I passed wisteria early bloom, honeysuckles full, rockets everywhere, cressleaf groundsel here and there, sweet Cicely, golden Alexander, wild phlox and geranium, late garlic mustard, late winter cress, late and lanky tangled catchweed, pokeweed up to three feet, hemlock to seven, huge fat mullein, wild lettuce. Burdock foliage the size of the well-developed rhubarb in the north garden. Grasses pace the height of the garlic mustard now, past three feet and dense. Nettle chest high. Early wild dark purple spiderwort in patches, first yellow wood sorrel, first wild raspberries flower, one pink trillium grandiflorum, one May apple in bloom. Elms and maples full leafed, oaks maybe half size, wild cherry blossoming, the canopy overhead sometimes a fourth filled, sometimes three-fourths to complete.

2001: First rhododendrons blossom along the south fence. First mock orange blooms. Korean lilac and spreading dogwood full bloom. The canopy is closing quickly. Fox seen between

Chillicothe and Washington Court House.

2002: Locusts opening in Dayton. Beech tree red with new leaves. First purple rhododendrons bloom in the south garden.

2005: First cardinal at 4:45 a.m., first dove at 4:53, green frog at 4:55. Here and there along the way to Washington Court House, neglected fields are yellow with winter cress. The corn and soybean fields are smooth and rich brown, disked and seeded.

2006: First skipper, black swallowtail and yellow swallowtail seen today.

2007: Mock orange beginning to open, honeysuckle completely full, hawthorn with buds ready, more iris in bloom in town. I saw a red admiral butterfly, the first of the year, as I was transplanting cosmos in the south garden. The first tropical storm of the year – three weeks early, is moving toward north Florida and the Carolinas.

2008: The late tulips disintegrate in the rain as the lilacs rust. The last of Don's pink magnolia petals are falling. I transplanted a handful of basil into the vegetable garden today. A field on the south side of town has been taken over by winter cress. Donna and Al Denman sent a message from Birch Creek: "We saw a mother wood duck with six ducklings today."

2009: Home to Yellow Springs from Maumee Bay State Park: Here, the viburnums, the catmint and the hyacinths are in full bloom now, and many allium and chives. Full Korean lilac and honeysuckle, fragrance filling the back yard. Full hawthorn in the park, full silver olives along the roads. Standard lilacs are done, bleeding hearts late. First mock orange, spiderworts, sweet Williams and first standard iris. Poppies on Elm street are out. Weigela is opening, Jerusalem artichokes are knee high. Red and pink quince completely gone.

2010: Privets budding, hawthorn in the park rusting quickly. Weigela remains in full bloom. The north viburnum has shed half its petals, and bridal wreath is just about gone throughout the neighborhood. Daisies are full, gathering momentum. Snow-on-the-mountain starting to flower.

2011: When I got up today, I found an adolescent camel cricket in the bathtub. I put him outside warning him to stay away from spiders and the cats. The red-bellied woodpecker is the most obvious songster this morning, and for the past week, as well. From Madison, Wisconsin, Tat says her daffodils are still holding in the cold and just one of her tulips is starting to open. First pure white moth by the porch light. Along Elm Street, the poppies are coming in, and all of the maples in town are well-leafed out. Azaleas and buckeyes and silver olive shrubs are in full bloom. Along Xenia Avenue, the sycamores have started, just a little ahead of the witch hazel by our south bedroom window. A toad sang in the pond all afternoon, and another yellow swallowtail came by while I was mowing the lawn. Zinnias planted in the evening.

2013: I got up about 3:30 in the morning. It had rained the previous evening. My window was open, and the air was cool and damp. I felt the anxiety and fear that sometimes greet me when I wake. I was still tired and wanted to stay in bed, but remnants of my dreams kept me from going back to sleep and finally pulled me up.

    I listened for birds at my window as I got dressed. Not a sound, not even a car passing on Dayton Street. And then I went outside with Bella, my border collie, to walk in the dark. The moonless predawn sky was completely clear, and I could see the constellations of an August evening, the Northern Cross, Aquila, Lyra, above me.

    I started south along High Street, at 3:50. I heard birds by the time I reached the streetlight at Limestone at 3:53: At first just sporadic chirping of robins, then their rhythmic singsong. When I turned down dark Stafford Street, I lost them altogether, had to go back the way I came to pick up the strand of chant.

    At 4:32, I heard the sharp vocalization of the first cardinal, then no other cardinals until they consistently joined the robins at 4:50. Song sparrows came in at 4:53, crows in the distance at 4:57, doves at , sunrise less than half an hour away.

And the sky grew lighter, and the sound increased around me. On the empty streets, down Davis and Phillips, robins, bold with lust, chased each other in the twilight down the sidewalks and the empty streets, seeming to me like startled crabs racing across the hard sand of the receding ocean tide.

By 5:10 I realized that the cardinals and sparrows and doves were so loud I could no longer hear the robins. And I was aware then that the worst of the night's phantoms had been sung away. The sinking feeling in my chest lightened, and my breathing deepened, my concerns washed in rhythms of the chorus.

House sparrows began their steady rhythmic chirp at 6:02. I came back to my house at 6:15, sat on the back porch and waited for the grackles: they joined the great symphony at 6:20. Then I waited as the sun came up between Lil's house and Jerry and Lee's house, until the red-bellied woodpecker called out at 7:00.

I watched all the color enter the trees and the flowers, revealing the violet of the hyacinths and the wisteria and lilacs, and then even the phantoms that had resisted the birds receded with daylight, the sun reaching the tops of the white mulberry leafing out and the box elder with its foliage complete.

In the afternoon, Bella and I stopped at the Upper Grinnell habitat and walked along its exotic paths lined with huge honeysuckle bushes. At the old quarry pool, a spread of cattails which were all about three feet high, large patches of ragwort in bloom, the part of the wetland area close to the path densely covered with touch-me-nots about six inches high. Down the steep way to the river: tall and common ragwort, sweet Cicely, phlox, geraniums, a pool with full-blooming watercress, giant white May apple flowers. Such a luminous glow to the woods, and all around the song of the brooks that ran beside and across the path.

2014: Sweet Cicely budded, petal fall accelerating – our red crab turning pale, the canopy developing quickly now. John Blakelock reports, disheartened, that his toads had not mated this year and that his robins were only about a tenth of what they had been. Bridal wreath full now along High Street. Paulownia has one-inch shoots, tree-of-heaven with bushy, new, short branches. The high tree line filling quickly, like Jekyll Island in late March. Poppies in the alley are still not open, but their bud stems are lanky, flower heads bobbing. The pink quince near the pond is shedding at the same rate as the red crab apple tree in the front garden.

2015: The circle garden is at its peak: full allium and blue wood hyacinths and the last blossoms of the Indian hyacinths. The new rhododendrons are cracking just a little. The great white viburnum is blanketed with white flowers, and the *Paulonia* has well developed leaves maybe a third of full size. A spicebush swallowtail zoomed in and then out of the yard up through the white mulberry tree. I transplanted a hobblebush along the north border, planted amaranth in the south alcove by the back porch. The amaranth I planted in the north garden has sprouted but is too small to thin and transplant.

2016: Jill's clematis started to bloom today, and bittersweet nightshade noticed in bloom winding through the honeysuckle hedge – as it has for as far back as I can remember. And a note from Jenny Cowperthwaite: "Since I last emailed (May 8th) we have seen 4 female RB Grosbeaks and I tried to get a photo of 7, yes, SEVEN males on our feeder plus 3 females all at the same time, but they are so wary it's hard to get close enough, even with a zoom, to get a decent photo. It's certainly been a magical year for us at he feeders, unlike any prior year and we've lived here for 11 years now. What delights us now through to October are the ruby throated hummingbirds, though the population seems to have dropped significantly in the last 4-5 years. It used to be we went though a quart of nectar per day, and at best count had 17 hummers but I think there we more. Last year we felt the number was more like 7 to 10 at most. "

2017: The viburnum on the north side of the house lost its final petals today, and the bright pink azalea is dropping petals all at once.

2018: Things are happening so quickly, and I can't keep up. Oak leaves, maple leaves, honeysuckle leaves, box elder leaves surging and filling in all the spaces left by March and April. Oakleaf hydrangea leaves reaching up like soft, pale hands. Pokeweed is six inches, milkweed almost a foot, hackberry buds just greening, trumpet creeper leaves an inch. More hollyhocks planted in the north garden, more dahlias in the north porch garden. As Jill and I walked the bike path, we saw May apple flower buds. And an American toad called out to us.

2019: This morning, I was surprised to see that yesterday evening's drive from Yellow Springs to Keuka Lake resulted in a windshield speckled with insects, the first time in several years that I have encountered so many insects at night.

2020: This morning, Shep said that four customers at his hardware store had seen Baltimore orioles this past week, and that two more had seen hummingbirds. Along High Street, bridal wreath spirea is open, and I saw sweet Cicely blooming down Stafford Street.

We looked far across the valley, to the green fields and the green of woodlands and the shadow of valleys, The air vibrated with birdsong, which is the great rhythm made palpable to the ear. All the senses tingled, alive with the season as the world itself is alive. Nothing was impossible. High achievement was all around us, beating on every one of our senses for recognition.

Hal Borland

May 10th
The 130th Day of the Year

But winter lingering chills the lap of May.

Oliver Goldsmith

Sunrise/set: 5:25/7:38
Day's Length: 14 hours 13 minutes
Average High/Low: 70/49
Average Temperature: 59
Record High: 94 – 1896
Record Low: 29 – 1966

Weather

Today's weather is almost always mild to warm, with just a 30 percent chance of rain. Highs in the 80s come 20 percent of the time, 70s come 45 percent, 60s come 35 percent. This is the first day since April 30th that chances of highs below 50 degrees are practically nil. The sun shines 85 percent of all the May 10ths in my weather history. Chances of frost: a light freeze comes once in a decade on this date, but after today, chances on a daily basis fall below five percent through the first week of June, after which they completely disappear.

Natural Calendar

This is Sweet Cicely and May Apple Blooming Season in the woods. Mayfly Season begins along the rivers and creeks. Weevil Season comes in throughout the local alfalfa fields. As Petalfall Season closes for crab apples, cherry trees and redbuds, Thrush Season, Catbird Season and Scarlet Tanager Season come to the bushes. It's Bullfrog Season in the swamp and Spitbug Season in the parsnips.

Daybook

1982: As the hydrangeas bloom, crab apple petal fall coming to an end. May apple and fire pink blossoming. Sweet Cicely has started its three-week cycle.

1984: This cooler year, a few bluebells and one toothwort found. Sweet rockets and fleabane budding.

1985: At the pond, hemlock was heading up. Plantain was blooming at Wilberforce. Canadian thistle was up to my chest, budding. Last garlic mustard fading, like in Arlington Virginia on April 26, but still chest high, dominating the undergrowth. Sweet rockets full, columbine full. Canopy complete here. Daddy longlegs on the hobblebush. Yellow swallowtails mating, almost tame. First forget-me-nots and corn salad. Wild phlox fading.

1987: Cascades: Ducklings seen big and fat, at least two weeks old. Last of the trillium. May apple blooming. Robin's fleabane full bloom. Yellow stargrass full. Water cress, ragwort, garlic mustard still dominate the woods. Spring cress and betony done. Golden Alexander along the paths. First maple-leaf waterleaf in bloom. Shooting star fading, columbine late full. Blue cohosh still holding (gone by the 12th). Some poppies full bloom in the village. First black raspberries flower. The village maple canopy is complete. It's summer in town before it is in the woods, seasons depending as much on species as on the weather. First yellow swallowtail seen (one seen on March 24 in Mississippi, 1989). Patches of iris in full bloom.

1988: Redbuds faded suddenly today, their leaves replaced flowers almost overnight. Daisies bloomed by the south wall.

1989: Buckeyes full. Garlic mustard just starting. Waterleaf budding. Jack-in-the-pulpit still strong. Wild lettuce has huge basal foliage. Sweet rockets budding. Virginia creeper has been leafing this past week. A third of the high canopy is in. Only a few spring beauties left. Squirrels eating the new green mulberries. Rose of Sharon leafing. Viburnum full leaf and bloom. Purple deadnettle yellowing. Sedum early full in the yard. Pink honeysuckle full bloom in the village, mine still budding.

1991: At South Glen, orchard grass and delicate brome are at their sweetest, late garlic mustard flowers at their tips now, sweet rocket strong. Ginger hidden but full bloom, full waterleaf. Touch-me-nots huge, pacing wood nettle to my thighs. Phlox being overgrown. Silver olive trees full bloom. Last of the yard's tulips coming undone. Dogwoods hold. Osage leafing, maybe a fourth size, sycamores a little ahead. First spitbugs seen in the yard. Wild cherry and locust in bloom. Canopy closing quickly. Center of hydrangea season.

1993: Air sweet with pollen (the most pollen in 20 years, reported on the news). First rockets opened today, one seen at the turnoff to Grinnell, one in the south garden. Early patch of purple iris along Xenia Avenue. At Wilberforce, gum trees are dropping their flowers, leaves half size. Maple seeds falling. In the river valley, the canopy is flushed, quickly maturing, still luminescent, fresh, adolescent, scanty. Bright blue egg shell on the sidewalk at the sunken garden. Junipers have new two-inch growth. One honeysuckle full bloom at Jim Oldham's. Some redbuds are leafing, their flowers deepening, then becoming overwhelmed by foliage. Aphids found on two budding rose plants tonight.

1994: Now the dark purple dwarf iris have started in front of the house, and taller varieties first opening along Dayton Street. Some late yellow and red tulips are still in full bloom. Ranunculus, golden ragwort, water cress, garlic mustard, violet wild geranium, winter cress, spring cress, light purple phlox at their best, peonies with large buds, first pyrethrum unraveling at the same time the first columbine is opening. It's early fleabane, sweet rocket, and sweet Cicely time, last days of miterwort, redbud and dogwood. Bleeding hearts are getting old. Honeysuckle bushes are starting, oaks in bloom. Last solar eclipse of the century today. It was dark outside at noon even though the sky was clear and the sun was shining. The whole yard seemed to be in the shade.

1999: Now mock orange, daisies, pyrethrum in the garden push out simultaneously. Six leaves on the water lily. Tadpoles getting medium sized. Catalpa leaves a third developed, pacing the black walnuts. Thyme and horseradish both full bloom in the garden.

2000: Sixteen leaves on the pond's water lily. Tadpoles large and now have spots. Red admiral butterfly seen along the north path today. Yesterday, a small, orange fold wing butterfly.

2001: Peonies are out in Xenia. Blue flag iris and comfrey suddenly blossom along the north border. First reddening strawberry found. Wild black raspberry full bloom. The puppy, Bella, found another snake skin today, this one under the peony bushes. Goslings big and fat on all the ponds.

2002: Angelica waist high, nettles knee high. Orchard grass perfect for pulling and chewing. First mock orange flowers.

2005: Hawthorns bloomed today at the triangle park, but even the bushy crab apples, late to flower, are losing their petals in the 80-degree days. Black walnut trees are producing small leaf clusters, and the high locusts are emerging. Mountain maples are coming in at the Antioch School. Iris are budding here, blooming around town. Honeysuckle buds are ready to blossom any minute.

2006: Hawthorns at the peak of their bloom in the park, Korean lilacs in the yard. The first blue flag and the first iris flowered in the north garden this morning. The last bluebell blossom faded by the shed, lungwort long finished. Pink spirea has small bud clusters in the south garden. Mateo's weigela started opening today.

2007: The second yellow swallowtail of the year seen this morning. Coleus planted under the apple tree. The hawthorn at the triangle park was in early bloom. More iris and all the poppies in town blooming. The tree line was completely pale green on the way to Octa this afternoon. Many corn fields had sprouted, sprouts about three inches tall. Winter wheat here was strong, maybe eight to twelve inches high. Fat, fuzzy goslings seen at Dewine's pond.

2008: The first sweet rocket in town seen at Don's this morning. Bridal wreath spirea in full bloom at Katie's. Ranunculus in early bloom by the house. Red double peonies noticed along Elm Street.

2009: Locusts are blooming in Wilmington, and fleabane.

2010: Jeanie reported a baby sparrow begging.

2012: To Dayton: Many catalpa trees seen in full bloom, more yellow poplars blooming, and early nodding thistles open.

2013: A brown toad with a light stripe down his back (like in a photo I saw of a Western Toad) was sitting on the front step when I came home from walking Bella this morning. Now that the front red crab apple and the pink quince in back are completely done blooming; the bright pink azalea holds the dooryard space together. Rick brought over a milkweed plant, six inches tall.

2014: In the yard: The red crab apple and the pink quince have dropped all their petals. Indian hyacinth and tall allium and star of Bethlehem in full bloom, last bluebells, first spiderwort, early ranunculus, peonies an inch across. Hackberry finally leafing, Jeanie's river birch filling in slowly, pale April green. The trumpet vine is putting out a few leaves, and the forsythia is budding. The redbuds that did not flower have tiny red leaves. At Ellis Pond: one sweet Cicely open, silver olive shrubs in bloom, toads calling, wild cherry budded, yellow buckeye and red horse chestnut in full flower, mountain ash full white flower clusters, *Halesia Jersey Belle* white with bell-like flowers, ginkgo leaves two inches, sycamore leaves one to two, scarlet oak three inches. In town, snowball viburnums open everywhere. Only scattered geese nesting in the fields, the great flocks of fall, winter and early spring broken and scattered for mating and raising their young. Some cornfields show their sprouts.

2015: All the honeysuckles are blooming all at once. It seems they came in overnight. As I jogged down Phillips Street at about 5:45, I approached a pileated woodpecker that was working at the rotten wood of a tree stump. He let me get within just a few feet before he flew off. Through the village: azaleas and Korean lilacs and bridal wreath all around.

2016: Scattered inventory: the village flowering just like last year, with poppies and sweet rockets and many iris as well; in the yard, the first blue spiderwort and the first white and blue spiderwort have opened; honeysuckles, lamium, celandine, ranunculus, wild geraniums and allium are full; Indian hyacinths and wind flowers done; wood hyacinths starting to brown close to the ground; peonies straining to open – a few buds showing petal color; north side viburnum still bright white; the azalea, garlic mustard and star of Bethlehem late; waterleaf foliage very tall; some bamboo to twelve feet; rhubarb almost ready to pick for pie; the decorative grasses struggling through the weeds; trumpet creeper vines with feathery foliage; wisteria with numerous flower clusters, but still quite bare; hosta and ferns full size; Joe Pye weed to eighteen inches; red amaranth sprouted under the weeds perhaps a week ago, needs to be thinned; last tulips, the white ones, ready to collapse; in the dooryard garden, the yellow bell flowers are still open (came in maybe a week ago). In the fields, winter wheat is more than a foot tall, and the corn has sprouted.

2017: The first long-bodied orb weaver wove its web across the west end of the pond overnight. I saw the first silver-spotted skipper in the circle garden late in the morning.

2018: The ancient azalea in the dooryard garden is putting out a few blossoms. Above it, the red crab apple blooms are fading. The south border hackberry is leafing. In the north side of the village: first iris, deep purple and first daisies. Dogwoods are in full flower in town, Jill's pink one delicate and almost draping against the front porch. Cressleaf groundsel colors the fields gold. Bridal wreath hangs across the dooryards. Pale rose-like petals of the quince float down to the surface of the pond.

2019: Heavy rains turn the local Miami River waterfall, the "cascades" into a thundering torrent.

2020: Blackberry Winter continues with raw winds and storms.

To be creative, man must relate to nature with his senses as much as with his common sense, with his heart as much as with knowledge. He must read the book of external nature and the book of his own nature, to discern the common patterns and harmonies.
Rene Dubos

May 11th
The 131st Day of the Year

And May has come, hair-bound in flowers,
With eyes that smile thro' the tears of the hours,
with joy for to-day and hope for to-morrow
And the promise of Summer within her breast!

Gerard Manley Hopkins

Sunrise/set: 5:24/7:39
Day's Length: 14 hours 15 minutes
Average High/Low: 71/49
Average Temperature: 60
Record High: 94 – 1896
Record Low: 33 – 1945

Weather

Today marks a another pivotal time in the progress of spring: Beginning May 11, the danger of frost at average elevations along the 40th Parallel diminishes sharply to less than ten percent per morning through June 7, when it becomes less than five percent. Highs rise above 80 degrees 50 percent of all the afternoons on this date, making it the day with the best chance of warm weather in the entire month of May. Twenty-five percent of the days heat up to the 70s, twenty more to the 60s, and only one day in a blue moon remains in the cold 50s or 40s. The sun comes out for at least a little while on 70 percent of all May 11ths; showers are relatively rare, occurring just 20 percent of the time, the driest of any May day in my history.

Natural Calendar

Scorpion flies appear in the garden. Bullfrogs call in the swamps. Minnows and chubs in the creeks have turned a reddish-gold for their mating season. Flea time has begun for pets, and spitbugs grow in the shelter of parsnips, announcing that the first cut of hay will soon be underway all across the Lower Midwest in average years. White cabbage butterflies and yellow sulphurs play and spiral above the rhubarb. Crappie fishing peaks in the shallows as the sun nears three-fourths of the way to summer solstice.

Daybook

1983: First purple iris seen on Xenia Avenue. Blue jays very restless. At Clifton Gorge, bluettes, ragwort, phlox, May apples, columbine, spring beauties, Jack-in-the-pulpit, sedum, water cress, white, yellow, blue violets, bedstraw, hairy waterleaf, sweet Cecily, golden alexander, swamp buttercup, Solomon's plume, henbit, wild strawberry, wild geranium, miterwort, nodding trillium full bloom. Trillium grandiflorum are pink and way past their prime, toad trillium and early meadow rue completely done, only one or two bluebells left. Thrush sings in the honeysuckle, leading me along the path.

1984: Jeni reports baby birds are out in Florida. Here at the Indian Mound: new pine cone growth noticed. Hemlock knee high, nettle waist high. Bright green beetle flies away from me. Dogwood and redbud still open. Thrush, catbird, wren, bluebird, scarlet tanager seen. Wild cucumber growing by the river, maple-like leaf on long tendril. First waterleaf comes in.

1986: Jacoby Meadow: Goat's beard early along Jacoby road. Buckeyes done blooming. Leafcup knee high, catchweed clumps waist high in the swamp. Canopy about a third complete. Fields of yellow buttercups. Heavy sweet scent to the air. Cowslips, geraniums still open. Next year's garlic mustard thick everywhere, grass wet and tall, reaching almost to my waist. Watercress lanky and toppling over, still full bloom. Lizard's tail leafing. Elms flowering, their leaves half an inch long. Mosquitoes biting. First daddy longlegs. It seems a totally different time of year, from only days ago.

1987: First plantain and meadow goat's beard seen in bloom.

1988: First meadow goat's beard. Cattail foliage waist high. Suckers mating below the Covered Bridge. Small school of sunfish a few hundred yards downstream, several carp in the main channel, migration full swing. Poison ivy leaves fresh, about half size, they pace the Virginia creeper. Purple deadnettle decaying, yellow. Comfrey waist high and budding. Bluebells done in the yard.

1989: First young doves seen out of their nest. At the Mill, wild hyacinth found full bloom, probably opened in April, its violet color adding to the deep purple of larkspur and the phlox and violets and geranium. Poison ivy a little ahead of Virginia creeper. Robin's fleabane open. First waterleaf. First parsnips. First crickets heard, the Northern Spring Field Cricket, the only chirping spring cricket in this region. First grasshoppers, hundreds of them clatter in the dry leaves. First sweet rocket. First clustered snakeroot buds. Sweet Cicely early full bloom. Mint and some zigzag goldenrod close to knee high.

1991: First standard iris in the yard. Blue flag iris have large buds. South garden in full flower: buttercups, poppies, sweet rocket, daisies, pyrethrums. First green-bottle fly seen. First orange skipperling in the iris.

1993: Only ranunculus and wood hyacinths in the south garden so far. Young squirrel and young groundhog killed on Grinnell Road this morning. Apple blossoms and redbuds suddenly gone in the 80-degree temperatures. First pyrethrum starts to unravel. Sycamores half leafed. Lupine buds in the garden pace the iris. First white clover seen at Wilberforce. John calls from New York Mills in Minnesota, says that they are a week behind Minneapolis, when usually they are two, and that peonies are ten inches tall, that tulips are open, lilacs and apples are budding, mosquitoes pesky, some dandelions open.

1995: First columbine opens this morning in the east garden as the azaleas are at their most beautiful. In the triangle park, yesterday's storms brought down all the apple petals. Along Dayton Street, periwinkles still in bloom; witch hazel leaves are half size. On Elm Street, an entire bed of orange poppies has come into bloom. Around the yard, ferns, lilies, comfrey, summer phlox all at about the same height, just below my waist. In New York Mills, John says that the trees are just barely budding, and the only sign of life in the ground is the emerging rhubarb.

1997: Azaleas full bloom in the east garden, along with the wild geraniums and the first small dark iris (bloomed two days ago), columbine budding beside them. Now the bleeding hearts, frozen down three weeks ago, are starting to come back with their hearts. Dead nettle is at its best. All the daffodils except the small ones have been dead-headed. The first fleabane has been open for a day or two. Sweet Cicely is budding. Rose of Sharon has finally started to leaf a little. Red quince fading in town. Apple petals falling heavily on Xenia Avenue. Daisies look ready to unravel this coming week. Pyrethrums are heading up. Ranunculus has opened. Pink honeysuckles full bloom along Grinnell, but home honeysuckles just budding.

1998: Meadow goat's beard all over the side of the road today. Middle of Late Spring now. Sycamores at least a fourth leafed, and Osage and black walnut, the last holdouts are filling quickly.

1999: First June bug.

2000: Wood hyacinths end a little after the creeping phlox, as the first bachelor's buttons come in. Small damsel fly, blue-tailed, at the pond today. Comfrey has opened up in the north garden, probably came in days ago.

2001: Into South Glen: second scorpion fly and second white-spotted skipper of the year seen (the first ones seen two days ago). First meadow goat's beard. Violet waterleaf flowers standing straight up like wild geraniums.

2002: First strawberry reddens. Scorpion flies seen. Silver olive and honeysuckle shrubs full bloom, pacing the poppies and peonies.

2005: Sweet rockets suddenly in bloom along Grinnell Road. Bridal wreath spirea is lush in Cedarville. One pollen spike has appeared on the wild iris rushes in the pond. Brown maple seeds are prominent in the trees, beginning to fall. Catmint budded at home, blooming downtown.

2006: The lilacs in the alley disintegrated overnight. Honeysuckles are in lush full bloom, some petals even falling in the rain. I either missed my sequencing when I wrote my April weekly overviews several years ago, or spring is advancing much more quickly than usual this year. Certainly, honeysuckle, viburnum and bridal-wreath spirea seasons follow directly after apple petal fall and the end of the redbuds. Kousa dogwoods follow on the heels of the standard dogwoods. First blue robin eggshell found on the sidewalk this evening in the park.

2007: The first sweet William opened in the night. Folded-winged butterflies noticed this morning speeding back and forth along the west border of the yard.

2008: A cold and rainy day in the 50s, the one day in a blue moon mentioned in my weather history for today. The pale spiderwort in the north garden does not care: two powder-blue blossoms this morning. At the park, hawthorn trees are fully budded with some blossoms spreading out. Wild cherry trees are open along Dayton Street, clustered snakeroot heading in the circle garden. The perennial salvia at the northwest corner of the yard has started to bloom. Peggy's iris, red purple, are opening. Jeni's pink dogwood is blooming in Portland, Oregon.

2010: First scorpion fly seen in the garden. Peaches about an inch long. First major thinning of the lettuce for lunch. First sprouts seen on two of the raspberry bushes set in during the first week of April. Toad seen when I was working on the new storage shed in the evening.

2011: Rome to Spoleto, Italy: Hillsides bright with yellow ginestra shrubs in bloom, many elderberries in full flower. Lilacs all rusted. Very late bloom of locusts near Rome, coming out more as we drove north. Red-orange poppies throughout. The land seemed dry.

2012: Cricket chirping outside the artisans' store at 6:15 this evening. Rick says his tadpoles are getting legs. Poppies in decline throughout the village, salvia and blue flags, spiderwort, sweet rocket, catmint full bloom (although the first sweet rockets faded over night). Jeanie cut back all the wood hyacinths this afternoon.

2013: On the way to Cincinnati, I discovered locust trees in bloom about halfway down, thirty miles south of Yellow Springs, the first I've seen this year. In the woods at the St. Clare Monastery, the only wildflowers were the full blooming May apples. All the lilacs there were rusted (ours at home definitely declining). A red-bellied woodpecker and cardinals called, and two other birds I couldn't recognize. Back home at Ellis Pond and the Kennedy Arboretum: Ashes half-leafed; sycamore greening, leaves about a couple inches long; bald cypress foliage spreading out now at about an inch; redbuds gone and dogwood fading; hemlock and dock heading up, having grown to three and four feet; the linden foliage is dense, maybe two-thirds of its mature size; full blooming lilac and garlic mustard and winter cress; the pawpaw has three leaves by each flower bud now; the pecan is flowering and has half-inch leaves; the buckeye and red horse chestnut are in full bloom; bur oak leaves are two to three inches; the sweetheart chestnut and the American chestnut that I thought would be very late have two-inch leaves; hornbeam seems fully leafed, as do the maples and the willows.

2014: First scorpion fly seen in the garden. First sweet rocket opening in the yard. Dogwoods still hold around town, but redbuds are definitely leafing now. Knotweed eight feet tall and bittersweet blooming in the alley. Spruce tip growth very prominent at Don's.

2015: Viburnum, about five-feet tall, planted along the south east bushes of the property, to fill a break in the foliage barrier there.

2016: One red admiral seen this afternoon. A short walk at dusk in John Bryan Park with Jill: tall and short ragworts, one Solomon's plume, many full-blooming May apples, wild phlox still open, one golden Alexander, a few tall angelicas, some poison hemlock stalks six feet high.

2019: Keuka Lake to Yellow Springs in the rain: the fields and hills glowing against the gray clouds. As we left, I noticed that the forsythia is quickly losing its flowers here in New York, and the flowers gradually disappeared altogether as we drove south. At home, Mateo's weigela had opened (ours, dying back, with only a few blossoms). They honeysuckles were in bloom, the wisteria putting out its dusky green foliage, the snowball viburnum near Jeanie's window gloriously full and filling the vista of the entire yard. On the living room wall, the first daddy longlegs of the spring. In the bathtub, a large brown hunting spider (possibly a *Tigrosa helluo*).

Think, bright Florella, when you see
The constant Changes of the Year,
That nothing is from Ruin free,
And gayest Things must disappear.
Think of your Beauties in their bloom,
The Spring of sprightly Youth improve;
For cruel Age, alas, will come,
And then 'twill be too late to love.

Poor Richard's Almanack

May 12th
The 132nd Day of the Year

Now Venus herself enters the furrows:
Love learns the rustic words of the ploughman.

Tibullus

Sunrise/set: 5:23/7:40
Day's Length: 14 hours 17 minutes
Average High/Low: 71/50
Average Temperature: 60
Record High: 90 – 1982
Record Low: 35 – 1938

Weather

As the third major high-pressure system of the month approaches western Ohio, today's chances of rain increase significantly over yesterday's. Showers occur on 45 percent of all May 12ths. Today is also one of the two cloudiest days in May: the 12th and the 25th bring completely cloudy conditions five years in a decade. Highs reach 90 ten percent of the time, warm into the 80s thirty percent, the 70s another thirty percent, the 60s twenty percent, and the 50s ten percent.

Natural Calendar

Mountain maples, lilacs and wild cherries flower. Poison ivy, like the Virginia creeper and wild grapes, develops to a third of its June size. The foliage of the green ash, rose of Sharon, ginkgo, sycamore, witch hazel, and sweet gum is all a third to half of full size. Last year's sweet gum flower clusters complete their fall as chives blossom.

Daybook

1982: Strawberries have green fruit. Sweet rocket seen blooming for the first time today.

1983: Most cherry and apple petals have fallen. Yellow wood

sorrel open at Wilberforce, chamomile too.

1984: First honeysuckle in the yard.

1986: Wood nettle and ragweed a foot and a half high now, other nettles and poke weed waist high. Ginkgo, leaves half an inch wide, getting round, brown seeds. Jacob's ladder done blooming. Wild onions heading. Poppies full bloom in Mad River. Fields of gray dandelions. Mulberry fruit just starting to form from the flowers.

1987: September's beggarticks are two to three inches tall now. First red-headed woodpecker seen since I was a boy in Marshfield, Wisconsin. First spitbug of the year noticed.

1988: Jacob's ladder full bloom. First poppies open in town. Maple seeds have been falling all week.

1991: Tulip tree budding, a few flowers opening. All the locust trees in town are in full bloom, flowers hanging down like white grape clusters. End of the lilac season. Wild grapes budding. Flicker still calling through the day. Mulberry fruit is full size now. Ginkgo leaves full size. Goslings the size of my boot seen at the south pond. Grackle in the back locust nest flies back and forth as if trying to lead its young from the nest.

1993: First pale violet iris opens in the yard, first lupine flowers with it. Purple deadnettle yellowing now. First black medic at Wilberforce. Hemlock chest high along Clifton Road. Buckeyes past their prime. Wild cherry full bloom. First honeysuckle blooms in the yard. Chives now in early bloom.

1994: East to New York and then back in a day. Winter cress common throughout. The canopy a week or two behind Yellow Springs in central Pennsylvania, dogwoods and redbuds full bloom too (almost all gone in southwestern Ohio). Great golden fields of April dandelions spread across the mountain pastures. The trees filled in rapidly as we moved toward the coast, dandelions all went to seed. New York City, like here, was almost completely leafed out. First of summer's yellow sweet clover seen in New Jersey, but just that one patch on the whole trip.

1995: Jacoby, 7:00 in the morning: Buttercups, cowslips, spring cress, ragwort, wild phlox still dominate the wetlands with violet and gold. The hills are white with garlic mustard. In the streams, water cress is past its prime, and chickweed has started to yellow by the paths. Wild geraniums have opened, the first white sedum and the first sweet Cicely. First gossamer webs of the year seen this morning.

A pair of geese with eight goslings (maybe a week old at most) swimming down the river. Further along, three wood ducklings playing in the water, waiting for their mother; she flies down, calling angrily (it seems) at them for being out alone. First star of Bethlehem is open by the vegetable garden trellis. This afternoon, I planted two flats of strawberries, two raspberry plants, two blackberry.

1998: Early morning robins still strong at 4:00 a.m. Forgot to note the other day, maybe two or three days ago: the first red admiral butterfly came to the garden. At the entrance to South Glen, toad trilliums have ended. First daddy longlegs seen. First scorpion fly. First buckeye nuts have formed. Purple waterleaf is in full bloom. First comfrey flowers.

1999: Bridal wreath, white *Spirea vanhouttie,* full. Black chokecherry, also white *Pyracantha* in bloom. And red horse chestnut, *Aesculus,* with buckeye-like leaves and reddish spike flowers in Troy.

2000: One tadpole with legs. They are secretive now, hiding out at the edge of the pond, difficult to find and catch. Soon they'll be gone. At the west end of the water, the first wild iris brought from Caesar Creek two years ago opened this morning in 85 degree heat. Arrowhead leaves are still small, having emerged a week or so ago. Over 20 leaves on the water lily today. First pink carnation opened, first snapdragons unravel, first pale pink peonies in the south garden. Almost all the clematis are blooming, the rhododendrons showing all their color. This afternoon, wild roses came in and the first blue flags in the north garden. In Columbus, crown vetch and patches of daisies open along the freeway. The canopy closing quickly.

2001: First dark pink peony in the yard. All the azaleas down. Buds on the privet and the spiderwort, locust flowers decaying.

2002: Sudden decline of the white bridal wreath spirea. Locust bloom spreading.

2003: I got up early Pentecost morning, made a cup of black tea, and went out into the back yard to watch the dawn. By 4:00, the robin chorus was faint but steady in the distance. The volume grew until cardinals began to sing at 4:37, and then the doves came in at 4:40, and then the blue jays at 5:48, and the red-bellied woodpecker at 4:56, crows at 4:59.

By the time the grackles woke up at 5:00, the bird chorus was loud and raucous. Then a sudden breeze passed through the trees, and, to my surprise, the grackles, adults and fledglings, became more boisterous, their calls drowning out the other songsters as the sun came up.

Earlier in the month, the birds had become quieter after sunrise, but that Pentecost morning, it seemed to me, the grackle babies had all hatched at once, and the entire community of grackles was aroused and excited.

The wave of their language grew and grew as though every grackle that lived in our woods had been filled with a great message, and that each one knew it was time to speak.

I sat there wondering, as I sipped my tea and listened to this grand gathering of creatures, if maybe the human saints were gone, the apostles and their fervor long decayed, and, in their place, these joyous birds had now received the overwhelming wind of Revelation, and were clucking and cackling, in universal, earthy tongues, the good news of summer and rebirth.

2004: Hawthorns at the little park on Dayton Street are in full bloom. Locusts started yesterday throughout the countryside, and wild cherry blossoms are coming in. Most of the maples have full-size leaves. Hemlock is up to my neck. The deep purple clematis is blooming, and one patch of daisies is open. One strawberry is reddening.

Driving to Washington Court House, I watched the mist rising from the dark, moist fields. Near Jamestown: great patches of golden cressleaf groundsel stretched to the horizon. At night, small long-bodied spiders have started to weave their webs across the pond.

2005: To Dayton: Locusts are in full bloom throughout the city. Silver olives blossoming along the freeway. In the afternoon, I found honeysuckles opening along the north border, and the first iris was blooming in the yard.

2006: To Dayton: Locusts in full bloom again this year.

2008: The first sweet rocket has opened overnight in the rain, pink.

2009: Maple seeds collecting by the side of the highway. Tight bittersweet buds and large leaves. Indian hyacinths fading quickly. New spruce growth an inch to two inches. American beech leaves to two inches.

2010: The yellow iris Tat gave us in Madison opened this morning. A new (or returning) toad has found the pond, began to sing about 1:30 this afternoon. On Dayton Street, the lilies-of-the-valley are rusting and disappearing. The kousa dogwood at the park has green flower petals.

2011: Tour of Spoleto and Monte Luco with Neysa and Ivano: Ginestra, wild locust, tea and rugosa roses, lily-of-the-valley, giant buckeye trees, elderberries, black medic all in bloom. Cottonwood cotton floating through the valley (placing the cottonwood season about three weeks ahead of the average in southwestern Ohio, linden trees with berries. Small zebra swallowtail seen. The valley fully green, the canopy seeming complete.

2012: Sage has bloomed overnight in the circle garden, alliums and chives still holding well there. This morning when I was transplanting ferns, Rick brought over a bottle full of tree frog tadpoles, a few with legs, for the pond. I seeded one flat of zinnias, a few marigolds and tithonias. Jennifer in Portland, Oregon, says that her tadpoles don't have legs yet.

Liz writes: "Zeitgeber for today! A black swallowtail butterfly has been resting on a hosta stem all day, hardening its wings. I accidentally discovered it because I sprayed some water in that direction, and must have knocked it off of wherever it was. It frantically shook its wings over and over, especially the right one, and then very delicately found the nice stem to attach itself to, and just be still. It has been such a meditative day for me, knowing that it was there preparing for its final stage of life. It is awe-inspiring to think that it came out of its chrysalis so very competent, and of course, so very beautiful."

2013: One sky-blue spiderwort opened yesterday, and Don's rhododendrons are beginning to flower. Neysa in Italy said she saw her first small wild orchid today. Some progress in the trees at Ellis Pond. The bald cypresses are greening up now, and all the oaks except the English oak (which had been planted for Vern Hogans, the famous Yellow Springs cat fisherman) have one-to-three-inch leaves (the scarlet, the red, the white, the sawtooth, the shingle, the chinquapin). The hickory still only shows flowers. Ashes are filling in, sugar maples all full, butternuts and black walnuts sparse still.

2014: I noticed a sudden change in violet bloom today, so many of the flowers disappearing with the dandelions. And throughout town, dogwoods are losing their petals. The honeysuckles started to blossom in today's 80-degree heat, the rich, sweet smell filling the dooryard garden. I saw poppies in bloom in the alley and on the way downtown, and Mateo's weigela is emerging. In Italy, Ivano reported that five merli (the Italian blackbirds) eggs had hatched, the mother covering them with her wings in the rain.

2015: Yesterday, the warm spell was broken up by wind and rain. Now this morning, the locust trees in the back yard are suddenly in bloom. Daisies are blooming at Peggy's, and the first flowers on Moya's mock orange are opening. Indian hyacinths almost gone from the circle garden. One spiderwort bud seen, some phlox budding, primrose getting tall enough to flower.

2016: This afternoon, I found the first scorpion fly, and saw the first beetles eating the phlox, penstemon, mint and primroses. Wood frogs heard close the bike path, steady chant.

2017: First scorpion fly found, first orange beetles (nymphs of the four-lined plant bug, *Poecilocapsus lineatus*) eating the phlox. In the shed, the spiders have woven their webs and are ready.

2018: A Baltimore oriole visited the hummingbird feeder at about four this afternoon. I planted the last of the zinnias with Tat. First peonies seen today on the way downtown, a full shrub of pink blossoms, a buckeye tree open by the old tennis courts. No beetles eating the phlox. Throughout town, dogwoods and bridal wreath spirea are blooming. In the North Glen with Tat: giant skunk cabbage leaves, ragwort, violet wild phlox, wood betony, fat, white May apple blossoms, spring cress, white violets, golden alexander, waterleaf, small deep-purple larkspur, the last trillium grandiflorum pink and drooping, sweet rockets.

2019: In the field west of Ellis, orchard grass is covering the Early Spring wildflowers, but meadow goatsbeard is nodding above it; parsnip and curly dock are ready to open; hemlock stalks have shot up past my shoulders, budded.

Stroke her daisy,
make his hay:
May will never
come again today.
Smell her rose,
snatch his bouquet:
Love will never,
ever
come again this May.

bf

Bill Felker

May 13th
The 133rd Day of the Year

The shepherd's swains shall dance and sing
For thy delight each May morning:
If these delights thy mind may move,
Then live with me and be my love.

Christopher Marlowe

Sunrise/set: 5:22/7:41
Day's Length: 14 hours 19 minutes
Average High/Low: 71/50
Average Temperature: 60
Record High: 87 – 1896
Record Low: 34 – 1901

Weather

Ten percent of May 13ths rise to the 90s, thirty percent to the 80s, twenty percent to the 70s, thirty percent to the 60s, and ten percent to the 50s. Frost is rare, and this is the last time in May when the chances of rain are only 25 percent. All the remaining days bring at least 30 percent, with some going as high as 50 to 60 percent. That increased frequency of precipitation carries the name of the "Strawberry Rains," a period during which local strawberries begin to ripen and are especially vulnerable to wet conditions.

Natural Calendar

When Yellow Springs azaleas lose their petals, daisies, clematis, and the first cinquefoil open all the way, the first strawberry ripens, and swallowtail butterflies visit the star of Bethlehem and bleeding hearts. The last quince flowers fall, and lilacs decay. Morel season is over in southern Ohio, but is just beginning in the Upper Midwest at higher elevations and in the far West. The bright yellow arrowleaf balsamroot is flowering in the Rocky Mountains as cottonwoods fill out there. Elk migrate north into higher summer ranges, and cutthroat trout are ready to spawn in mountain streams.

Daybook

1983: First June bug on the front screen. Snowball viburnum continues at full flower. First sweet rockets seen. Dogwoods magnificent. Grass knee high.

1984: First fleabane blooms, buds on the iris.

1986: Snow-on-the-mountain opens in the yard.

1987: Comfrey blooms. Black medic, white and red clover noticed at Wilberforce. Locusts full bloom along Corry Street. Milkweed six to nine inches high. Canopy closing quickly. Chicory getting lanky. Many hemlock budding. Early Summer yellow sweet clover: some tall and budding. Groundsel becoming overgrown in the pastures. Groundhog activity continues high (judging, at least, by the number of road kills).

1990: First poppies and mock orange bloom. Almost all the trillium grandiflorum are gone.

1991: First hemlock is in bloom. Some of the wild cherry trees have completed their flower cycle. The small green ash is full of flowers by my window at Wilberforce. Locust full bloom, the last step before the catalpas blossom and the canopy is filled in. A mother possum and her babies were killed on Wilberforce-Clifton Road last night.

1993: First red pyrethrum is just about fully emerged now. First spiderwort. The Glen canopy is maybe three-fourths full: complete where maples dominate, still delicate and thin where there are more oaks and sycamores.

1995: At the triangle park, small pinecones have fully formed on a few of the spruce. Seed pods on some of the silver maples are turning brown, some falling. At Antioch School, the mountain maples are in full bloom.

1998: To Dayton last night for the symphony, Beethoven's 9th. The roads were lined with locusts in bloom. When we got home, the first June bug was lying on the porch rug.

1999: Wood hyacinth remains lush. Ten leaves on the water lily. Purple rhododendrons full. Spiderwort opens. Tadpoles gone overnight.

2000: In the city, salsify blooming in the sidewalks, and then out east along the freeway, more, and one parsnip and Canadian thistles open from the summer-like heat of the past week. At the nursery, I saw the first locust flower cluster on one of their small trees planted near the driveway.

2001: Nodding thistles starting to open, first yellow sweet clover seen, parsnips early full along the road to Dayton, first small darner seen at the pond.

2002: First cardinal song at 4:58 a.m.

2003: Home from Madison, Wisconsin: Lily-of-the-valley now mostly gone. Daisies, comfrey, and spiderwort came into early full bloom while we were gone. Mock orange and the rhododendrons are all the way out. More sweet Williams are opening. The first peony is starting to unravel. The first scabiosa, multiflora rose, and snow-on-the-mountain blossomed. Catmint is full bright blue downtown, less bright in our yard. Catalpa leaves are half size. Wood hyacinths are starting to lose their luster.

2004: The first multiflora roses opened last night. Day and night, the air is thick with the sweetness of honeysuckles and mock orange and lilacs.

2005: At South Glen: Sweet rockets, wild phlox, Jack-in-the-pulpit, nodding trillium, white violets, garlic mustard, silver olive, sweet Cicely, one meadow goat's beard. Black snakeroot and corn salad budded. At home and through most of the village, the late tulips are done blooming. The white late daffodils on the north side of the arbor hold, but they are in decline. Korean lilac is full and fragrant; the purple lilacs along the south border are starting to break down. Mock orange buds are cracking.

2007: First blue flag at the west end of the north garden. Rockets, allium, chives, honeysuckle, Korean lilac, mock orange are in full bloom. Blue wood hyacinths starting to fade. Snow on the mountain flower stalks are tall, a few in bloom. Many rose of Sharon leaves a fourth of their mature size. The high canopy seems complete except for the sycamores, the locusts and Osage.

2008: Spring field crickets singing in the evening. The first of our purple iris has opened. The roadside canopy on the way to Columbus is still pale April green, March in southern Georgia. Redbud trees hold only a dusky remnant of their color now. First patch of daisies seen on the way to Wilmington. First locust flowers seen on the way home from Dayton. Wheat heading. Fleabane blooms in the yard.

2009: Inventory: Indian hyacinths completing their season. Red tulips hold. More rockets unravel. Late sweet Cicely, late garlic mustard. Wild lettuce waist high. Light leafing on the bamboo. Full bloom allium. Full fragrance of the Korean lilac. Full weigela, full buds on wisteria. Mother cardinal left the nest yesterday, no babies seen. Wheat is pale green across the countryside, hemlock heading, lamb's ear heading, snow on the mountain budding. First orange lily open on Davis Street. Pentstemon heading. White clover an black medic blooming.

2010: Large pink bush roses in bloom in the alley, and Mrs. Timberlake's peonies are coming in. Locust flowers are still full, but they seem to be darkening with age. Osage budded. Redbud seeds about an inch and a half long, thin. White clover and yellow sweet clover all along the roads, and first red clover noticed. First blue flags in the north garden. Azalea, Korean lilac and viburnum flowers almost all gone, honeysuckle and locusts starting to fall around then neighborhood. Penstemon and pink spirea budding. White bleeding heart opened under the honeysuckle in the back. Full mock orange, full chives, buttercups. The toad is singing in the pond as the temperature rises above 80 degrees and the local weather station announces a tornado warning.

2011: Italy: Riding in the country with Ivano and Neysa to Montefalco winery, then lunch at the Montefalco square. Haying seems complete in the Umbrian countryside, buttercups, hawkweeds and sow thistles fill many pastures. Pie cherries are ripe (almost a month ahead of the average in Yellow Springs). Wheat is tall, headed, a dusky green. Brome and foxtail grass nod in the wind. Thistles are budded but not really open yet. Nettles waist high. Comfrey found in bloom, and many azaleas.

2012: Roses in full bloom throughout Dayton, many stella d'oro lilies are out. Along South College Street in town, the catalpas are maybe a third in bloom, the phase quite early. Above the trellis, pale red-violet clematis flowers opening. All along the freeway, the locusts are finished, their foliage finally filling in. Along High Street, black walnut flower clusters and one small, furry nut fallen to the sidewalk. Comfrey is still in full bloom in the Phillips Street alley, as are the poppies.

2013: Phil Hawkey called: He had seen his first male tiger swallowtail at 7:10 in the evening. It was all bright and new, lying in the grass, he said, like it was in "HD."

2015: The first pale violet spiderwort opened overnight in the northwest garden, and the last Indian hyacinth went to seed in the circle garden (but wood hyacinths and allium holding). First white-spotted skipper seen near the white-flowered viburnum. Throughout the village, locusts are in full bloom. Running several miles in John Bryan Park around 4:30 in the afternoon, I saw bluettes, May apples, Solomon's plume, ragwort (a few with puffy seed heads), wild phlox, spring beauties, dwarf purple larkspur.

2016: Snowball viburnum: white petals falling into the bed of spent tulips, into the tall ferns and hostas. Deep red-violet redbud leaves match the red-violet of the shed. Algae gradually taking over the pond. No buds on the Japanese water iris this year, the first time ever, I believe. Into John Bryan Park with Jill: Lush foliage, canopy half filled, pileated calling, river high and fast, wood nettle thigh-high, late ragwort, many wild phlox, rockets, Solomon's plume, flowering May apples and tall white violets, fleabane, some swamp buttercups in the muck, Jack-in-the-pulpit being overgrown with grasses, a couple of small dark-purple larkspur, chickweed on the slopes collapsed and yellowing, catchweed lanky and still in bloom, black raspberries flowering, the air heavy with the smell of honeysuckles.

2017: I was having lunch on the back porch when I saw the first red admiral butterfly, then a Baltimore oriole, and then a catbird. In the honeysuckles, robins are guiding their young with peeps and chirps. At the shop downtown, the Kentucky coffee tree is in full flower. A dreamy, fragrant late afternoon in the Covered Bridge habitat: sweet rockets, corn salad, catchweed, a wild multiflora rose bush starting, wild geraniums full. Late garlic mustard, sweet Cicely, ragwort, a few phlox and white violets, parsnips large and budded, many bright buttercups, wood nettle knee high, sycamores only about a third leafed, tulip tree blossoms on the ground, the high canopy much thinner than the maple canopy of the village. Another red admiral butterfly seen, visiting beside us on the riverbank. The water was calm and silky near dusk, sun all over the far shore, the honeysuckles, all in flower, glowing. Coming home, I found a small grass snake had come in the back door that I had left open; he disappeared into the storage cabinets.

2018: Tat saw a Baltimore oriole in the back yard this afternoon. I noticed several weigelas open around town and mock orange buds on the old bush near the shed. Scott Stolsenberg photographed a rare King Rail at the Glass Farm pond.

2019: Pale sugar maple seeds cover Jill's driveway and the sidewalk down High Street.

2020: Finally a mild afternoon with sun and in the 60s, only the second nice day this month. Ranger and I went walking at the Old Mill path, found first blooms on catchweed and sweet rockets, lush full bloom of wild geraniums, groundsel, sweet Cicely, white violets and garlic mustard, many wild phlox and ragwort, some swamp buttercups. May apples, mock orange and wild raspberries were budded. I saw two red admiral butterflies and two cabbage whites. At home, lilacs hold, but their best is over. Hyacinths are still at their peak, and the allium is trying to open (even though Liz's allium has been completely open for a week). Fecal sacks noticed in the pond: the grackles have hatched.

One of the best things for me when I went to the hermitage was being attentive to the times of the day: when the birds began to sing, and the deer came out of the morning fog, and the sun came up....
                    Thomas Merton

Bill Felker

May 14th
The 134th Day of the Year

Late Spring keeps the promises of April: mock orange wide open days before peonies, iris and poppies, daisies and the first clematis, meadow goat's beard and red pyrethrums, ginger and sedum, comfrey and stitchwort, silver olive and the honey locusts flower all the way; strawberries ripen on the high tide of purple rockets and golden buttercups.

bf

Sunrise/set: 5:21/7:42
Day's Length: 14 hours 21 minutes
Average High/Low: 72/50
Average Temperature: 61
Record High: 89 – 1962
Record Low: 36 – 1920

Weather

The chances of sunshine on the 14th of May are high: a full 80 percent. Rain, however, falls on 35 percent of the days, a ten percent increase over yesterday's odds. Highs in the 50s are infrequent on the 14th, occurring only once in 15 or 20 years. Temperatures climb to the 60s on 20 percent of the afternoons. Seventies are the most common, coming 45 percent of the time; 80s and 90s round out the spectrum at 25 percent and five percent respectively.

Natural Calendar

Almost all the Midwestern field corn has now been planted in drier years. Half of the soybean and half the sugar beet crops are in the ground, along with two-thirds of the potatoes and a fourth of the tomatoes. Commercial sunflower planting time begins as the chances of a light freeze fall well below five percent. In the salt marshes of the South, fiddler crabs emerge from their tunnels in the creeks and estuaries. Across the Atlantic Ocean in the fields of Great Britain, apple orchards are usually in bloom, bulbous buttercups and bluebells, too.

Daybook

1983: First two comfrey flowers.

1984: Crabapples still holding their petals in this cold spring.

1985: First strawberries for breakfast today. Osage flowers falling, every poppy, sweet rocket, and mock orange open. Blue flag and sweet Cicely fading. Garlic mustard gone and bowing. Full rockets everywhere. Tall meadow rue and angelica buds completely emerged. Wingstem two feet tall. Canopy virtually in place.

1986: First parsnips flower in Dayton. Hummingbird seen at the frog pond along Grinnell Road. Yellow sweet clover, red clover, black medic at Wilberforce.

1987: Very first mock orange opened in the yard today.

1989: Still no poppies, no mock orange, no strawberries.

1990: My nephew John reported his first strawberry blooming in New York Mills, Minnesota, 800 miles north of Yellow Springs, 30 days from the first strawberry bloom here, right on schedule, spring moving north at the rate of approximately 25 miles per day.

1991: First blue flag opens. Tulip tree in bloom at the Covered Bridge. The air sweet with flowers. Honeysuckles falling. Canopy complete.

1993: Bright orange geum starts to open. First comfrey and pyrethrum fully open. First patches of poppies suddenly full bloom along Grinnell Road and Elm Street. Dock heading on Xenia Avenue and along the fields. Lupines fat and blue now, flags budding. Scorpion fly on the window screen this evening. Orchard grass well developed.

1998: First blue flag unravels in the garden.

1999: First orange daylilies open along Grinnell Road. The bridal wreath spirea suddenly declines, honeysuckles and locusts stay at their peak. First blue flag opens. First skipper butterfly seen. Tadpoles discovered hidden in corners and under rocks of the pond. The bathroom suddenly full of huge black flies.

2001: Multiflora roses open in the garden, poison hemlock seen in bloom along the highway to Dayton.

2002: Robins suddenly constantly peeping in the yard. Orienting their young? First spiderwort and columbine bloomed today.

2003: First blue flag iris and stella d'oro lily opened in garden. Bridal wreath spirea almost gone. Snowball viburnum flowers hold. Poppies full bloom in Clifton.

2004: Multiflora roses reach full bloom overnight. In the woods, geese are honking. No insects seen. Waterleaf is blossoming, and the first meadow goat's beard is open along the path in the butterfly preserve. Late garlic mustard, full sweet rockets, sweet Cicely dominate the fields. Ironweed, jewelweed and wood nettle are past knee high. Poppies and iris flowering all over town, but not in the south garden. Weigela is in bloom now.

2006: The first dark blue spiderwort was open today. Bright red azalea in the east garden holding, but the allium has passed its best, and the late season tulips are almost gone.

2007: Allium strong, azaleas and tulips gone. Mateo's violet weigela is in full bloom. Star of Bethlehem ends suddenly. Herb plants set into the circle garden.

2008: The perennial blue salvia in the far northwest corner of the garden pulls my view out from the violet hyacinths, the violet flax and the red-violet allium in the circle garden, then back to the pink deadnettle and the pale blue spiderwort between them. The one purple iris to the left, more hyacinths to the right fill my vision. In the alley this morning, all the lilacs were gone, and a small flock of grackles was making a ruckus in someone's back yard.

2010: Blueberry bushes have two buds. Dutch iris early full, Indian hyacinths all to fat seeds. First daddy longlegs seen, clustered snakeroot blooming, pollen gold, roses and campanulas opening. First peony opens at home, meadow goat's beard full bloom in town and along the highway south, locusts starting to fall. Multiflora roses coming in.

2011: Long walk in Spoleto around the hills that surround La Rocca. Sunny and mild, light wind. Rondini (swallows) in the valleys, wild fennel all along the paths. Purple wild cyclamen in the hilly shade. Cuckoos and merli sang in the distance. White campion, bladderwort common, spitbugs on a number of plants, several St. John's wort in full bloom, large late euphorbia on the hillsides, and something similar to blueweed.

2012: Liz wrote again about the black swallowtail: "The butterfly stayed until today...was still here this morning, then gone when I came home from work. Two days of total stillness before setting off on its adventure. A sesshin!"

2013: Goshen, Indiana: Many fields of dandelions still bright, but many also gone to seed. Crab apples mostly gone. Redbuds and dogwoods fading.

2014: At the parking lot near the grocery store, Neysa and I saw one very small gosling with its parents in the grass. One meadow goat's beard was open by the side of the road.

2015: First dark violet spiderwort bloomed in the north garden. If I had enough rhubarb plants, I could have a pie; the stalks on my only plant are big enough to cut. Wood hyacinths, Korean lilac and allium holding, poppies full in Liz's garden, and Mateo's weigela is in full flower (must have come in with the locusts and mock orange and honeysuckles). Creeping phlox in decline downtown. In the North Glen: sweet rockets, catchweed, Solomon's plume, ragwort, May apple, phlox, watercress, white violets, small yellow sedum. Touch-me-nots knee high.

2016: Large patches of wild daisies along Dayton-Yellow Springs

Road, winter wheat tall and mellowing. The yellow climbing rose at Liz's is in full bloom. My weigela early bloom, starting to anchor the west end of the north garden near the house; Mateo's weigela loaded with blossoms. Honeysuckle flowers falling in the cold rain. On the steps to the Cascades, wood betony.

2017: The first peony in the yard opened overnight, three more in the afternoon. Weigelas are holding strong. First locust petals starting to fall. At Clifton Gorge, Solomon's plume (more than I've noticed in other walks), waterleaf and white violets are the main plants in bloom. Leafcup is waist high, all the undergrowth lush. A third red admiral butterfly came by the circle garden.

2018: I keep feeling left behind by the speed of spring, and so in this backwater of flowers in which I find myself, confused, surrounded by the full-beautied detritus of the flood of May, I stumble through the woods and garden, picking up pieces, seeing this, seeing that, not knowing where to begin, knowing that it doesn't matter, knowing that it does. And even though the markers of this time of May are never quite the same from year to year, they are similar enough to offer a kind of stability to my own history and to the history of the landscape and climate, a collection of floral trivia making sense of larger and smaller things.

2019: A walk in North Glen with Jill: the undergrowth lush, wild phlox, waterleaf (*Hydrophilum appendiculatum*) and wild geraniums common beside the white violets. One red admiral butterfly came by, and I saw a sulphur when I went jogging with Ranger in the early afternoon. At home, the first wisteria flower has unraveled. Dennie sent Jill a video of bees swarming at her farm.

2020: Blue jays calling and calling, fledglings out of the nest. One yellow sulphur butterfly. One common fleabane in bloom. Only a handful of honeysuckle flowers open (a gauge of how cold this spring has been). Pink quince flowers falling to the koi pond. I went to look for Liz's yellow rose, but the plant was no longer there. Mosquitoes attacked me on the back porch for the first time this spring. Thunderstorm at 5:15 this afternoon, dark clouds and wind sweeping across the woodlot. Finally, Aida called to say she had seen an American redstart, a relatively common migrant in the middle of May.

It is Nature's rutting season. Even as the birds sing tumultuously and glance by with fresh and brilliant plumage, so now is Nature's grandest voice heard and her sharpest flashes seen. The air has resumed its voice, and the lightning, like a yellow spring flower, illumines the dark banks of the clouds. All the pregnant earth is bursting into life, like a mildew, accompanied with noise and fire and tumult. She comes dripping rain like a cow with overflowing udder.

Henry David Thoreau

May 15th
The 135th Day of the Year

I cannot meet the Spring unmoved –
I feel the old desire –
A Hurry with a lingering mixed,
A Warrant to be fair.

Emily Dickenson

Sunrise/set: 5:20/7:43
Day's Length: 14 hours 23 minutes
Average High/Low: 72/51
Average Temperature: 61
Record High: 92 - 1900
Record Low: 32 - 1910

Weather

With the arrival of the third major high pressure system of the month, the 15th of May often brings cooler temperatures than those days on either side of it. While a five percent chance of a high in the 90s exists, the possibility of 80s drops to just ten percent. Seventies occur 50 percent of the afternoons, 60s on 30 percent, 50s on ten percent. Rain can be expected an average of once every three years on this date, with completely overcast skies covering most of Lower Midwest more than 40 percent of the time.

The Weather in the Week Ahead

High temperatures are usually above 60 degrees the week ahead, with the chances of 70s or better rising to 70 percent, a ten percent increase over last week's chances. Cold in the 50s occurs rarely, but if it does appear, it is typically on the 21st and 24th. Chances of frost are low, but tender plants are in some danger after the passage of May's fourth cold front on the 15th and fifth cold front on the 20th. The 18th, 19th, and 22nd are the wettest days in the period; the 20th and the 21st are the least likely to bring precipitation.

Natural Calendar

When azaleas lose their petals, daisies and the first clematis and the first cinquefoil open all the way, the first strawberry ripens, and the first swallowtail butterflies visit the late star of Bethlehem and bleeding hearts. The last quince flowers fall, and lilacs decay.

The yellow heads of meadow goat's beard appear along the roadsides next to the sweet clover foliage spreading out for June. The pink and violet of sweet rockets replace the purple wild phlox in the woods and pastures. All of the buttercups blossom, and by the end of the week, the first pyrethrums presage the poppies. Horseradish and comfrey are budding.

Locust leaves emerge, their first flowers now open as the high canopy slowly closes in. Rich-scented four-petaled flowers of the silver olive are still open. Lizard's tail has at least three leaves now. Golden ragwort, wild phlox, pale violet Jacob's ladder, Jack-in-the-pulpit, columbine and wild geraniums are still in full flower. Multiflora roses and wild raspberries are budding. Black walnuts and oaks become the major sources of pollen. Cedar waxwings migrate up the rivers as the last buckeye flowers fall. Half the goslings are bigger than galoshes.

Daybook

1982: Meadow goat's beard is out. Evergreen growth is at least an inch on every branch.

1983: Red peonies and iris in bloom.

1985: Hemlock is tall and blooming now. Near Antioch School, one wild lettuce plant and a Queen Anne's lace are chest high, budding. Canadian thistles seem ready to open. Out in a field off Grinnell Road, the big nodding thistles are as tall as my waist. Japanese knotweed is over my head. Milkweed is two feet. In the village, iris, mock orange, and peonies are in full bloom.

1986: Canopy closing quickly. First peonies and blue flags.

1987: First poppy opens in the yard. Wisteria seen in bloom.

1988: First mock orange opens late in the day (before the peonies, about four days after the first iris). At Far Hole, hunchback chubs caught, all bristly for mating. Tall meadow rue is knee high, pacing the angelica, unfolding. Sweet rockets have replaced the violets. Tallest canopy still in bud. Lizard's tail has three leaves now. Goslings maybe two weeks old, size of my shoe. Wood nettle six to eight inches. Multiflora roses budding.

1989: Horseradish bloom time, apple petals all fallen. Red and pink quince still hold a little. Most tulips gone, a few late ones and a couple of the smallest narcissus hold on. Star of Bethlehem full. Cardinal seen building nest. Last bluebells fade. Peonies now tall with large buds, select iris budding. Lesser stitchwort discovered in bloom on the lawn at Wilberforce.

1990: First pyrethrum opened today. Viburnum has gone now. Locusts pace the oaks. Gum tree near full, ginkgo also. Rhododendron flowers on West Center College Street. Lilacs over for the year.

1991: The air heavy and fragrant: mock orange dominating the yard, and the locust flowers all over town. Hydrangea still full. Peonies bloomed today in near record heat. Second day of blue flag. Yucca seen heading in Xenia. Parsnips in bloom along the highway south. Hemlock has been open for several days. Azaleas losing their petals, daisies full bloom, pyrethrums and iris. First strawberry ripening. First yellow and black swallowtails noticed.

1992: First pyrethrum opens. First daisy not far behind. Rockets full. Two poppies. Snowball viburnum. All the buttercups in bloom. Locust branches white with blossoms. Mock orange almost ready. Canopy nearly complete. Cherries half formed. Blue jays loud and nervous. Orange geum half out. Full budding of the blue flags. Horseradish and comfrey full bloom.

1993: Lilacs turning brown, shriveling. Geum opens more. Locusts full bloom all the way to Kettering. Horseradish and snowball viburnum full bloom. Some ferns up to my chest.

1998: First pale pink peonies opened overnight, the first blue spiderwort too. The back locusts are in full bloom. Mock orange, honeysuckle, daisies, pyrethrums, poppies, iris, rhododendrons everywhere. First water lily buds reach the surface. Buds on the privets. First mosquitoes bite. Geese fly over 6:40 a.m.

1999: Pale violet flax and deep red pyrethrums are in full bloom as first pink peonies open in the south garden, and wood hyacinths decline. Bridal wreath spirea and daisies open more. Star of Bethlehem still makes a white border in the north garden. The first blue flag opens. The first skipper seen yesterday, last lilac. Tadpoles discovered hidden in corners and rocks of the pond, shyer now, getting ready to live under rocks.

2000: First poison hemlock flowers along the bike path. Honeysuckles past their prime now. Several buds getting ready to open in the pond. Pink spirea budding, star of Bethlehem gone, snowball viburnum falling apart.

2002: Robin chatter continues through the day. First bud on the water lilies and water iris, first pollen spike too. Peak of iris, clematis, and coral bells at Park Meadows. Wheat is heading and turning pale on the way to Washington Court House. In the wet fields, bright vistas of cressleaf groundsel. Azaleas end in the east garden. Late hawthorns at the triangle park are in full bloom.

2004: One cardinal sang at 4:45 a.m., but the other cardinals waited until about 6:00. The red azaleas in the east garden fall quickly now. The first pale pink peony is unraveling slowly in the cool rain. Poison hemlock has come into full bloom.

2005: The very first mock orange and purple clematis blossoms opened today. The violet iris in the north garden and the catmint across from the Korean lilac have several blooms now. Sweet rockets opened yesterday along the fence.

2007: First new Dutch iris opened overnight. First locust blossoms seen on the way to Xenia and Dayton. Indian hyacinth at the end of its blooms. Long dry spell continues. Chives and allium continue at their peak. Baltimore oriole was singing in the back trees this morning, its partner sitting on the high branches of a rose of Sharon. Toad lily planted.

2008: A wonderful green stability these days, the cool weather keeping the blue hyacinths, flax, Indian hyacinths, and the Korean lilac in bloom. The Dutch iris are fully budded, but a ways away from flowering. A few mock orange buds are stretching to open. Yellowing wild deadnettle at Katie's in the alley.

2010: Roses coming in around the yard, red and yellow.

2012: Lace vine in bloom today as the iris and mock orange wind down throughout the village. Out in the countryside, thin-leafed waterleaf found in full bloom, a white campion, parsnips, and several golden Alexander plants in flower. One black swallowtail, one red admiral seen.

2013: Inventory before leaving for Wisconsin: Myrtle leaves red and about half an inch; first sweet William opening; first yellow tiger swallowtail; azalea holding bright; geranium still full; perennial salvia coming in; paulownia leaves four to five inches; Indian hyacinths and silver olives finally gone; dogwoods losing petals; highest trees thin but still greening.
    On the road to Goshen, Indiana: Silver olive flowers reappear about an hour north of Yellow Springs; bridal wreath seen full near Celina; apple trees gone in Van Wert; redbuds coming back near Fort Wayne; apples and lilacs coming back near Goshen, and patches of dandelions in full flower, along with patches all gone to seed; wheat a foot tall and bent in the wind.

2014: Ivano reports from Spoleto (Italy) that the merli (blackbird) fledglings have left the nest. Libby said she saw a firefly tonight.

2015: Mild in the upper 50s, no wind, barometer slowly dropping. I began running at 3:40 a.m., heard the very first robin at 4:11, the chorus starting a minute later, a cardinal joining in at 4:15 as I turned down High Street to head home. No crickets heard. When I walked downtown at noon, I saw the village in full iris, poppy, weigela (ours must have just bloomed overnight), and bridal-wreath spirea bloom, new peonies in some yards. Buckeyes were the size of a pea. One catmint plant was starting to flower. A scorpion fly noticed in the spiderwort yesterday. A white spotted skipper flew by as I was updating this information.

2016: On the way to the Cascades, wood betony all to seed.

2017: Three yellow male tiger swallowtails seen this morning, one downtown, and two in the peonies at home. Parsnips are in flower on the way to Xenia. Peter said that his hummingbirds arrived late this year, the first male on May 7, the first female on May 12.

2018: Pale sugar maples seeds clustered on the tips of their branches, and fallen, too, onto Davis Street this morning, and then I found more maple seeds, many days old, on Limestone Street. Snowball viburnums full in Fairborn. I saw the first scorpion fly of the year along the overgrown west garden hostas and pachysandra.

2019: Osage branches show a little green now. The first large ants have appeared in the studio. For the first time, English plantain (*Plantago lanceolata*) is flowering along the path beyond Ellis. I saw a few more red clover blossoms, too. Jill's first poppy bloomed today.

2020: Leslie reports a six-spotted green tiger beetle today and the first June bug at her window tonight.

There is a time when spring's new leaves are just opened, the grasses are growing to their first tallness, violets – yellow and blue, cowslips, crowfoots, woodruff, false Solomon's seal are in bloom, the woods are dense against the evening sky, but not yet as dark as in late spring....

August Derleth

May 16th
The 136th Day of the Year

Summer set lip to earth's bosom bare,
And left the flushed print of a poppy there.

Francis Thompson

Sunrise/set: 5:19/7:44
Day's Length: 14 hours 25 minutes
Average High/Low: 72/51
Average Temperature: 61
Record High: 94 – 1900
Record Low: 32 – 1904

Weather

A morning below 32 degrees, which could be expected at least one day in seven around the 4th of the month, can be expected only one day in 70 on May 16. Average highs stay in the 70s, and typical lows come into summer-like 60s for the first time since September. There is a 70 percent chance of a high above 70, and a 95 percent chance of a high above 60. The sun shines 85 percent of all the days. The chances of a shower are one in three. Wind is not uncommon today, as the fourth high pressure system of the month moves across the Lower Midwest.

Natural Calendar

The first June bug clings to the screen door when the first firefly glows in the lawn. Orchard grass and tall meadow rue is knee high now in the wetlands and fields, pacing the angelica. In the rivers, lizard's tail has three leaves. July's wood nettle is a foot to two-feet tall. Deep red ginger has replaced the toad trillium close to the ground around the small open fingers of white sedum.

The Stars

Cassiopeia has moved deep into the northern night sky behind Polaris, the north star, by this time of May, and Cepheus, which looks a little like a house lying on its side, is beginning to come around to the east of Polaris. When Cepheus is due east of the north star, then it will be the middle of July. When it lies due south of Polaris, then the leaves will be turning. When it lies due west of Polaris, it will be the middle of Deep Winter.

Daybook

1982: First peonies and columbine seen, and first mock orange bloomed today (remained until June 10).

1983: First white clover seen at Wilberforce. Purple deadnettle yellowing along the roadside. At the Covered Bridge: fire pink, sweet Cecily, star of Bethlehem, golden Alexander, mallow.

1984: Mill Habitat: First June bug. First ducklings seen on the river northeast of the mill. Then a few hundred yards farther upstream, a pair of geese with seven huge goslings swimming between them. A few bluebells left. May apple, rue anemone, phlox, watercress, ragwort, violets, spring beauties, geraniums, spring cress, crowfoot, catchweed, garlic mustard, Jack-in-the-pulpit in bloom. Redbuds and buckeyes still in bloom, yellow poplar budding. Grasses up to my knees. Buzzards in their tree at the bend of the river, wings outstretched to the sun. Sycamores have one-inch leaves, some oak leaves at about the same size. Canopy pubescent, half finished in a tantalizing middle season between spring and summer.

1986: First hemlock flowered today. Earliest field crickets heard. Aloe buds are opening in the greenhouse.

1987: First strawberries for breakfast after a morning walk by the Covered Bridge. I saw hundreds of suckers and giant carp swimming slowly up the Little Miami River. When I threw in my line, I caught a shiner, a chub, a sunfish, a bluegill and a rock bass, all very small.

1988: First hemlock flowers. High canopy full green now, but some oaks and sycamores hold out. Locusts in full bloom, mock orange in early bloom as the first comfrey blossoms. Hemlock very tall, first flowers seen in Mad River. Connie writes that water lilies have opened at Crystal Lake, and it's the best year yet for *Iris pseudacorus.*

1990: Locust and wisteria in full bloom, and all the grasses. Dogwoods almost completely gone. Waterleaf fills the woods floor, in bloom by today every year on record. First rhododendrons seen in town.

1991: Petals of the locust are falling today, the last wild cherry blossoms disappear: the beginning of the last days of Late Spring. The star of Bethlehem has just ended, garlic mustard at their final buds. The canopy has closed almost everywhere (with Osage, walnut, sycamore, a few oaks holding back). Red clover and blackberries full bloom, foxglove just starting.

1993: Mother-in-law's-tongue full bloom in the greenhouse for the past week. Several bright orange geum now completely open beside two wide daisies. Very first mock orange unravels.

1994: Spiderwort opens in the south garden. At South Glen, sweet Cicely and purple larkspur are in full bloom beside the last of the wild phlox and wild geraniums. In town, bridal wreath spirea is completely gone.

1995: East to New York City: Now is the time for the grasses to dominate, and all the fields and fence rows are growing tall with brome and orchard grass and timothy. Yellow winter cress appears in the pastures from Yellow Springs into New York. At the lower elevations, the canopy is half complete, cottonwoods parallel to the gums, the ginkgoes, and the oaks. In the mountains above 1,800 feet, dogwoods and redbuds are still in full bloom (the redbuds have just leafed out in Yellow Springs), coltsfoot plants are marked with dandelion-like seed heads, and there is more gold in the tree line than in Yellow Springs. May apples seem just to have emerged, and fields of dandelions are still flowering near 2,000 feet. At Somerset, Pennsylvania, 2,300 feet on my altimeter, I saw white daffodils. A yellow swallowtail butterfly flew in front of the car there. At the peak elevations, near 2,500 feet, the high trees are almost bare, and it seems I've driven back into April. Descending the Appalachians, daisies appear in the roadsides coming into

Harrisburg. In New Jersey, the wheat is turning a week or two before Greene County's crop.

1996: Rain and flooding for weeks, the ground saturated, the garlic as tall as can be, rhubarb immense. Peonies have large buds. In the south garden, the first pyrethrum opened in a shower last night. Rockets and buttercups have been blooming for days, and the pale lavender hyacinths are just starting. In the east garden, the dwarf iris and columbine are coming in, the azaleas at their best. At Wilberforce, the dandelions were all going to seed yesterday. No farm planting has been done so far. In the Great Plains, the wheat crop has been destroyed by drought; here, the corn and soybean crops will suffer from a late start.

1998: Honeysuckle time is ending quickly now. Full bloom of bittersweet nightshade. Wood hyacinths wilt suddenly.

2000: Mountain maple full bloom at Antioch School yesterday. Spiderwort opened in the south garden, flags early full, achillea seen along North High Street. This afternoon, several large black flies in the bathroom, the same kind that appeared on May 14 last year: the world on schedule.

2001: First spiderwort opens. Wheat heading. Full bloom of water iris in the Grinnell wetlands. First June bug found hanging on the screen door when we got home from the symphony tonight at 10:45.

2004: The pale violet wood hyacinths are turning brown. The red azalea in the east garden is gone. The Dutch iris are coming in. The allium still holds tall and purple. Sweet rockets and sweet Williams now give color to the long north garden. The Korean lilac has peaked, its flowers collapsing all at once. Scorpion flies are suddenly everywhere this afternoon. Red and white clovers and yellow sweet clover are blooming by the side of the road. One nodding thistle is beginning to show pink near Byron.

2005: Peak of blue wood hyacinths, pale blue-violet iris and the Korean lilac.

2007: Last night, rain for the first time this May, a hard rain at first with thunder, then soft, lasting until near dawn. In the lawn, I noticed that white clover has followed the seeding of the dandelions. Bittersweet budded. Almost all of the wood hyacinths are gone now, but the golden ranunculus by the east side of the house are in full bloom. The garden mirrors what I noted here May 16 of 2004. Near the peach tree, the new Dutch iris continue to unravel: one blue and yellow, one pure yellow.

2008: Weigela in bloom in Wilmington and here. Hawthorns stay white with flowers. The circle garden keeps all its blue and violet, the same as in 2005. Mock orange struggles to open, but the day remains in the 60s, still a little cold.

2010: Grackles loud at 6:00 a.m. Judy reports white campion and meadow goat's beard in Goshen, Indiana.

2011: Spoleto, Italy: Walk along the bike path near Pontebari: Thistles (*Cardo mariano*) are starting to flower here, a plant with wide leaves that have light, spreading veins. A plant very similar to poison hemlock is in late full bloom.

2012: June bug found while I was transplanting zinnias. On the way to Fairborn, coreopsis seen open. All along the roads, daisies and yellow sweet clover, full blooming parsnips and hemlock. Catalpas flowering in the city and country. In the garden, our yucca is well budded, stalk high. Liz writes: "I saw two male Baltimore orioles squabbling through air and tree in the Whitehall neighborhood today...what flashes of color!"

2013: Madison, Wisconsin: Yellow leafy spurge rife throughout the roadsides and fields, bromes and orchard grasses and vetch vines blowing in the strong south wind. Full dandelion bloom, full apple bloom, some pears still holding petals, but mostly leaves; tulips and daffodils, Solomon's plume, bellwort, lilacs, geums, Virginia bluebells, anemone, wild cherry, bridal wreath, poppies flowering, a few trillium grandiflorum turning pink, toad trillium still in bloom, one May apple open, iris budding.

2015: At 9:20, a rainy wet evening, I went outside and I heard the rhythmic chrrr-chrrr of the Eastern gray tree frog (*Hyla versicolor*). No crickets heard yet this year.

2016: Light frost last night throughout the countryside, but no damage here in Yellow Springs. As this cold May continues: news that April was the warmest on record for the planet and that 2016 is forecast to be considerably warmer than last year.

2017: At the quarry habitat, tadpoles bask in the shallow pools, very few blooming plants, only wild daisies, some honeysuckles, dogbane waist high. In the afternoon, I completed the zinnia plantings, two plots: one maybe six by twenty, the other maybe twelve by twenty-five seeded around milkweed. Above me, wisteria flowers were disintegrating. Downtown, the Kentucky coffee trees have lost most of their blossoms. Along High Street, at the corner of Davis, blackberry bushes are in flower. Privet clusters are unraveling.

2019: Two silver-spotted skippers, a common buckeye butterfly, a red admiral and a sulphur seen today in the fields by Ellis Pond. White clover has opened overnight along my running path. The first spiderwort flowered in the north garden, and the first mock orange blossom from the struggling mock orange bush appeared by my studio window. More zinnias and dahlias planted. The news reports that this past April was the second-warmest on record.

2020: A trip to Erie, Pennsylvania (283 miles) to get Jill after she had an encounter with a deer that smashed her windshield. She was fine, but not the deer. I drove up in sun throughout the trip, watched the canopy thin to maybe half of that around Yellow Springs, and the return of the Great Dandelion bloom halfway through the trip. As I approached Cleveland, the roadsides filled with flowering crabs and cherries.

There she stopped to scent a peony:
My small glory, my flaxen head.
But there were many, blood and cream,
And solemnly she cupped each flower
With gracious care...buried nostrils deep
And long within the fragrant petal silk
As though one passed might feel offense
If she went by and did not take its gift.
Thus, slowly up and back the row
She walked, nor even missed the one,
Bird-broken, lying on the ground.
Quietly she took my hand to go
Then turned and said, "Good-bye."
I cannot help but think she spoke
To things akin: with beauty meant
To gather up in one short hour, love
To last the days when flushing petals
First curl close about the heart,
Then softly break with dew-fall
In the night.

"Judy" by her father, Robert Felker

May 17th
The 137th Day of the Year

The foolish fears of what might pass
I cast them all away
Among the clover-scented grass,
Among the new mown hay,
Among the hushing of the corn
Where drowsy poppies nod,
Where ill thoughts die and good are born
Out in the fields with God.

William Wordsworth

Sunrise/set: 5:18/7:45
Day's Length: 14 hours 27 minutes
Average High/Low: 73/51
Average Temperature: 62
Record High: 93 – 1900
Record Low: 33 – 1895

Weather

Highs in the 90s are rare on the 17th and 18th of May, but 80s occur 30 percent of the afternoons; 70s take place 40 percent of the time, and 60s twenty percent. Cold 50s take the remaining ten percent. Under the influence of the fourth high-pressure system of the month, skies are often partly cloudy to clear today, and there is only a 15 percent chance of completely overcast conditions. Rain showers occur one day in three.

Natural Calendar

The center of Late Spring is already closing the canopy. Sycamores, Osage, cottonwoods and oaks are leafing out, and white mulberries and buckeyes blossom. Along the sidewalks, iris, poppies, sweet William, and florescence of bridal wreath spirea and snowball viburnum have appeared. The delicate Korean lilacs take over from the fading standard lilac varieties, and bright rhododendrons replace the azaleas. Serviceberry trees have small green berries now. In the alleys, scarlet pimpernel comes in beside the thyme-leafed speedwell.

Columbine is open on the cliffs, and throughout the deep woods, Solomon's seal, false Solomon's seal, bellwort, wild phlox, trillium grandiflorum, wild geranium, golden Alexander, wood betony, early meadow rue, swamp buttercup, ginger, Jacob's ladder, water cress and golden seal are blooming. White garlic mustard and sweet Cicely still dominate the deep woods; violet sweet rockets increase throughout the fields and glades.

On most Midwestern farms, the corn is up and soybean planting is underway in average years. Orchard grass is heading. A little alfalfa is budding. Red and white clover blossom in the pasture. In the garden, it is the center of pepper, tomato, bean, cantaloupe and cucumber planting time.

Daybook

1982: Lilacs done, comfrey blooming, first red clover seen.

1983: Daisies blooming at King's Yard. Jumpseed and Canadian thistles nine inches long at South Glen, waterleaf early bloom, pink trillium grandiflorum holding. May apple, toad trillium, phlox, sweet Cicely, catchweed, golden Alexander, sweet rockets, geranium, henbit, winter cress, celandine, fleabane, chickweed, small flowered buttercup, spring cress, wild ginger, swamp buttercup in full bloom. The tree line still yellow and brown rather than the glowing greens of Late Spring and summer. A black butterfly, with orange and white on its wings: a red admiral.

1984: Chives blooming in the garden. First firefly seen glowing in the night lawn. Dandelions finished.

1986: First firefly seen, but not glowing. Robins and blackbirds loud all day.

1987: First damselfly by the river, and first bite by a horsefly. Wild cherry, black walnut and locust still in full bloom, and the rest of the canopy complete. Some parsnips coming in by the roadsides. Angelica is past knee high, pacing the wood nettle. Orchard grass is excellent for chewing, will soon be past its prime and hard to pull. Dock flowering at Middle Prairie. A big red-horse sucker caught at Far Pool; it got off the line as I brought it to shore, eluded me, flopping in the grass, and then jumped back into the water.

1989: First daisies. Black walnuts and oaks becoming the major sources of pollen.

1991: Lily-of-the-valley and bleeding heart seasons are over.

1992: Locust full bloom, mock orange holding, sweet rockets full. One young squirrel exploring, got stuck on top of the utility pole in the back yard, finally came down. Canopy near complete, cherries half formed. Blue jays and crows loud like they have been for the last two weeks. Poppies and iris, comfrey, and horseradish full bloom. Siberian iris full budding.

1993: First purple clematis, first red sweet William today. All the Siberian iris are budding. Buttercups, iris, and rockets full bloom. Quince gone. Wild onion heading. First yellow and black tiger swallowtail seen on Wilberforce-Clifton. At South Glen, waterleaf has tall violet flowers, all open. Twinleaf and toothwort and early meadow rue have their seed pods. Toad trillium is tattered and decaying. Jack-in-the-pulpit, wood nettle, touch-me-nots, and leafcup are all up to my thighs, the undergrowth surging up as the canopy closes in.

1994: Spanish scilla/blue wood hyacinth is in full bloom in the south garden today. The first daisy opens, first iris, first sweet William. Siberian iris budding. Poppies and peonies seen in Xenia. Along the river, the lizard's tail is up about six to nine inches, three leaves on each plant. First red admiral butterfly seen along the south wall.

1995: The last clumps of creeping phlox have completed their bloom now. Their best time is April.

1996: Brief stop at the mill with Buttercup and Fergus, the bulldogs. I saw meadow goat's beard and corn salad opening there, catchweed and wild geraniums full bloom, parsnips heading, wild phlox at their last. Foliage of ironweed and thin-leafed coneflower is up to my knees.

1998: First two red water lilies opened in the pond overnight. Across from them a lavender water hyacinth is flowering. Along the east fence, the first foxglove is open. At Antioch School, Jeanie saw the first yellow swallowtail of the year and a white spotted skipper. Out on the road in Greene County, the first yellow sweet clover seen. White clover is blooming in the grass. Hemlock is blossoming and the first parsnips. Some of the locusts are falling. Blue Siberian iris in the north garden are full now. A flea bit Jeanie when she was working in the yard.

1999: First sweet William. Robin calling at 4:00 a.m. Jeanie gives me a yellow poplar blossom. Sweet Cicely to seed.

2000: Up at 3:00 a.m. this morning, I listened for the whinny of the screech owl, but it didn't come. Is that call only for late winter and early spring? Out in town, the yellow roses are in full bloom, have been for some time. Wild grapes open, perfection of iris, blue flags, peonies, poppies. Sweet Cicely gone to seed. First water lily opens in the pond this afternoon.

2001: Tulip tree and lupines full.

2002: Sudden end to the wood hyacinths. Orchard grass was too tough to pull today, a pivot to summer. And the first of June's gold-collared blackflies.

2003: First strawberries are ripe in the garden.

2004: The first purple spiderwort opened today. In the north garden, the white flowers of the lily-of-the-valley have started to brown, the Korean lilac rusting above it. In the triangle park, the Kousa dogwood blossoms have taken form.

2005: Robins quiet at 3:40 a.m., began to chirp very faintly at about 3:45. By 4:00, they were in full song. Doves were singing at 4:45, cardinals late at 4:50. First scorpion fly noticed on the parsley this morning.

2007: Mateo's multiflora rose has started to come out. Blue eggshell noticed on the walk in front of the house. Hemlock blooming on the way to Dayton.

2008: To New Kensington, Pennsylvania, and return: Locusts and wild cherry trees blooming from here into western Pennsylvania. Rhododendrons and azaleas and dogwoods and weigela full bloom throughout the area. Garlic mustard at about the same age as in Yellow Springs. White chestnut flowers seen.

2009: To Yellow Springs from Madison, Wisconsin: Yellow sweet clover and red-winged blackbirds all 500 miles. At home. All the aliums were open, the first Dutch iris, full rockets, full late hyacinths, most sweet Williams open, Korean lilacs faded, more groundsel open, full locusts here and throughout the area, variegated weigela open, clematis purple, end red tulips, falling viburnum flowers, full standard iris, late hawthorn, first peony unraveling, first gold stella d'oro lily in the redbud garden, full mock orange, privet budded. At sundown, grackles and robins strong.

2010: Heavy honeysuckle flower fall in the rain, early full peonies bowing, locust petals coming down with the rain. Baby cardinal begging to be fed.

2011: Italy: Into the mountains north of Spoleto to purchase cheese: At higher elevations, the canopy is suddenly thin, April green, luminescent. Dandelions and lilacs appear in full flower, and wisteria is in bloom. Forget-me-nots and buttercups throughout the lush hillsides, watercress in the streams. Iris is budding in the mountain gardens, open down in the city. At Vallo de Nera, catchweed and red clover seen in full bloom. First jasmine petals coming out in Spoleto.
Riding up into the mountains above the Spoleto valley, I can see the elevation show, within just a few miles, a month of seasonal difference taking me back to April in Yellow Springs as well as in Rome. `

The advanced state of the foliage in Spoleto accelerates Yellow Springs time ahead a month, and somewhere halfway up these mountains, central Italy and southwestern Ohio are almost in sync, elevation compensating for the position of the sun and continental climate differences. The many similar species and a sense of their trajectory from bloom to seeding tie together the 5,000 mile distance between Spoleto and Yellow Springs, reducing horizontal distance to seasonal time, and seasonal time to color and scent.

2012: Flower clusters fall from the Osage orange trees near the shed in the back yard. Dark mulberries have fallen to Dayton Street. Pie cherries ripening on Dayton Street and Stafford Street and High Street, too. Pink spirea open at the Lawsons' and in front of Gerard's, ours lagging behind. In the circle garden, the penstemon has opened, and the broad-leafed waterleaf along the west edge of the property.

2014: The hyacinths, the honeysuckles and the allium remain just past their prime now. The poppies have reached full bloom. My milkweed plant from Rick has grown fat and a foot tall. More spiderwort is coming in, including the pale ones at the west end of the garden. The last Virginia bluebells fall to the ground; beside them, the lungwort has lost its blossoms. The hostas cover so much now, seem to have reached their full spread. Most dogwoods are coming down, most lilacs gone.

2015: Running at five in the morning after rain, the air soft, and the sky light enough for me to see a parsnip budding, hemlock and cressleaf groundsel in bloom by the stream at Ellis Park, winter cress at the end of its flowering, garlic mustard almost gone, snow-on-the-mountain with bright umbels, dock heading up, orchard grass fully formed, and blue grass, black walnut blossoms covering the road under each leaning tree, honeysuckle flowers scattered from the rain, sycamore branches with small pale new leaves, the town gardens covered with hostas, and the canopy almost complete. In the circle garden at home, the allium and the wood hyacinths are finally browning and starting to be tattered. The old north garden of twenty years ago had blue flag iris and sweet

Williams to fill in before lilies. And the circle garden then, of course, was only the apple tree with a few hosta around it. In Dayton, sow thistles are in bloom now, and trefoil has appeared along Dayton-Yellow Springs Road (and a boot-sized new gosling). Red flowered chestnut tree full at the Bergamo Center, and a hawthorn with tiny berries.

2016: Another cold day in the 50s, but peonies noticed in flower along Elm Street across from the school playground, and the first blossoms of snow-on-the-mountain in the dooryard garden.

2017: All the zinnias planted yesterday with perfect daytime sun and mild night temperature in the 60s. In the back yard, the red peonies have come in now. Lack of yard maintenance, however, is getting out of hand: bushes, lawn, weeds, transplanting, landscaping. Honeysuckle flowers, all dark after pollination, fall to the sidewalk in front of the house, at the same time that the locust petals come down (spun and tumbled by the wind) and azalea petals are almost gone. Early spirea seen along Dayton Street, a few snow-on-the-mountain flowering here. Red oak acorns are twice the size of a BB in front of the Catholic church. Throughout the village: poppies and iris.

2018: All the zinnia, Mexican sunflower, hollyhock and dahlia seeds planted a week ago have sprouted.

2019: Rain after several mild and clear days. Honeysuckle flowers seemed to darken with age overnight and have started to fall. Black walnut catkins have come down onto Greene Street near Jill's house. Poison ivy with giant leaves covering the old shed in the Stafford Street alley starting to bud. A catbird visited Jeanie's river birch as I sat in the afternoon listening to the waterfall. Tonight near the college, the steady, cenobitic rhythm of tree frogs chanting.

2020: I found a June bug on my front screen door this morning. The first white-spotted skipper played in hyacinths late this afternoon.

Today, Father, this blue sky lauds you. The delicate green and orange flowers of the tulip poplar tree praise you. The distant blue hills praise you, together with the sweet-smelling air that is full of brilliant light.

Thomas Merton

May 18th
The 138th Day of the Year

A garden or nature journal becomes an autobiography, the act of watching becoming watching the self, and forming the self out of and in front of nature. I am this person who is observing leaf after leaf, field after field. Following these seasons, I become myself.

bf

Sunrise/set: 5:18/7:46
Day's Length: 14 hours 28 minutes
Average High/Low: 73/52
Average Temperature: 62
Record High: 93 – 1962
Record Low: 35 – 1973

Weather

Today is often the beginning of a wetter-than-average period during May, the time of the Strawberry Rains. Between the 18th and the 29th, the average likelihood for precipitation grows to near 50 percent. There are a few times, however, in the next dozen days when fields may dry out a little: the 20th and 21st, the 24th, and the 28th. Today's chances are not so good: 55 percent chance of showers by nightfall. Highs in the 80s on this date come 20 percent of the time, 70s fifty percent of the time, 60s twenty-five percent, and an occasional day just in the 50s comes once every 15 years or so. Almost 40 percent of May 18ths are completely overcast.

Natural Calendar

Iris Season, Mock Orange Season and Peony Season reach above the 40th Parallel as May deepens. Locust Blossoming Season sweetens the winds. For gardeners, it is Clematis Season, Rhododendron Season and late Star of Bethlehem Season (but Flea Beetle Season, too). Strawberry Ripening Season arrives, marked by the earliest days of Swallowtail Season and Monarch Butterfly Season. Along the roadsides, find Meadow Goat's Beard Season and Sweet Clover Season and Buttercup Season. At your screen door, it's June Bug Season. Meadows host Tall Meadow Rue Season and Angelica Season.

Daybook

1984: At the Covered Bridge: A flock of cedar waxwings along the river. Most buckeye flowers done blooming, falling to the ground. Two geese seen with five goslings. The upper path shows its Late Spring undergrowth, colored with the purple of phlox and geraniums, and the gold of ragwort. Ginger has replaced the toad trillium close to the ground. First poison ivy seen. A few wilting bluebells. Jacob's ladder still in bloom, swamp buttercups too. Sedum open, columbine still blooming on the cliffs, redbuds fading, locusts starting to flower.

1986: First catbird in the yard. In the Vale, blackberries and wild roses opening. Very early hemlock, and curly dock, cinquefoil budding, and yarrow, and privet. Wild lettuce, wood mint, and wingstem up to my waist, the railroad tracks lined with sweet rockets and old honeysuckle, fading garlic mustard, yellowing toothwort leaves, new clustered snakeroot. Almost all the canopy complete. Indian hemp and touch-me-nots are knee high. The plumes of smooth brome sway in the wind.

1987: Great mullein thick-leafed and huge, past knee high. First yellow sweet clover seen at Wilberforce. Fleas appearing on the animals.

1989: First mock orange barely opening. First iris seen in town. First meadow goat's beard seen on the way to work.

1990: South Glen: Wood nettle almost full grown now, waist high, cohosh berries forming, goldenrod, touch-me-not, wingstem, and dogbane two feet tall. Star of Bethlehem still open, last of the phlox, ragwort still strong. High canopy still thin. First daddy longlegs seen. Red admiral butterflies everywhere: this is the first day of their first cycle. First cricket heard, the Northern Spring Field Cricket. Sweet Cicely almost gone. Mulberries are setting fruit. Yarrow budding, leaning into the sun. Wind in the clover and orchard grass. First azure butterflies, a pair of them, seen in the garlic mustard.

1991: First bowl of strawberries from the garden.

1992: Grackles talking back and forth: guttural coaching of the parents and the imitation from the young. Continual chatter, encouragement, demonstration, excitement, panic in the old dying locust. In the south garden, it is full season for sweet rockets, poppies, daisies, pyrethrums, geums and ranunculus.

1994: First goat's beard noticed today, and the lupine opened overnight. Bainberry discovered along the path to Grinnell Pond.

1995: Clematis comes in all at once. Now the daisies are starting. Overnight, the snow-on-the-mountain sent up its flower umbels.

1998: Summer headlong. A grasshopper flying and a lightning bug found.

1999: Now sudden full comfrey, now the peonies, pyrethrum, daisies, poppies in full bloom, locusts and honeysuckles, mock orange holding, rhododendrons full, thyme full. Some locust petal fall begins. Multiflora roses have been open for the last few days. Rhubarb and horseradish to seed. First lamb's ears blossoming. Full bloom flag iris. In the pond, arrowhead is about six inches and very spindly. Loosestrife full size at three feet. No tadpoles seen today.

2000: First ditch lilies opening along Grinnell Road.

2001: First water lily in the pond. Blue eggshell found under the apple tree.

2002: First daisies in the yard.

2003: Snakeskin found by the side of the pond.

2004: Coral bells are blooming. The first periodic cicada of the cycle found by John Sturm along the bike path.

2005: Purple lilacs end today. Toads or frogs calling in the distance at about 10:00 p.m.

2007: Fringe tree in bloom throughout middle May in the village and at nurseries.

2008: The first of the Korean lilacs has started to rust. The earliest hyacinth has decayed. The first mock orange flowers, the first white spiderwort and the first sweet Williams opened yesterday or overnight. Sweet Cicely and sweet rockets provide color to the southeast garden area. Deep fragrance from the honeysuckles throughout the back yard. The Osage trees are finally leafing, and the high locust seems to have small blossom clusters. As I stood by the pond, two fledgling grackles struggled to keep their balance in the rose of Sharon bushes, the mother nearby in the red mulberry, changing her vantage point as I moved. The lettuce and spinach planted a week ago have finally started to sprout.

2009: Very light frost this morning on the car windshields. Bridal wreath in the alley has rusted, only a few flowers remaining. New winterberry leaves are darkening now, and the poison ivy beside them has full-size foliage. At Dayton Street, Don's black walnut tree has filled out maybe a third of the way. In the park, the hawthorn flowers are holding at maybe half. First scorpion fly is out.

2010: The first spider web seen above the pond this morning. Black walnut flower stems lie all across the sidewalk along High Street. Foxglove in bloom near the park. Zinnias sprouted under the east windows last night. Grackles cackling in the evening.

2011: Italy: Walk all day from Pontebari to Spoleto, sunny and mild: Spindly white achillea, purple bush clover, tall purple mallow, budded hollyhock. More open jasmine, comfrey, iris. Locusts still out but fading.

2012: Four fledgling sparrows drowned in the pond over night. Foxglove is in full bloom throughout the area, catalpas, peonies, daisies, snow-on-the-mountain, roses and privets continue. Cattail foliage is tall in the ditches, roadsides bright with yellow sweet clover. Four orange Asiatic lilies have opened now. Cardinals and robins singing at sundown. Peggy's lamb's ear has just opened.

2015: Inventory: The snowball viburnum and the azalea are shedding quickly, and the honeysuckle blossoms, darkened from pollination, are collapsing onto the sidewalk. A few buds have appeared on the ditch lilies, the Anna Belle hydrangea and the stella d'oro lilies. Spiderwort has a few more flowers, the perennial salvia and the sweet rockets are full, the ancient mock orange bush is finally full of blossoms, the catmint has several open spikes, and the backyard peonies are straining to open. The penstemon is almost ready to bloom.

At about 8:00 this morning, grackles mating. Along High Street, privet bushes are budding. In the village, catalpas are budding, iris full, honeysuckles still strong, hemlock and parsnips and a fringe tree starting. Good-size goslings across from Ellis Pond, and a snapping turtle, shell maybe a foot long was crossing Polecat Road. I nudged him over into the grass. Up the bike path, most of the black raspberries have recently set fruit.

2016: Very much like last year except that the old mock orange no longer blooms, and some plants in the new milkweed patch are two feet tall. The very first locust blossoms seen on my backyard trees; Jill said she saw one lush with full blooms yesterday.

2017: Grackles, chickadees, sparrows and the red-bellied woodpecker feed constantly throughout the day. Steady robin peeping at dusk. Locust flowers falling quickly.

2018: Locusts full bloom, Jill's maple seeds spinning to the driveway, Mateo's and my weigelas are covered with blossoms, the mock orange (reviving) has several buds, some open, honeysuckle, sweet rockets, iris strong, poppies still early full, some bridal wreath rusting. When I went out to feed the koi at about 9:30 this morning, light rain falling, I startled the first tiger swallowtail of the years in the peony bushes, and it fled flying low to the ground.

2019: To Oxford, Ohio: Locusts full bloom throughout, and all is the same as last year, except for the tiger swallowtail. And I saw several patches of peonies all open. Roses budding at the Interfaith Center. During my morning walk with Ranger, robins were still singing and running around in the lawns and streets. When I fed the koi, I saw the first spider web across the pond.

2020: In last night's rain, the first honeysuckle flowers fell on the sidewalk in front of the house, and more red and silver maple seeds all down Limestone Street. Jill's first poppy opened, and the old mock orange bush by the shed produced its first blossom. Heavy rain in the afternoon, tornado warning. The first tropical storm has formed in the Caribbean.

For us, the winds do blow,
The earth doth rest, heaven move,
and fountains flow.
Nothing we see but means our good,
As our delight, or as our treasure.

George Herbert

May 19th
The 139th Day of the Year

Resurgent May, softness with energy,
Warmth after cold, reunion after loss.

Vita Sackville-West

Sunrise/set: 5:17/7:47
Day's Length: 14 hours 30 minutes
Average High/Low: 72/53
Average Temperature: 62
Record High: 92 – 1962
Record Low: 37 – 1894

Weather

Chances of rain are high today: over 50 percent. Completely overcast skies come one year in three. Highs in the muggy 90s occur five percent of the afternoons; 80s are recorded 30 percent of the time, 70s on 30 percent of the days, 60s on 30 percent, and 50s the last five percent. As the fifth high pressure system of the month approaches, the barometer is usually dropping, and the wind is down, conditions which typically improve prospects for fishing as well as for allergies.

Natural Calendar

Pheasant, grouse, and turkey chicks appear along the fence rows. Half of the season's new ducklings and goslings swim the creeks. Bullfrogs call all along the rivers. Catfish, bullheads, northern pike, bluegills, largemouth and smallmouth bass, white bass, spotted bass, striped bass and crappies spawn when the water temperature reaches about 65 degrees.

Daybook

1982: Clustered snakeroot has small yellow flowers now.

1984: On the way to Indiana, white chestnut flowers seen along the freeway, sweet clover foliage prominent but no blossoms yet.

1986: English plantain in bloom, probably began a week or so ago.

1987: Cardinal singing at 4:07 a.m. Peaches one inch in diameter, apples half an inch, cherries maybe a third grown. Rhubarb blooms done, snowball viburnum and bridal wreath spirea fade. First peony opens (gone in the yard by the 30th of May).

1988: Ferns almost completely unfurled now.

1993: Lupine full bloom, spears of violet and blue. Some bridal wreath browning. First sweet William opens in the north garden. Opossums half grown, three killed in two days on Grinnell Road. From northern Minnesota, John says that peony buds are half an inch across, lilacs are budding, strawberries starting to bloom, rhubarb pie size.

1995: Mock orange and the first iris opened together today. Osage was beginning to leaf out. North to Norwalk: Lilacs were still in full bloom there, a hundred miles or so due north of Yellow Springs. The green of the tree line was less conspicuous. A few apples were still in bloom, fields of late dandelions still in bloom, some tulips and some oaks, redbuds all still flowering. Ten to fifteen miles equaled a day of spring progress: Norwalk was back at the end of Yellow Springs April or the first week of May.

1997: First lupine is blue today. Honeysuckles coming in now. The Siberian iris put out buds two days ago. Mock orange still holding back. Dogwoods still keep their flowers. The first pink azalea petals fell. On the way to work, I almost hit the first monarch butterfly of the year! In the courtyard at Wilberforce, tall cressleaf groundsel in full bloom. At Jacoby, buckeye blossoms are aging. May apples in bloom, the last spring beauties, fading late yellow toad trilliums. Among the giant skunk cabbage leaves: water cress, spring cress, golden buttercups and ragwort full bloom in massive patches at the swamp. The canopy maybe a third complete. This is the finest of Jacoby, so bright. Up the ridge, purple waterleaf late full, a few purple violets, lots of purple phlox, toothwort foliage bleached pale yellow, new sweet rockets pink and violet. And a flock of crows above me screaming.

1998: Lamb's ear opens overnight. Young grackle or starling in the lawn.

1999: It is full Early Summer, and I am ambivalent. The air is heavy and sweet with the scent of honeysuckles, mock orange, and locusts. Poppies, clematis, spiderwort, daisies, and the first roses are open. Peonies have unraveled. Lupines pace the iris. Yellow poplars and catalpas are ready to bloom. In the woods near my house, ragwort and watercress hold over from early May. Sweet Cicely has replaced the wild geraniums. Columbine, waterleaf, and parsnips are strong. Wild grapes are blossoming. Tall hemlock is budding.

This is what I wait for every year, the completion of the promises that began in January with the days lengthening and the cardinals starting to call. My emotions always follow the seasons. This week they tell me it is time for things to be coming together. All of the delays of this long cold spring are over. All the seeds purchased in February can be planted. There is no chance of frost. All of my expectations have materialized, and all of the projects saved for these warm afternoons are waiting.

Still, part of me balks at action. I have heard the voice of self-sufficiency, the call to work, the call to build. I have also heard a conflicting voice, one more ancient, that says it is time to enjoy each moment, to wander the paths of summer, to take things as they come. It's almost berry time. The river is warm, the fish are biting, and the shade is cool.

On the one hand, summer calls my bluff. It says: "This is what you've always wanted. This is the top of the tide. Life is short. This June, these furrows, and these chances will never come again. Redeem your April ambitions." On the other hand, summer seduces me to a sensuous lethargy: "There is more time than you can ever imagine," it tells me. "The leaves will never fall. June will never end. There can be no true self-reliance without joy, without abandon. The world is beautiful beyond your wildest winter longing. Give in to its careless magic. Lie in its arms."

2000: Honeysuckle flowers suddenly decline. Pond iris are open. End Late Spring.

2001: First sweet William.

2002: Frost on the grass this morning, but the first of summer's yellow sweet clover opened, and nodding thistle buds showed a little pink.

2003: Driving south thirty miles to Washington Court House, I saw the first parsnips, first yellow sweet clover, first red clover. There were still great fields of golden cressleaf groundsel, and the wheat was turning a pale gray green. At South Glen, sweet Cecily is almost gone, wood nettle knee high, the canopy full. At Antioch School, cecropia moths were mating.

2005: The iris in the north garden is completely open. The first sweet William has flowered. Hemlock is six feet tall and budded. Rhododendron is starting. Asian ladybugs seen in the undergrowth.

2007: Mateo's Jerusalem artichokes are past knee high now, and all the geraniums at Mrs. Timberlake's are done blooming; her poppies are still strong. Meadow goat's beard was opening in front of Don's house. Mock orange still full bloom, honeysuckle flowers starting to fall.

2008: At South Glen, the canopy still very spotty. Rockets, honeysuckles, waterleaf and May apples are in full bloom. Meadow goat's beard is open in the meadow where the old barn used to stand. Grasses, wood nettle, wingstem past knee high, hemlock shoulder high. A red-bellied woodpecker called once as I entered the woods, but I didn't hear it afterwards. Two pairs of geese at the carp hole, but no goslings. The first scorpion fly seen in the north garden this morning, along with a lady bug. Comfrey, iris, hyacinths, rockets, spiderwort, snowball viburnum full flower; mock orange and sweet Williams gathering momentum. One overgrown purple clematis flower unfolding in among the forsythia. Peaches less than half an inch in diameter, maybe almost an inch long. In the alley, bridal wreath holds. The heavy scent of the Korean lilac lies sweet across the yard. Locusts in flower throughout the area.

2010: Osage flower clusters have fallen in the rain.

2012: A young skunk came to the back porch this morning around 6:15. Most of the blue flags are gone in the yard, but Peggy still has many. Many ninebark shrubs in bloom along Dayton-Yellow Springs Road now. This year is about three weeks ahead of 2008, but not so far from this date in 2010. The first tropical storm has formed in the Caribbean. And the last twelve months have been the warmest on record in the world. Certainly this May is shaping up to be way above average, maybe five to eight degrees.

2013: Aida called to report that both an American redstart and a yellow-rumped warbler had flown against her screen door, had been stunned from the impact, and, saved from the cat, flew off to continue their migration. The redstart is typically seen only during May and September in this area. The yellow-rumped warbler passes through the area from early April into middle May, returning in October, and Aida probably saw one of the last on its way north.

2014: To South Carolina: Milkweed two-feet high in southern Ohio. Canopy thinning in the mountains of West Virginia. Hemlock tall and starting to open near the Virginia border (Yellow Springs actually a few days ahead). Full rockets, early multiflora roses, purple vetch and poppies as we approached North Carolina. Moth mullein flowering at Columbia (and well advanced at Santee-Cooper). At Eutawville on the reservoir, full elderberries, catalpas, large magnolias, yuccas, daisy fleabane, sow thistles (tall, prickly alternate leaves), several ripe blackberries (the vines sprawling with the kudzu), and a new plant: five tiny violet petals, square rough stem, opposite, thin, rough, toothed leaves. Wild onions, some blooming, some all to seed. Corn is past knee-high, and wheat is pale tan, seems ready to harvest in North Carolina as well as at Santee Cooper. Black swallowtail, white spotted skipper seen at the canal. On the lake, fish were not biting for John and me, and we didn't see any fish taken by other boats.

2015: Many purple flag iris in bloom throughout the village. In my east garden, the last wild geranium and azalea flowers fall. In the south garden, the first light pink peonies opened. Spitbug noticed on a primrose plant. Milkweed plants two-feet tall, arrowhead six to nine inches, lizard's tail to a foot. And I noticed that the purple bittersweet nightshade (*Solanum dulcamara*) was blooming in the old forsythia bushes at the southeast corner of the property. A nodding thistle showing some pink seen on the way to Dayton this afternoon.

2016: Walking through the village with Jill: Many purple flag iris, a locust tree in early bloom, many standard iris, catmint tall and in full purple flower, privets and lamb's ear budding, forget-me-nots still common and strong, the high canopy almost filled in. In the dooryard garden, the wild geraniums are almost gone, and the snow-on-the-mountain is coming in, the rockets helping to replace the color lost as the pink azalea collapses. At the quarry yesterday evening, we wandered along paths that were bordered by dense hedges of honeysuckle, creamy white with blossoms. We saw tadpoles in the shallow pools and the first yellow sweet clover on the hill, creeping blackberry vines in bloom, and I dug a few wild daisies from the waysides.

2017: Hard storm in the night, the Strawberry Rains continuing, most of the honeysuckle and black walnut flowers down, the first privet flowers on the sidewalk. Some zinnias have survived the rain, sprouting in patches. Buds becoming prominent on the stella d'oro lilies. Robin vespers strong at 8:00 p.m.

2018: Mild and rainy, honeysuckle flowers coming down, and the viburnum is almost done shedding, covering the tulip garden with white petals. Through the alleys last night, locust flowers fat and fragrant, flag iris in full bloom, deep purple, pale yellow and violet. Buds have grown out of the stella d'oro leaves, sweet Cicely has finished its blossoming, fleabane is wide open near the pond, the golden ranunculus (remnants revived from the first south garden of almost forty years ago) color the ragged east garden next to the house. From Spoleto in Italy, Neysa sent a photograph of a wild orchid on the hillside of her property.

2019: Some locust petals falling in the wind on Davis Street. The flowers of the snowball viburnum on the north side of the house have suddenly lost their vitality, some darkening.

2020: Rain and cool. The hackberry trees in my yard are finally showing green. The snowball viburnum on the north side of the house holds its petals. In the countryside: one wheat field seen only a foot or so tall, deep green. Rick came over in the afternoon with some tiny praying mantises that had just hatched from their ootheca. I let some go in the greenhouse and the rest in the circle garden to make their way.

Something must be lost or absent in any narrative for it to unfold: if everything stayed in place there would be no story to tell.

                        Terry Eagleton

Bill Felker

May 20th
The 140th Day of the Year

There is joy in the woods just now,
The leaves are whispers of song,
And the birds make mirth on the bough
And music the whole day long.

Claude McKay

Sunrise/set: 5:16/7:48
Day's Length: 14 hours 32 minutes
Average High/Low: 73/54
Average Temperature: 63
Record High: 90 – 1977
Record Low: 37 – 1894

Weather

Today and the 21st can offer relief from the late May rains 65 percent of the time as the fifth major high pressure system of the month moves through the Midwest. Wind speed often picks up throughout the day, and the sun shines through the cumulus clouds. Frost is not common with this fifth cold front, but morning temperatures drop into the upper 30s once in a decade. Highs reach above 80 degrees 35 percent of the afternoons, the first time chances have been so good for heat since May 16. Mild 70s come 50 percent of the time, with highs staying in the 60s ten percent of the afternoons, and in the chilly 50s five percent. After today chances of highs in the 80s or 90s do not fall below 30 percent until the middle of September.

Natural Calendar

This is the time the Sun comes into Gemini, and when the Sun reaches that constellation, then ragweed has grown two feet tall, and cow vetch, yellow sweet cover, wild parsnips, poison hemlock, angelica, motherwort, wild roses, locusts, blackberries and yarrow are flowering, and the last of the leaves come out for summer. Under the closing canopy of the 40th Parallel, spring's garlic mustard, chickweed and catchweed die back, their yellowing foliage accentuating a major decline of April growth.

Daddy longlegs are all over the undergrowth now, partial to clustered snakeroot and its pollen. Wild strawberries wander though the purple ivy and the sticky catchweed. Wild iris blooms in the wetlands.

Middle Summer's wood nettle is past knee high. Wild lettuce, wingstem and dogbane have grown up hip high. Grasses along the river banks are waist high. Poison hemlock reaches chin high, angelica more than six feet.

By this time of year, slugs usually roam the garden. Flies bother the livestock. Bean leaf beetles are common in the fields. Alfalfa weevil and leaf hopper infestations become more troublesome. White-marked tussock moths attack the elms; May beetles find the oaks; scurfy scale comes to the lindens. Tadpoles become toads and frogs and finally move to land. Cricket song grows louder. Ducklings and goslings swim beside their parents. Mosquitoes become more pesky. Dragonflies appear along the river. The earliest fireflies come out to mate.

Fawn births peak as the wild roses fade. Elderberry bushes and panicled dogwoods reach full bloom. Bottle grass is fresh and sweet for chewing, and a few mulberries are ready to pick.

Daybook

1982: The latest of the tulips has dropped its petals. First red strawberry in the garden. First daddy longlegs.

1983: Siberian iris and roses with large buds. Mock orange blooms today (lasts until the 12th of June). First meadow goat's beard noticed.

1984: Cascades: Toad trillium and dogwoods holding. Shooting star, white baneberry, dwarf larkspur, golden alexander, meadow parsnip full. Trillium grandiflorum are pink and old now, nodding trillium tattered. First spitbug seen, first spider in a web. Jacob's ladder fading.

1985: In this warm May, mock orange is almost done blooming. At the Covered Bridge, parsnips, hemlock, clustered snakeroot, and angelica are in full bloom. First striped cucumber beetle seen. First cricket heard, first black damselfly seen. Daisy fleabane tall and budding. Ragwort going to seed, the last of Late Spring in the swamp. Bugle (*Adjuga reptans*) almost gone under the pussy willow.

1986: Locusts in full bloom, Osage and mulberry leaves getting near summer size.

1987: Bluegrass identified, *Poa sylvestris*, in flower as orchard grass comes into full bloom with its yellow and tan heads. Siberian iris and the first orange ditch lily opened today. Hemlock and parsnips in bloom. Garlic mustard almost done for the year, its lanky stems bowing to set their seeds.

1988: Wild cherries full bloom, parallel with the locusts. Connie reports goat's beard and cinquefoil open at Medway, ten miles north of Yellow Springs.

1989: Orange blight well established on the black raspberries. Mountain maple full bloom. First raspberry flowers in the late afternoon. First cinquefoil blooms. The last quince flowers fall, and lilacs decay. Star of Bethlehem in full bloom, and most honeysuckles and snow-on-the-mountain. In the Vale settlement south of town, I found clumps of wild red columbine along the railroad tracks and wild grapes budding. Honeysuckle and sweet rockets full, corn salad early, yarrow and hemlock budding. Fire pink and dogwood full. Hackberry finally leafing.

1990: Mock orange and rhododendrons are in full bloom, following the hardy azaleas with just a little overlap in perfect sequence. Osage is budding. First strawberry ripens. Red admirals continue all around the yard. Purple spiderwort opens.

1991: Wild grapes full bloom. First foxtail grass seen.

1993: Frost on the roof this morning, with airport temperature officially 40. John calls, says there was snow in New York Mills, Minnesota, on Saturday, the 15th. The first of his strawberries are flowering, his rhubarb full grown.

1996: Spring has finally come. The cold and gray disappeared three days ago, and highs have been in the 80s and 90s. Poppies and iris are out in town. Strawberries have large green fruit now. Comfrey is budding. The east garden is at its best, with the columbine and late azaleas and bleeding hearts, dwarf iris, dead nettle. Rockets and buttercups and deep red pyrethrums blossoming in the south garden. The daisies are about to open (have already seen some in town). Along the west wall today, the clematis bloomed, three purple flowers all at once. At South Glen this evening, soft glow of dusk and violet rockets, wild phlox, honeysuckle. Found the rich scented four-petaled flowers of the silver olive, wild at the Butterfly Preserve. The woods floor is speckled with tiny petals from the locust trees above.

1999: Crows 4:51 a.m. Fishing with John in the afternoon: six catfish, three carp, lost four big cats. Yellow swallowtails common. Canopy complete except late locusts.

2001: Grackle feeding its baby across the street in the driveway.

2003: Doves and cardinals calling at 4:55 a.m. Multicolored Jacob's coat rose in bloom, and some dark reds. Yellow multifloras seen about town.

2004: Seventeen-year cicadas common at Antioch School.

2005: At South Glen, waterleaf is declining, sweet rocket, bedstraw, corn salad, sweet Cicely full. Half-inch fruits have formed on the buckeye branches. Goslings maybe a week old seen in the undergrowth with their parents. Locusts full bloom throughout the village, even the late locusts in the back yard. Dahlias transplanted to the east garden. The frog sang in the pond this afternoon before the rain.

2007: Blackberries blooming in the alley, black raspberries setting fruit. The first pond iris bloomed overnight, and the first peony in the yard opened. Growing color from Dutch iris and flags, sweet

Williams, sweet rockets in the north garden. One flower cluster on the porch wisteria is starting to flower. Lettuce thinned in the evening, looking good.

2008: Daisies open in Lil's yard. A large bush of pink peonies in Wilmington. Hemlock tall and budded just as wheat heads and starts to pale. Robins and grackles agitated tonight, herding their young. Black medic in the lawns. Iris, hyacinths, allium, flax, red azalea, hawthorns, locusts, snowball viburnum, bridal wreath spirea all hold. Three white daffodils left in the next yard past Lawsons'. The first blue Dutch iris opened along the north garden.

2009: End of the Korean lilac. Full Dutch iris. Fields of daisies and iris. First pond iris. Hemlock in bloom just north of Wilmington, and yellow roses seen there. Parsnips golden in Old Town.

2010: First Japanese honeysuckle noticed today, and poison hemlock was in early bloom all along the highway to Xenia. Privet buds are white now, almost flowering. The first white penstemon is open in the circle garden and the first orange ditch lily (*Hemerocallis fulva*) in the northwest corner of the north garden (the earliest I have recorded for those lilies in the yard).

2011: Italy: To Gary Jo Gardenhire's house in the hills near Spoleto then up the mountain to Pettino for lunch. Gary's garden had full blooming columbines, *Vinca minore,* roses, thyme, mock orange, budded oakleaf hydrangeas, late purple hydrangeas, the last remnants of money plant flower, taxus shrubs done flowering, tall allium late, some seeded. A red admiral, a small black swallowtail and several sulfurs seen. Up the mountain, numerous oxalis and low yellow varieties of plants in bloom, along with a paulonia-wisteria kind of tree or shrub with hanging yellow flowers. One garlic mustard plant, very old, had faded leaves. Lilacs in full flower near the cow pasture at Pettino. The elevation throughout the trip kept foliage and flower time close to that of an average Yellow Springs.

2012: All the mock orange petals have fallen. Peonies hold, sweet rockets fading now, garden sundrops budding. Honeysuckle flowers have turned to berries. Catalpa flowers have covered the radio station parking lot. At Ellis Pond, hawthorn flowers are almost all gone.

2014: Shulamit reported that she encountered the first chigger of the year last week, likening these insects to "sunsoaked and sundrunk performers" racing about in red leotards "soundless in modern dance formations, their choreographer gone mad."

Carrying the theme a little further, she added, "In the wings, covert in the grasses, they nip at my ankles. Furtive and quick, ravenous and ravening, they strike as I brush by. Then rush to catch their cue ...."

2015: Common mallow full bloom. Last flowers on creeping phlox. Downtown at the Village Artisans shop, two fine yellowwood trees (*Cladrastis kentukea*) are in late full bloom. I have lived here since 1978 and must have passed these trees in flower so many times but never noticed them, even though their blossoms are dramatic and elegant. In King's Yard alley, two stella d'oro lilies are opening, and two yellow sweet clover stalks have flowers. High-pressure moves down into the Lower Midwest tonight, Lilac Winter forecast.

2016: Robin chatter throughout the day, guiding the fledglings, bird seed disappearing by late morning, ravenous grackles. Multiflora roses flowering along Stafford Street. This year's Lilac Winter ending. A swarm of bees reported in town this afternoon.

2017: To Oxford, Ohio: Some fields partially under water. Yellow sweet clover and hemlock in full bloom. At home, I went to sleep as a storm moved across the yard, soft lightning, distant thunder, rain against the tin roof.

2018: The season of locust flowers and iris and peonies and mock orange and sweet rockets and poppies continues so strong.

2019: The tiny petals of the burning bush fell overnight in the wind and rain. Beside them, bridal wreath spirea has rusted, and snowball viburnums are bare. The first peonies open in my garden, not so far behind others in town. I saw a pair of catbirds in the honeysuckle by the studio this morning. In the field behind Ellis Pond: one Eastern black swallowtail, the first sighting of the year.

2020: Cold 50s today, time in abeyance. A clump of daisies has opened along Dayton Street. Mateo's weigela continues in full bloom. Hemlock starting to head. White clover appearing in the lawn now. Honeysuckle flowers and maple seeds cover the streets, so many fragments of time, fallen, made visible.

The first in time and the first in importance of the influences upon the mind is that of nature. Every day, the sun; and, after sunset, Night and her stars. Ever the winds blow; ever the grass grows.

Ralph Waldo Emerson

Bill Felker

May 21st
The 141st Day of the Year

Perchance the beginning of summer may be dated from the fully formed leaves, when dense shade begins. I will see.

Henry David Thoreau, *Journal,* May 20, 1852

Sunrise/set: 5:15/7:48
Day's Length: 14 hours 33 minutes
Average High/Low: 74/53
Average Temperature: 63
Record High: 92 – 1902
Record Low: 32 – 1907

Weather

As the fifth high-pressure system of the month becomes fully entrenched, today brings a slight increase in the possibility of a high just in the 50s: ten percent of the years get that cold. Most of the time (85 percent of the time), however, May 21 is in the 70s or 80s, with 60s occurring the remaining five percent. Two years out of three, the Strawberry Rains let up on May 21, and this date records just a 35 percent chance of showers. Skies are at least partly cloudy 70 percent of the time.

On May 21 in 2014, up to five inches of rain fell in the village and in much of southwest Ohio in the span of just a few hours, the most rain in one day during the years for which I have records.

The Yellow Springs Torch of May 24, 1895 noted that on this date (May 21) and the next in 1883, snow fell intermittently for 18 hours, bringing a total accumulation of seven inches in the village: a hard Lilac Winter. This is the latest record I have of local snow in May.

Natural Calendar

This final week of May, the dense shade has moved up all the way from its source along the Gulf of Mexico high into the northern United States. Osage and black walnut flowers come down in the rain across the East Coast as leaves continue to expand. In the South, Spanish moss grows its small flowers in the axils of leaves.

Out in the sun, elderberry bushes flower along the highways. Cow vetch, wild parsnips, poison hemlock, angelica, motherwort, blackberries, yarrow and the rough Canadian thistles bloom. Black raspberries set their fruit. The corn has usually sprouted in the fields, and farmers are taking the first cut of alfalfa.

When the canopy of leaves is complete, then flea beetles attack beet greens in your garden. Aphids multiply on heliopsis. Damselflies and dragonflies hunt the ponds. Leafhoppers, corn borers and armyworms assault the crops. Flies are bothering the cattle, ticks roam the brambles, cricket song grows louder, and the earliest fireflies flicker in the lawn. Along the coast of the eastern Atlantic, sea turtles begin to come ashore to lay their eggs – their season lasting until middle August. In the Georgia and Florida swamps, male alligators bellow out their courtship calls beneath the full, high trees.

We see it like Thoreau saw it: this is, perchance, summer for sure.

Daybook

1981: The mock orange opened today.

1982: First peonies today. Bridal wreath through for the year.

1984: First white clover at Wilberforce. First black flea beetles noticed in the garden.

1985: Catalpas bloom.

1986: First four strawberries picked.

1988: First poppy and first peony today at home.

1993: First poppy opens in the yard, well behind others in the village. Clematis full boom now. First patches of red clover seen. First parsnip noticed at Goes Station. Geum now full bloom in the east garden, forget-me-nots lanky and old. Pair of catbirds in the back bushes, singles seen before but never a pair. In the windstorm this afternoon, last year's maple seeds fell all at once throughout the village.

1995: At Grinnell Pond, maple waterleaf is in full bloom, its pale violet flowers pushing up above its leaves. Honeysuckle flowers are all out, heavy and lush along the path. The canopy overhead still needs its high locusts, Osage, and sycamore to be complete. In the east garden, columbine are still all out, astilbe keeps reddening, bleeding hearts are almost gone. The first strawberries ripen in the new patch. In the south garden, the red pyrethrums and dusky sweet rockets are all open, daisies coming in, yellow ranunculus still full, that garden's finest time. Along the north row, half a dozen blue Siberian iris in bloom, the other iris, white, pale gold, purple have come in, sweet William underway, lupine just starting.

1997: Throughout town, bridal wreath and poppies are in full bloom. In the north garden, the first sweet Williams open, and the lone purple iris unravels. Honeysuckles full bloom. By St. Paul's church, oak leaves are about a fourth of their full size, the shagbark hickory leaves beside them maybe a sixth or seventh of their full size. Along Corry Street, the tree line of the Glen is pale green, with the canopy filling in to perhaps a fourth.

1998: Flickers mating in the back tree 6:45 a.m. Hard mock orange petal fall. Japanese honeysuckle full bloom in the forsythia hedge.

1999: Full crappie season continues at the lake. Starlings still building nests. Dragonflies, small and large. Frogs croaking. Cressleaf groundsel full bloom. Lots of geese pairs but no goslings. Two catfish caught and two large ones lost. Along the roadsides, full blackberry, early full parsnip, early hemlock. First of our garden roses blooms, but the yellow roses in town were open more than a week ago.

2001: Osage flower stems falling. First dark purple Japanese water iris opens in the pond. Another young grackle seen in the yard.

2002: First pale pink peony. Very last Korean lilac flower falls.

2003: Korean lilac now done, but pale pink peonies and blue flags are in full bloom. The ramp leaves have disappeared, replaced by a thin three-inch stalk and a reddish, elongated bud. The tall purple allium loses its color in Liz's garden as locust flower clusters come down in the wind. In Dayton, the very first pink spirea is open along First Street. Poison hemlock seen open on the way south to Washington Court House.

2004: The first privet, peach-leafed bellflower, white penstemon, lamb's ear and lady's mantel bloom today. First pink flowers noticed on the spirea on Limestone Street. Tall rhubarb stem with flowers noticed in the Stafford-High Street alley. Casey's red-flowered buckeye past its best.

2005: Viburnum budding in the pine forest. Dwarf larkspur in bloom in the North Glen.

2006: Jeanie reports that one of her students showed her a giant cecropia moth emerging near school.

2007: To Clifton Gorge with Jeanie: A few last wild geraniums seen, a few white sedum flowers, clustered snakeroot common, maple waterleaf and thin-leafed waterleaf in full bloom providing some of the only real color to the forest floor, one fire pink bud just showing red, a few Solomon's plume left, a few white violets, Solomon's seal with triangular seed pods, miterwort with seeds, tulip trees in bloom, two of their fallen flowers on the path, bluets seen on the high path, foliage gone and their petals white, daddy longlegs in the snakeroot and the wood nettle (which was waist high). In town, most of Liz's poppies are done for the year, her alliums all going to seed. Iris are in full bloom all around the village, privet bushes budded along High Street. Honeysuckle coming to the end of its season, mock orange holding well so far. Tall yucca stalk seen on Davis Street. Each day brings more to notice than I have put in the entire year's journal.

2008: A young grackle sitting by the birdbath this morning. Tall coneflower foliage is waist high in the alley. Three Dutch iris in bloom today.

2009: Yellow poplar flowers full bloom. First deep peonies in the yard. Hawthorn ends bloom as wild rose reaches its peak.

2010: Daisy fleabane budded in the alley. Robins there peeping orientation calls to their young.

2011: Italy: To Assisi: Some corn just sprouted, some fields maybe six to nine inches. Wheat seen turned golden green. At the Fountain of Clitumno, some new ducklings, some adolescent.

2012: Rick reports the first fireflies of the year in his backyard this evening, and young toads in the muck.

2013: Inventory on return from a five-day trip to Madison, Wisconsin: Robins chirping at 3:45 a.m., the first cardinal at 3:47. All kinds of changes: two peonies, two roses and a yellow iris open (iris full throughout the village), and all the locust trees, and the mock orange; almost all the hyacinths and wild geraniums are gone, and the pink azalea is dropping its leaves, the snowball viburnum littering the ground with its white petals; the first sweet Williams have come in; pink and violet sweet rockets and clumps of spiderwort anchor the south garden; bluebells and lilacs (full in Madison) are completely gone here; the bamboo has started to leaf, continuing to drop its sheaths; clematis and catmint and all the weigela (ours and Mateo's) of the neighborhood are flowering; the buttercups of twenty years ago have started to come back near the pond; honeysuckle (just starting in Madison) has so many darkened flowers, many falling; the last of the trellis wisteria fades, but the Japanese wisteria is in full flower; the one rhubarb plant has sent up a huge flower stalk; dead nettle (lamium) has stopped blooming; the garlic mustard inflorescence is at the top of its stalks, and sweet Cicely is done for the year; poppies are open in front of Liz's house on Stafford Street; the first white-spotted skipper seen; wild grapes starting to bloom in the east shrubs.

2014: Unusually heavy downpour throughout the village, about five inches in two hours, flooding. DeWine's pond overflowed, many streets full of water, many photos and videos on Facebook.

2015: Robyn saved a starling fledgling from a cat, but it was in shock, didn't make it.

2017: More Strawberry Rains. In the northwest garden, the first buds have appeared on the ditch lilies. Lamium still in flower, more spiderwort budding, more stella d'oro lilies and ditch lilies budding. Liz's alliums are done blooming; I have only two left. Her yellow rose is almost finished. Jill's poppies fading. And Maryellen Jacobson wrote from Springfield: "I saw the first of my praying mantis hatchings today. They were about a third of an inch long and thinner than a cat's whisker – perfect little replicas of Mom and Dad. They are feasting on whiteflies, aphids and spider mites (of which there are plenty)."

2018: My first two peonies flowered this morning, small white, the first blossoms of the plants I transplanted there two years ago. On top of the fountain at the pond, a cluster of five young sparrows fluffing and drinking, learning, perhaps from their parents. I saw and listened to a medium-sized gray bird that looked like a catbird, had a beautiful, syncopated burble song, but had no meow-like calls.

2019: The Eastern black swallowtail was exploring the groundsel and orchard grass again today. First scorpion fly found hiding in the bee balm. Two silver-spotted skippers seen today near the circle garden. All the Indian hyacinths have gone to seed now. Don's oakleaf hydrangea has sent out buds. Maggie sends a photo of a patch of lady slippers in full flower in the preserve near her house.

Journal

At the beginning of Early Summer, the Northern Spring Field Cricket begins to sing in Ohio Valley pastures. This cricket is the easiest of all the crickets to identify because it is the first and only species to appear at the end of spring. Overwintering as a nymph, it comes out as the canopy closes, when rhododendrons, peonies, and mock orange bloom, and the first strawberries ripen.

By the middle of July, when the other crickets are just starting their seasons, the Northern Spring Field Cricket has completed its cycle. By then, writes Vincent Dethier in his book, *Crickets and Katydids*, "the crickets of Early Summer, have sung their lays, courted, consummated their love, and died. Their consorts have laid eggs in the soft soil and died in turn."

As autumn approaches, the number of cricket species multiplies, and the task of identification becomes more challenging. Entomologists like Dethier have found that the shape of a cricket is less helpful in naming its species than the insect's call. "Appearances," he writes, "are neither distinctive nor meaningful, but an acoustical signal to which the female can orient and home is essential. And the song must be correct in order to lead the female to the genetically compatible mate, otherwise consummation, even if completed, is fruitless."

Like Dethier, I find little use for outward appearances as I reflect on the subtle differences in the species of men and women. There is, I think, something radical and violent that separates us, either some vastly complex design, or else a primordial mix-up that once set our evolution out of kilter, a cosmic banishment that scrambled our voices and scattered us like children of Babel; and in order to find our partners and friends, to break the isolation and loneliness, to be fruitful, we have to sort through a planet of neighborhoods and habitats. We have to study where we might belong if we were really ever to find home, and then we have to listen and listen until we can hear the song meant only for us.

And the world cannot be discovered by a journey of miles, no matter how long, but only by a spiritual journey of one inch, very arduous and humbling and joyful, by which we arrive at the ground at our feet and learn to be at home.

Wendell Berry

Bill Felker

May 22nd
The 142nd Day of the Year

It was the time of summer, in the month of May, when the days are long, and the nights are still and sweet....

Aucassin et Nicolette

Sunrise/set: 5:14/7:49
Day's Length: 14 hours 35 minutes
Average High/Low: 74/53
Average Temperature: 63
Record High: 92 – 1902
Record Low: 32 – 1883

Weather

The likelihood of precipitation rises sharply to over 50 percent, but temperatures are typically warm: 80s on 40 percent of the days, 35 percent in the 70s, a fourth of the days in the 60s. The sun shows through the clouds three days out of four.

The Weather in the Week Ahead

The final week of May is typically a wet one, with completely overcast conditions more common than during any other time of the month. On the 25th, 26th and 27th rain falls almost half the time, and the 29th is one of the rainiest days in the whole year. Average temperature distribution for this time of the month is as follows: five percent chance of highs in the 90s, thirty percent of 80s, thirty percent of 70s, twenty-five percent of 60s, and ten percent of 50s. The brightest days of the week are usually the 27th and 30th.

Natural Calendar

The last week of Late Spring (the last week of May at average elevations along the 40th Parallel) offers the best of Sweet William Season, Multiflora Rose Blooming Season, Siberian Iris Blooming Season, Privet Blooming Season, Yellow Poplar Blooming Season and Spiderwort Season. In the woods, Gold-Collared Blackfly

Season and Green Six-Spotted Tiger Beetle Season.

Along bikepaths and old railroad right-of-ways, it is Blackberry Blooming Season and Black Raspberry Blooming Season. In the garden, Leafhopper Season and Scorpion Fly Season open Early Greens Season. Grasshopper Season and Northern Spring Field Cricket Season bring the fields alive. Butterfly seasons include White-Spotted Skipper Season and Red Admiral Season. It's Fledgling Robin Season in the yard, Young Groundhog Season in the fresh grass along the highways.

Daybook

1982: First Siberian iris opens. Wild parsnips bloom.

1983: Wisteria full bloom. First red clover seen. Catalpas and Osage starting to leaf along King Street. Poppies full bloom, lily-of-the-valley late full.

1987: Siberian iris have all come in at once. Snowball viburnum gone, locust flowers disappearing, Osage flowers at their peak.

1988: Middle Summer's wild lettuce, wingstem, and wood nettle are as tall as my hip, grasses past my waist, sweet Cicely gone to seed, phlox worn. Mosquitoes pesky. First damselfly. White-spotted skipper. Ragwort with fluffy white seed heads. First wild rose open.

1991: First sweet William opens in the yard.

1992: At home, the peonies all opened at once this morning, iris near full bloom. Into South Glen, gold-collared blackflies are out. The last of the garlic mustard is blooming. Full late phlox, late star of Bethlehem. Rockets continue near perfection, wood nettle past knee high. White violets blooming. Late and tall catchweed, lanky and falling, tinted with yellow. Chickweed tangled and old, henbit bright blue and gangly, honeysuckle still full, damselflies and daddy longlegs common. A few late sweet Cicely. Seed pods on the wild geraniums, angelica six feet and headed, locust still blooming, parsnips, blackberry flowering. Lots of white clover, some very late winter cress. Continuous songs of cardinals, robins, warblers, finches. Red-winged blackbirds whistle. Wild cherry full, rich, heavy fragrance, wingstem up to the bottom of my pocket. The canopy is complete but still not mature; there are shadows, patches of paler green all along the tree line. Some Canadian thistles budding. Spitbugs on the goldenrod, yarrow heading.

A blackbird female hovers above me as I walk; I'm near her nest. First brilliant green tiger beetle of the year seen. Dogbane up to my thighs. Sweet clover budding. In the deeper woods, full bloom of the blackberries. Wild strawberries climb, bright yellow through the blue ivy and the dying catchweed. Sycamore leaves still just half size. Queen Ann's lace and teasel mostly small, basal leaves only, wild lettuce still basal plus a foot or so. One high ragwort, the last, and the last spring beauty. Blue-eyed grass found. Clustered snakeroot with golden pollen, fields of rockets and corn salad, hundreds of yards ahead and back as far as I can see, giant tall buttercups, full meadow parsnips. Three carp, one white sucker, one bluegill caught in the weed bed at Far Hole, constant bites for an hour and a half. Coming home at five o'clock, I heard the first cricket of the year.

1993: Iris at their best now. Violets noticed gone; I always miss the end of their season, they are so strong for such a long time. Flicker call heard this afternoon for the first time in weeks.

1994: First clematis opens along the west wall, first poppy in the south garden. Lupines and iris full bloom, last of the bleeding hearts. At South Glen, owl heard in the late afternoon calling, "Who cooks for you? Who cooks for you?"

1996: The locusts and wild cherries are in full bloom all over the county. The first mock orange unraveled today. The first iris bloomed last night. The daisies are coming in early full now, and the rockets are at their best. Garlic mustard late but strong. Violet hyacinths in the south garden hold, columbine hold. Honeysuckles still full, bleeding hearts almost gone. The cressleaf groundsel is in full bloom scattered throughout the pastures from Fairborn into Wilberforce, maybe three feet high.

1998: End rhododendrons. Most mock orange fall. Peonies decline, many Siberian iris.

2000: To Caesar Creek with John: One catfish in two days, ten bluegills yesterday, but none today. Hundreds of carp mating in the backstreams. Zebra swallowtail, tiger swallowtail, black swallowtail, and a viceroy seen. Rockets and cressleaf groundsel are the flowers in bloom. River willow trees shedding their cotton now, tufts gathering in the sloughs. The yellow-headed warbler just seen once yesterday, not at all today. Geese still loud, but bird activity much less this time than my last time out earlier in May. Canopy of leaves appears complete here. Bullfrog calling.

2001: Cardinal calls in the rain at 5:35 a.m. Doves at 5:50. Blue flags gone now. Full bloom of white clover in the fields at Washington Court House. Tulip tree flowering at Antioch, catalpas in Dayton. Privet just barely opening. Red admirals and skippers have been out maybe a week and a half.

2002: Robins still talking back and forth to their young. First nodding thistle opening on the freeway to Dayton.

2003: First dark purple iris blooms in the pond. One water lily bud has appeared. The rhododendrons are declining.

2004: First water lily opened at home today. On Kelleys Island, wild grapes and cottonwoods have budded, willows and honeysuckles are in bloom, mulberries just half size (half Yellow-Springs size). A flower similar to hemlock parsley is in late bloom all along the banks of the lake. Balsam ragwort identified, the dominant plant on the quarry floor. Wild madder is in full bloom, as is herb Robert and a pale violet penstemon.

2005: Many blue flags fully budded. First yellow swallowtail seen in the honeysuckles this morning, the first large butterfly all year. Ranunculus is flowering in the south garden, and the first pale pink peonies.

2006: First pale pink peonies have opened. Bittersweet above the sidewalk at the corner of Limestone and High Streets is blooming, flower hulls falling to the sidewalk. Under the apple tree, the first sage blossoms have appeared. Kousa dogwoods are coming in at the triangle park. Iris, locust, mock orange full bloom everywhere in town. First scorpion fly noticed near the pond.

2007: Moya, our next-door neighbor, reported that the deer that lives in the woods behind our houses gave birth to a fawn about a week to ten days ago. At the park, all the crabapple trees that were so hurt in the April freeze have recovered most of their foliage – but have never flowered. In the back yard, our Osage and locusts are leafing but not complete. Spiderwort now full bloom, purple-stemmed penstemon budding, first candy lily just barely starting to unravel, peak of Dutch iris, reddening of astilbe, budding of purple coneflowers. Mallow dug up and moved yesterday, suffering in the 80-degree heat today.

Notes in 2007 for the *Yellow Springs News* on the Possible Effects of Global Warming in Yellow Springs

Bruce Stutz's *Chasing Spring* notes that the growing season in Europe now begins eight days earlier than it did in 1970 and that North American tree swallows lay eggs nine days earlier than they did in 1959. "Worldwide studies of more than 1,500 species," says Stutz, "show that frogs mate, birds nest, and trees bud on the average more than a week earlier than they did 50 years ago."

Reports this year from places as diverse as the Shanghai Botanical Gardens and the New York Botanical Gardens emphasize the unusual nature of this past winter-spring season. The first four months of 2007 in Yellow Springs brought extremely early blooming of trees and perennials, as well an unfortunate freeze that produced the only April in recent memory without significant color from redbuds and crabapples.

And that was enough of a surprise to send me to my daybook to look for more evidence that our climate might be in flux. Although my phenological records of the past quarter century in Yellow Springs are not exactly rigorous (I did not record blooming or leafing dates for many species some years), they offer an interesting perspective on blossoming times since the early 1980s.

To test the hypothesis that some flora are flowering earlier than they did 25 years ago, I checked my first blooming dates for common shrubs that grow in my yard, shrubs for which I have the best records: forsythia, redbuds and mock orange.

I recorded the first flowers of forsythia as early as February 25 in 1998 and as late as April 3 in 2001, with March 25 the mean blooming date. Among the earliest years, three occurred in this century, four in the 1990s and three in the 1980s. Among the latest years, three occurred in this century, none occurred in the 1990s, and six occurred in the 1980s and 1970s. Although an easy progression was not clearly visible, more forsythia have bloomed before March 25 since 1990.

I came up with similar results when I checked my notes on redbud blooms. While earliest flowers occurred as early as March 17 in 1990 and as late as April 21 in 1989, with the mean of April 13, almost all of the earlier flowering occurred after 1990.

Most striking because they displayed the clearest progression were my notes on first blooming dates for mock orange. The earliest day I have recorded for mock orange is May 5 in both 2006 and 2000. The latest date is May 25 in 1984, with the mean being May 15. Ten out of 12 of the earlier dates occurred after 1990. Seven out of 12 of the later dates occurred before 1990.

The results of this unofficial overview? Yellow Springs may be experiencing the same kind of changes already noted in so many other locations. Even though every spring is different, it appears that 1) forsythia is more likely to flower before March 25 than it was in the 1980s), 2) that redbuds are more likely to flower before April 13 than they were in the 1980s, and 3) that mock orange bushes are more likely to bloom around May 8 instead of around May 18, the expected average date in the middle 1980s.

2008: Yellow roses early to mid bloom at Liz's yard. The air along Stafford Street is heavy with the scent of locust flowers, the high trees white with blossoms. One cardinal sang outside our window this morning at 3:50 EST. No red-bellied woodpeckers today. The top few inches of three Jerusalem artichokes in the garden had been eaten off overnight. Rabbit? Deer? Violet locust tree in bloom at Stutzman's nursery. Pond iris budding. On the way to Wilmington and back, great patches of ivory locust blossoms, some entire woodlots in bloom. Pineapple weed (*Matricaria discoidea*) seen at school – years ago I had identified it as chamomile. Jeanie cut back the New England asters today. Blue-flowered bittersweet nightshade seen in bloom along High Street. Four Dutch iris in bloom today in the north garden. Berries fully formed on the hackberry, Osage budded. Robin singsong at dusk.

2009: Kousa dogwood opens as the hawthorn ends. American beech now fully leafed.

2010: Cedar waxwings feeding in the mulberry tree late this morning, robins peeping to their young, toad singing in the pond, red admiral butterfly in the circle garden, sun coming through the clouds, cool northwest wind. Water iris fully budded. Yellow swallowtail comes by. Porch wisteria fading, some yucca six feet tall. Lamb's ear full bloom, many crab apples full size.

2011: Italy: Ninebark flowering in the hills around Spoleto. Pink spirea in bloom at the apartment.

2013: First scorpion fly seen in the garden, first buds noticed on the stella d'oro lilies, fleabane noticed full.

2015: The Japanese wisteria at the porch has three flower clusters; the trellis wisteria is putting all its energy into leaves and tendrils. Kathy's strawberries are still in bloom, only a few with berries, all green. A male Baltimore oriole appeared in the north honeysuckle hedge this afternoon, the second one this year. And Robyn said she saw a pair today as she was driving to Fairborn.

2016: First bee fly noticed. First golden bi-wing skipper.

2017: Don's dark-leafed ninebark remains in full bloom. Corry Street lined with fallen petals from the Kentucky coffee trees. Pie cherries on the Stafford Street tree are ripening, a few ready for pie. Pink spirea early bloom on Dayton Street. Jill's poppies are gone, but Peggy's are still all open. The very first mulberries are turning along the west border of the property. In the dooryard garden, the first astilbe has come into bloom. Cottonwood cotton wisps floating down near Jill's house.

2018: Early blooming of the poison hemlock on the road to Xenia, locusts falling. Peggy's clematis in full flower. At home, the wisteria flowers fell in the night storm. The purple spiderwort gathers momentum. Small green mulberries have formed, privets are budding.

2019: Another silver-spotted skipper seen today. On Davis Street, a yucca stalk just starting to emerge from its core. At Ellis, the bald cypresses are almost all leafed out with their feathery foliage. Moya's mock orange, Peggy's iris, Jill's poppies all full flower. This afternoon, a scarlet tanager came to the feeder.

2020: A day trip to Erie, PA, the second in about a week: most fields planted now, some sprouting. Roadside daisies seen, and ditches of wintercress. Last week's lush flowering trees were far less prominent.

Now Venus herself moves to the beckoning fields,
And Love learns the country words of the ploughman.

Tibullus

May 23rd
The 143rd Day of the Year

Doest thou not see the little plants, the little birds, the ants and the spiders, the bees working together to put in order their several parts of the universe?

Marcus Aurelius

Sunrise/set: 5:14/7:50
Day's Length: 14 hours 36 minutes
Average High/Low: 75/54
Average Temperature: 64
Record High: 90 – 1939
Record Low: 33 – 1889

Weather

The chances of rain decline from yesterday's 55 percent to 40 percent, and the likelihood for sun increases to 85 percent. Highs in the 80s come 30 percent of the time; look of 70s on 65 percent of the days, and 60s the remaining five percent. There is a very slight possibility of light frost tomorrow morning and on the morning of the 25th, since the sixth high pressure system of the month is due on the 24th.

Natural Calendar
*Trees and fields now flowering appear,
the woods full of leaves, greenest of the year.*

Virgil

When mulberries ripen and box turtles lay eggs and winter wheat turns pale gold green, then it is the first week of Early Summer, and the whole time of warmth lies ahead. Blue chicory flowers in the waysides. Catalpas and privets and pink spirea bloom as the first cutting of hay gets underway. Nodding thistles, Canadian thistles, the first daisy fleabane, the first great mullein, the first Asiatic lily, the first orange trumpet creeper and the first tall meadow rue open.

Daybook

1981: Peonies bloom. Columbine is almost done blooming. Wild parsnips are open, Jack-in-the-pulpit gone, phlox gone, watercress almost done. Fire pink discovered, wild onion flowering.

1982: First black damselflies seen.

1984: Mountain maple full bloom.

1986: First spring field cricket heard.

1987: Cardinal sings at 4:04 a.m. The 17-year cicadas, the red, spotted cicadas, emerged after the last of the yellow poplar blossoms fell. Peonies early full bloom.

1988: Honeysuckles are declining with the garlic mustard, Osage flower clusters falling, village iris in late bloom, birdsong lighter.

1992: The first rose opens: it's the Peace Rose, says Ruby Nicholson from down the street.

1993: Catbird pair seen in the back honeysuckles. Daisies, iris, and sweet William fall over in the rain: another sign of summer, the lodging of lush growth. The very first deep red peony was opening this morning along Dayton Street. In the yard, the first pale pink peony started, and wild mallow opened. At Wilberforce, the leaves on the Virginia creeper around my window are complete, and new tendrils are a foot long, beginning their outward summer reach. In southern Wisconsin, Maggie says the lilacs and bluebells are almost done, wild geranium just beginning.

1995: At Grinnell Pond, Solomon's plume is in full bloom. May apples are done flowering. Along Wilberforce-Clifton Road, the wheat turns a little now, becomes pale and warm.

1998: The yellow poplar flowers are in full bloom along Livermore and Herman Streets. The blue flags come to an end, the sweet

Williams and the foxglove still full. No more bleeding hearts. Late rockets. Blackbirds mating in the back yard, flying back and forth with nest material. Around the township, green frogs are calling, and the gray tree frogs are starting to sing.

1999: At the pond, swamp iris heads up. Pink and orange poppies full late, last ranunculus, full spiderwort and daisies, fleabane, early lamb's ear, late toad flax, late full rhododendrons, red wild strawberries, late full peonies and mock orange, flags, sweet rockets, clematis. Very last bleeding heart, late lungwort. Wild geraniums have disappeared, last days of locust bloom.

2000: Purple rhododendrons ending, white beginning, honeysuckle gone, mock orange nine-tenths fallen, Siberian iris suddenly completely wilted, pond iris full bloom, poppies and standard iris declining quickly, lamb's ear early, fireflies glowing faintly in the night grass.

2001: First gold-collared black fly. Pokeweed six feet high, wild garlic heading up.

2002: First pale violet pond iris opens in the pond.

2003: First water lily blooms in the pond.

2004: On Kelleys Island, robins began singing just a minute after 5:00 a.m.

2006: Yellow floribunda roses seen in full bloom at Liz's house this afternoon. Her purple allium bed is still holding.

2007: Jeanie saw a cedar waxwing in the mulberry tree this morning at about 9:00 a.m. One yellow swallowtail and one black swallowtail came by early this afternoon. Allium and Indian hyacinth now completely done, and mock orange flowers are shedding quickly. Peonies are still full, as are the Dutch iris.

2008: A bright sky of orange and pink at six this morning; I exercised outside in short sleeves. Doves and robins all around.

Now more clouds have moved in, the day cooler. Some blue wood hyacinths starting to turn in the circle garden. Eight Dutch iris in bloom. The very last Indian hyacinth flower fades. In the park, the kousa dogwood is opening as the hawthorns start to rust. Wild geraniums are dropping their petals in the east garden, and lily-of-the-valley is aging at Greg's house. First white-spotted skipper of the year seen in the front honeysuckles.

2009: Five pond iris are open today, first pink spirea downtown. One black swallowtail, first hibiscus stalk emerging, very first privet flowers, lance-leaf plantain full bloom. Smoke bushes flowering, heavy locust and mock orange petal fall, first dragonfly. Burning bush (green, four-petaled flower) has been blooming for maybe a week or so.

2010: Cedar waxwings in the mulberry before dawn. On a drive to Dayton: Catalpas and nodding thistles flowering. Tulip tree and pink spirea full across from the school. Long-bodied spider seen weaving above the pond for the first time. Four pale-violet pond iris in bloom.

2011: I was digging in the garden, had worked up a sweat and was resting in the shade of the back porch, sipping a glass of iced tea. Sparrows were chirping steadily in the honeysuckle bushes nearby, the sky was clear blue, a light west wind moving the high trees.

My pulse was up from the garden work, and as I rested, I checked my heartbeat with the second hand of my wristwatch, 75 beats a minute. I rested a little more, looking out over red and violet Sweet Williams and the pale blue spiderwort, and listening to the birds.

And the sparrows were so loud, and so steady. And then I realized that they were chirping at about the same rate as my heart was beating. I checked my watch and I timed their song. Their vocalizations were almost a metronome matched to the beating of my heart, an audible affirmation of my existence, my life force tracked not by technology or even by self-awareness but by the companion birds.

That evening, I was walking Bella through the neighborhood and I noticed robins chirping their familiar, up-and-down singsong call, and again I timed my rhythm and the robins' rhythm and found they blended almost perfectly.

2013: Pink spirea only budded. Privet buds straining. Very first growth, less than an inch, showing on the hibiscus. The pink azalea petals are gone. Weigelas continue full bloom. At the old school house, mulberries are blushing. At least half of the honeysuckle flowers have darkened, their pollination complete.

2014: Locust trees noticed in bloom throughout southern Ohio as John and I returned from our trip to South Carolina.

2015: Many locust blossoms still hold throughout the area, but their brightness is gone. Honeysuckle flowers prominent but receding like the locusts. Along the road to Oxford: yellow sweet clover full, wheat fields a soft gray green, a fringe tree seen in full bloom. Returning home at supper time, I found that the first penstemon flowers had opened. Luna moths and periodic cicadas reported in southern Illinois.

2016: A black swallowtail, the first of the year, flew through the yard as I was cutting the grass this afternoon. Privet buds showing white along High Street. Rhododendrons, iris, poppies lush throughout town.

2017: Privets full bloom, fragrant, replacing the sweetness of the mock orange. Honeysuckle flowers have all fallen. Chris Moore reported an abundance of tree frogs calling at night in the area. John Blakelock said that frogs and toads were arriving frequently at a small pond he had made for an acquaintance.

2018: First blackberry bush in bloom seen on High Street. A swallowtail zoomed through the yard as I was weeding this afternoon. Peonies, mock orange, poppies, weigelas and iris remain lush. Locust flowers are browning. Flowering of all the apples and the home viburnum is complete.

2019: Blackberry bushes in bloom at High and Davis Streets. A small black swallowtail visited the north garden late this morning.

Aida reported cedar waxwings feeding in her serviceberries. As Jill and I walked down High Street at dusk, gray tree frogs were calling, intermittent medium-high trills lasting just a few seconds.

2020: Heat returning. Honeysuckle shrubs all in full bloom around the yard. Bluegrass tall and seeding, The first spiderwort, a white one, opened. Zinnias and tithonias planted, followed by heavy rain!

There is no other land, there is no other life but this, or the like of this.

Henry David Thoreau

May 24th
The 144th Day of the Year

Many of the events of the annual cycle recur year after year in a regular order. A year-to-year record of this order is a record of the rates at which solar energy flows to and through living things. They are the arteries of the land. By tracing their responses to the sun, Phenology may eventually shed some light on that ultimate enigma, the land's inner workings.

Aldo Leopold

Sunrise/set: 5:13/7:51
Day's Length: 14 hours 38 minutes
Average High/Low: 75/54
Average Temperature: 64
Record High: 90 – 1975
Record Low: 36 – 1925

Weather

The sixth high-pressure system of the month is due today, and statistics show some of its strength. There is a 15 percent chance of an afternoon high only in the 50s, and another five percent of 60s. Although that leaves plenty of room for warmth (80 percent chance of 70s or 80s), the risk of light frost does enter the realm of possibility for the next 72 hours. Rain on May 24 is usually light, with only a third of the days bringing precipitation, and skies are mostly clear on this date three days out of four.

Natural Calendar

After peonies come in and the flowers of the yellow poplar open, past the decline of poppies, the last leaves of the canopy cover Yellow Springs. When the high foliage is complete, then wild multiflora roses and domestic tea roses bloom, clustered snakeroot hangs with pollen in the shade, and parsnips, goat's beard and sweet clovers take over the fields. Swamp valerian blossoms along the creeks, timothy pushes up from its sheaths at South Glen, and orange daylilies come in down Grinnell Road.

Middle Summer's wood nettle is past knee high. Wild lettuce, wingstem, and dogbane have grown up hip high. Grasses along the riverbank are waist high and seeding. Poison hemlock reaches chin high, angelica over your head. The dusky violet smoke bush is in full bloom.

Daisies, golden Alexander, cressleaf groundsel, sweet rocket and common fleabane still hold in the pastures, but the violet heads of chives and allium decay. Wild onions and domestic garlic get their seed bulbs. Petals of mock orange, honeysuckle, lupine and Dutch iris fall to the garden floor. Osage and black walnut flowers come down in the rain. Under the closing canopy, Late Spring's garlic mustard, columbine, geraniums, ragwort, chickweed and catchweed die back, their yellow foliage dividing May from June.

Leafhoppers, corn borers and armyworms assault the crops. Flies bother the cattle, ticks roam the brambles, cricket song grows louder, and the earliest fireflies flicker in the lawn. Half-grown squirrels explore the maples, and almost every gosling has hatched.

Daybook

1982: First wild roses seen, and yarrow open by the railroad tracks.

1984: South Glen: First bloom on the parsnips, waterleaf still full, wood nettle reaching up to replace it, sweet Cicely and garlic mustard still dominant, violets gone, yarrow budding, canopy still not complete.

1985: First motherwort blooms.

1986: Connie reports cottonwood cotton at Crystal Lake.

1987: Mayflies everywhere along the river, and gold-collared black flies mating. Angelica over my head, budding, first Japanese honeysuckle flowering, English ryegrass discovered in early bloom. Garlic mustard droops, closes the path with its seed heads. Chickweed and bedstraw are pale and dying back. Sweet Cicely gone to seed. First wild roses. No chiggers yet.

1990: At the Covered Bridge, sweet rockets are still full bloom, tall buttercups cover the swamp, angelica and parsnips coming in, wild garlic heading, first damselfly seen, poison ivy budding, sweet Cicely gone, white violets holding, yellow poplar flowers falling to the path, red admirals still common, late honeysuckle, very late garlic mustard.

1991: Flock of cedar waxwings in the reddening mulberries today. Last of the Siberian iris and mock orange in the yard.

1992: Hemlock full bloom along Dayton Street. Siberian iris early full today, mock orange full.

1993: The first Siberian iris was beginning to flower before I went to work; after a day of wind and light rain, four were completely open. The first strawberry reddened today. A small cluster of locust flowers fell to the lawn, its scent piercing and beautiful. When I was out walking later, the night wind was full of locust bloom.

1995: First ripe strawberry eaten today. All the azalea flowers have fallen in the rain. Peonies and locusts blooming in Xenia.

1997: At 5:00 a.m. birdsong is still strong, and continues past dawn. Honeysuckles are in full bloom in the yard and everywhere. The two violet iris in the yard are closing just as the first two mock orange flowers open. Canopy still far from complete, Osage holding back, locusts. Azalea flowers half fallen. Wild cherry trees seen in full bloom along the freeway. First yellow sweet clover. Early locusts seen. Many other species with only half-size leaves. First June bug came to the screen door after dark.

1998: Robins, cardinals, doves, crows loud at 5:00 a.m. No letup in birdsong this morning! If there is a decline of calls in late May, it wasn't evident today. Purple water iris blooms late this morning. In the pond, the tadpoles have changed their habits over the past week or so. First they began to feed together in three or four large groups. Instead of their haphazard independence, each going in its own direction, they seemed to have developed a sense of solidarity. And now over the past two days they have become secretive, suddenly moving to the edges of the pond and hiding and feeding in the algae there.

1999: First miniature turban lily opened today as blue flags decline.

2000: The turban lily didn't open today, in spite of 80 degree heat. That measures this year a little later than last.

2001: First cardinal at 4:27 a.m., faint bird chorus then. Doves joining by 4:47. Japanese honeysuckles opening up now. High locusts and the last of the high canopy filling in. The air is fragrant with roses, honeysuckles, mock orange, privet, peonies. Early peak of Japanese iris in the pond, and the other plants are spreading quickly. No turban lily this year, the plant probably swallowed up by weeds.

2002: Black walnut, angelica, and parsnips early full bloom. First blackberry and sweet William flower seen. Thrush heard.

2003: At South Glen: blackberries and first orange daylilies are in bloom, wild cherry finished. Brome grass and orchard grass are up to my waist.

2004: First yellow primrose (*Oenothera fruticosa*), first short, orange Asiatic lily bloomed today. Pollen heads on the native fern. Rockets fading rapidly. Allium, pale violet clematis and garlic mustard done. Seeds have formed on the redbud. Scabiosa full bloom. Blue flag iris disappeared as quickly as they came, less than week of bloom.

2006: Multiflora roses suddenly open in the alley as the snowball viburnum rusts. Momentum gathering in the blue flags. Sweet rockets and iris full. Snow on the mountain budding. Greg reported that a mother skunk was transferring her babies one by one from his yard to underneath the neighbor's shed. Jeni, visiting from Portland, says her azaleas have just ended, and the rhododendrons have just started blooming. This is rose festival time in Portland, too, she says.

2007: First privet flowers seen on our walk this morning. The white clematis continues full bloom along the east fence. One of the new poppies opened over the night, and more are budded. More lilies are budding: the season should start in a day or two. Cedar waxwing heard in the back yard this afternoon.

2008: A sense of the quieting of birdsong these mornings after dawn. Two long-jawed orb-weaver spiders have woven webs across the pond overnight. Fourteen Dutch iris now in bloom. Seeds well formed on the back standard redbud. Stella d'oros seen in bloom in Xenia on the 22nd. Some of the ones I transplanted last year have small buds now. The first two peonies opened in the yard today, and I saw a few in bloom along Elm Street near the school. Three purple clematis flowers in the forsythia hedge, another three in the garden trellis. Daisy fleabane budded. The red azalea flowers are wilting all of a sudden as the weather warms. Gary at Stutzman's nursery mentioned that this was the best year he could remember for hawthorn blossoms. In the alley, Don's multiflora rose came into bloom today or yesterday. Throughout the back yards of the alleyways, hostas provide foliage color, sweet rockets most of the accents. Heavy scent of locust blossoms all along my walk. Caladiums planted in pots this afternoon. Soft, rhythmic call of wood frogs after dark.

2009: First black damselflies, full hemlock and yellow sweet clover, loud grackles at 8:00 p.m. One gosling seen with parents by the university. Heavy honeysuckle flower fall. Lush ranunculus, first pentstemon.

2010: Mulberries reddening in front of Gerard's on Dayton Street. The pond toad sings all day. Rick Donahoe wrote this morning: "Hey Bill, We've got a real problem, and although you're not directly responsible, I do think you should share some of the guilt for speaking this one into existence: fecal sacs. What started out last year as an occasional fecal sac in our birdbath (which can no longer be called such) has mushroomed into an onslaught, with there often being more than fifty popcorn-sized sacks by day's end.
 Moreover, these grackles have lined the rocks around our pond with white sacks, and sometimes don't even bother to land,

bombarding the pond on their way over. One result, we surmise, is that our pond is getting too much nitrogen, why water from the waterfalls is frothing white."

2011: The landscape, always in transition, keeps balance and stability within its layers, and the coincidence of plants at different stages of growth and decay throughout the village and the Glen creates a message of unity and coherence.

Here at the edge of June, as the canopy closes quickly overhead, the woodland floor reveals its parallel seasons, simultaneous birth and death, reminiscence and prophesy.

I can see them all together in an hour's walk: entangled with the blossoms of the present (the pink sweet rockets, the yellow swamp buttercups, the pale blue waterleaf, the violet wild geraniums, white Solomon's plume, deep purple spiderwort and larkspur, the golden-pollen clustered snakeroot), full-grown skunk cabbage from February, sprawling chickweed from March, aging trilliums from April, seeding ragwort from early May, black raspberries and blackberries blooming for June, prickly wood nettle knee high for July, lanky goldenrod stalks for August, spears of wingstem and ironweed for September, aster leaves for October.

In village gardens, the floral year is equally apparent: this week's peonies and mock orange, early roses, Kousa dogwoods, Japanese honeysuckles, weigelas, and pink spirea bloom beside the floppy snowdrop foliage of February, the toppled bluebells of March, the April forsythia and crab apples now fully leafed, the last six-petaled star of Bethlehem of May, the long drifts of lilies waiting for June, the coneflower clusters for July, the stonecrop stems for August, the artichoke shoots for September.

Not only is each season formed in sequence and context; each contains maps of mutual genesis and destiny, supple connections and byways that bundle the days together, softening their transience with communal meaning, and promising their return.

2012: The first yellow primrose (*Oenothera fruticosa*) opened in the north garden overnight. The first oak leaf hydrangea flowers came out this morning, and the first Queen Anne's lace is unraveling near the fence. Along the freeway, chicory is no longer a rarity; now the asphalt is edged with blue as well with yellow from the sweet clover. More mulberries falling to the sidewalk near Lawson Place. Privet, peonies, Japanese honeysuckle aging, Siberian iris gone.

2013: Way back behind the waterleaf, under the drooping honeysuckle, one orange daylily came into bloom today. Now the oakleaf, the hobblebush and the Annabelle hydrangeas are all budded. Japanese honeysuckle has buds, roses just starting. Peonies, sweet William, weigela, Japanese wisteria, common honeysuckle, mock orange, perennial salvia, late allium, yellow iris, and sweet rockets all full bloom in the north and south gardens. White berries have developed on the raspberry bushes. In front of Liz's house, pink coral bells are all out beside the poppies. At the corner of Limestone and Stafford Streets, a clump of daisies in flower. Throughout the day, the red-bellied woodpecker called and called. And for the second evening in a row, a downy woodpecker attacked the south wall siding, the rapping echoing through the greenhouse.

At Jeff and Kit's house, chives, sage and peonies in bloom. Iris throughout Cedarville and Yellow Springs. Our peonies the best ever, it seems. The white fringe trees are in full bloom along Corey Street, locust flowers rusting above them. The yellow roses and purple flag iris are flowering on Stafford Street, tall angelica in the wetland across from the Covered Bridge. Meadow goat's beard in bloom near Fairborn.

2014: Inventory on return from Santee-Cooper: One stella d'oro barely opening, a handful of peonies, white and pink, half open, privets along Dayton Street budded and straining, honeysuckle flowers mostly darkened from pollination, iris and Dutch iris still full bloom throughout the village, poppies fading, hyacinths collapsing quickly, Asiatic/Oriental lilies budded, cut-back roses recovered to two feet, perennial salvia bushy and full, sweet rockets, catmint and spiderwort providing violet markers for the north garden, the snowball hydrangea losing its petals rapidly, pacing the wood hyacinths. Weigelas and rhododendrons completely out, bittersweet flowering in the alley.

2015: Half an hour before dawn: full bird chorus, of course, peonies, poppies, blue flag iris, and multiflora roses most prominent as I jogged through the neighborhood.

2017: Cottonwood cotton in the wind. A few stella d'oro lilies open at Peggy's. Male cardinal feeding a female fledgling on the platform feeder this morning, and a robin competing with a grackle for something on the ground near the back porch. I transplanted the tall sedum (Autumn Joy) this morning, digging it up from behind a fat clump of spiderwort and moved it to the porch area, a west-facing strip of ground along side the brick patio. It was one of my few innovations since Jeanie died, and I liked the way it looked. I liked the fact that the space could be an autumn garden now – in place of the many failed plantings of bulbs there. As I set in the plants, I felt that Jeanie would approve, and I liked that.

2019: Tree frogs chanting near Dayton Street at about the same time Matt saw the first firefly of the summer. He wrote: "Walking the dog this evening ca. 9:30 p.m., I saw what I thought was either a headlight or low star through the trees, or — gasp! — a firefly! I had to be sure, so I stared for a long time to where I saw it last, it finally flew past my head and blinked four times. Sad little fly, looking for a mate who is still asleep…."

2020: Hottest day of the year so far, high 87. More zinnias and marigolds planted, a few vegetables, too. Small mating checkerspot butterflies seen in the north garden foliage. Walk at the quarry just before the Early Summer flowering: only a few honeysuckles still in bloom, a few yellow sweet clover, common fleabane and yarrow just starting, daisies budded. Tadpoles still swim the shallow puddles and pools. Red-winged blackbirds whistle from the cottonwoods.

Gather ye rosebuds while ye may,
Old time is still a-flying;
And this same flower that smiles today
Tomorrow will be dying.

Robert Herrick

May 25th
The 145th Day of the Year

I see a fearless generosity in the flowers and trees, in the way birds sing out at dawn, in the steady drumming of the rain. As I grew older and found I had things to protect, I forgot. I completely forgot that I had always had enough in the first place. Now I am trying to learn this once again—total abundance, nothing begrudged.

Sallie Tisdale

Sunrise/set: 5:12/7:52
Day's Length: 14 hours 40 minutes
Average High/Low: 75/54
Average Temperature: 64
Record High: 95 – 1911
Record Low: 33 – 1925

Weather

Even though 60 percent of May 25ths are in the 70s or 80s, a full 40 percent are not, making it the day with the most potential for chilly conditions since the 15th. A five percent chance of a high only in the 40s appears in my weather history for the first time since May 9. Fifties occur ten percent of the time, and 60s another 25 percent.

Light frost is a distinct possibility this morning and tomorrow morning, and along with the increased likelihood for cold, the chances of rain rise from yesterday's 35 percent all the way to 50 percent. Clouds dominate half the time, making today one of the two cloudiest days of the month (the 12th is the other). In 1895, the Yellow Springs paper reported that quail's egg-size hail fell for 15 minutes on this date and left two inches of ice on the ground.

Natural Calendar

In the cooler years, the last of Late Spring's seasons come to a close. Wood hyacinths and spring beauties disappear. Violets stop blooming until autumn. Dogwood petals are taken down by the rain and wind. The last of the lilacs turn brown. Early snowball hydrangeas lose their luster. Sweet Cicely goes to seed. Garlic mustard and winter cress weaken under the closing canopy. Spring phlox are getting old. Ragwort flowers turn to fluffy seed heads. Watercress falls over in the sun. The last tulips and latest daffodils are gone.

Daybook

1982: First ripe strawberries picked. Today marked the end of Hydrangea Season in the yard, the beginning of Yellow Sweet Clover Season along the roadsides. Wild mallow opening now in the north garden.

1983: At Clifton Gorge: Columbine, winter cress, ragwort, garlic mustard, black snakeroot, sweet rockets, fleabane, violets, sweet Cicely, pepper grass, and robin's fleabane found. Wild rose ready to flower. Except for a few of the tallest trees, the canopy is complete. The touch-me-nots are rising above the waterleaf, mosquitoes follow me back to the truck.

1984: Last lilacs disappear. First mock orange blooms.

1986: The first honewort discovered beyond the Covered Bridge, first flower of the completed canopy, sure sign of Early Summer. Lizard's tail was all leafed out, one to two feet tall. Boneset two feet. Garlic mustard almost all gone, tall and leaning now, the most obvious deterioration of spring growth. Clearweed nettle was up two inches, had sprouted maybe a week before. Tall meadow rue was ready. Sweet Cicely and catchweed gone to seed. Sweet rockets getting late. First gold-collared blackfly seen. Wild lettuce up to my waist. Rare *Anemone canadensis* blossoming, golden Alexander full, and henbit. Purple vetch in bloom. Spitbugs seen and the first mayfly. Canopy complete. Suckers in the shallows near shore. First motherwort opening at home.

1987: Japanese honeysuckle flowers.

1989: East to New Jersey for my nephew's wedding: Leaving Yellow Springs in the rain, the maple canopy full, sycamores light,

Osage barely leafing, first peonies opening. Along the freeway, daisies and rockets in full bloom all the way to the coast. Tree line stable into the mountains, then thinning in the higher Appalachians, to a week or two weeks earlier than in Yellow Springs. Across one meadow, dandelions were still in full bloom. In eastern Pennsylvania, sweet clover, rhododendrons, and purple vetch were open, canopy complete. On the other side of the mountains, the New Jersey countryside had yellow poplars and locusts in flower, parsnips and hemlock blooming, a few huge thistles opening.

1990: First ripe strawberry picked today. Full decline of the snowball viburnum.

1991: Catalpas full bloom, and Osage flowers fall, mulberries have turned red.

1992: Violet swamp iris in bloom across from the Covered Bridge.

1993: Dogwoods are gone; I missed their last days. Peak time of poppies, iris, daisies, buttercups, fleabane, snow-on-the-mountain. Astilbe spikes shoot up. The locusts increase in intensity, shading the new green canopy with their cream white flowers. First daylily opened along Grinnell this afternoon. Clematis full bloom.

1995: Spiderwort full bloom now in the south garden, with the daisies and sweet rockets and poppies and ranunculus.

1997: First dark blue spiderwort opens in the south garden. The red-violet spiderworts have produced one or two flowers this past week.

1998: A flock of cedar waxwings in the back locusts this afternoon. Now the roses are at the peak of their first bloom, reds and yellows and pinks.

1999: The first water lily is blooming today, 32 flat, round leaves encircling it.

2000: Half-red mulberries seen on the street.

2001: South Glen: Gold-collared blackflies and red admiral butterflies common, sweet rockets fading, angelica and white campion full bloom, some very late honeysuckle, first green-bodied black-winged damselflies of the year, orchard grass too tough to pull or chew, brome emerging, canopy above complete. At home, lamb's ear has been full now for a week, pacing the pollen spikes on the wild pond iris. Bridal wreath is done at Susi's. Glowing pink spirea started yesterday at Washington Court House.

2003: A flock of cedar waxwings in the white mulberry at noon today.

2004: The first encounter with local periodical cicadas (the *Magicicada septendecim*) was announced a few days ago to the *Almanack* by John Sturm: "This morning, May 18, 2004," he wrote, "I spotted one of the Brood X cicadas in Glen Helen. It was on the low trail back from the pine forest that runs along the Yellow Springs Creek. There is no doubt it my mind it was of the 17-year variety. I saved one from the 1987 emergence in a small plastic box."

By the next day, nursery school students at the Antioch School were finding the newly emerged insects in their play area. During the afternoon of the 20th, Eric Clark called the *News* from the Springs Motel to report his first sighting. Toward noon on the 21st, drivers of the Antioch School kindergarten field trip to the Cincinnati zoo had cicadas bouncing off their windshields.

I wasn't able to get to the woods until the 23rd, late Sunday afternoon. After all the reports, I felt that I would have a good chance of seeing the cicadas where I had discovered them more than a decade and a half ago.

Entering South Glen from Grinnell Road at about five o'clock, I made my way along the path above the river. Ash seeds and clusters of spent Osage flowers covered the ground. A few gnats and mosquitoes touched my neck and face. A broad-winged damselfly looked down at me from a box elder tree. An Alypia moth with white stripes on its wings fluttered back and forth in the undergrowth. New gold-collared blackflies explored the foliage and flowers of sweet rockets, multiflora roses and waterleaf.

But there were no cicadas. I wondered if I were too early, or maybe even too late to find Brood X.

Then a hundred feet or so from the road, I saw one of the telltale brown hulls of the nymphs from which the adult cicadas emerge. I walked a little farther, found half a dozen nymph shells hanging to the underside of hickory and honeysuckle leaves, then more on buckeye, elm, garlic mustard and sweet Cicely.

I started searching under the low, two-foot canopy of touch-me-nots and wood nettles. A fat toad hopped ahead of me down the path. Daddy longlegs crouched on the black snakeroot. Scorpion flies hunted for prey.

Then I found the elusive *magicicadas* themselves. They were resting quietly all around, waiting for me. They were an inch or two in length. Their wings were shiny and gold, their eyes red, their bodies black.

I approached them slowly, carefully stepping off the trail and entering the inner sanctum of their habitat. I reached down and touched one on the back, then stroked its soft wings. The creature remained still, seemed completely unafraid, and accepted my caress as though it had been expecting my curiosity.

I went deeper into the green waist-high world of touch-me-nots and nettle, and the cicadas allowed me to observe and handle them there, confident, perhaps, in their great numbers (my sources suggested there could be up to a million of them in the small forest glade I was exploring).

With only slight encouragement, one climbed up on my index finger and looked at me benignly while I studied its angelic wings, and wondered at its docility and its trust. In a week, I whispered to my guest, all of this soundless, contemplative, prepubescent innocence would be gone. He (if he were a he) would be mad with lust, loud and frantic, charging into trees and automobiles or plunging into the river. And she (if she were a she) would be watching, listening, waiting, loving the grand display.

2005: Northern Spring Field Cricket heard in the yard today.

2007: Two cedar waxwings seen in the white mulberry at about 8:45 this morning. Mock orange flowers are almost completely down. Purple columbines still strong throughout the alley gardens, some poppies and iris, some pink bush roses, some red. Blue flags and sweet Williams holding. New blue-purple midnight salvia planted on the west corner of the north garden. Very first achillea opening. Kousa dogwoods in full bloom throughout the village. Caladiums planted in pots this afternoon.

2008: First achillea opens. Most of the hydrangeas are budding. No cedar waxwings yet, and the mulberries aren't ripe yet. A black swallowtail, golden markings came to the allium at 1:30, this afternoon, two yellow swallowtails with black markings later in the day. One call of the red-bellied woodpecker heard about noon. Wild grapes in full bloom. Several Jerusalem artichokes transplanted to the south window garden. Jeanie saw the first young grackle begging for food from its parents under the bird feeder.

2010: Highs in the 80s once again, Early Summer here. The landscape is full of clovers and roses. The heavy scent of Japanese honeysuckles fill the dooryard garden. Mulberries are fat and sweetening. Orchard grass is in full bloom. Redbud seeds are full size. Privet is coming in. Mock orange petals almost done, and peonies have entered their decline. A few strawberries reddening in the garden.

2011: Yucca in full bloom along the steps to the *Musei capitolini* near the piazza de Venecia in Rome.

2012: Now the season is just a little ahead of 2010, maybe a week but not too much more. Catchweed is seeding now throughout the garden. In the alley, pokeweed seven feet tall and budding, low mallow with pink flowers. Hobblebush and Annabelle hydrangeas have opened parallel to the oak leaf hydrangeas, and the Endless Summers are budding. The first zinnia seeded in April is opening. Sweet rockets are fading very quickly, catchweed burs sticking to me when I do the weeding. Sage flowers holding. Clustered bellflower opened yesterday. Grackles no longer come to the feeders since we have changed the feed to sunflower and safflower seeds. One fledgling seen in the south yard, though after lunch. A green-bodied damselfly came to the pond while I was adjusting the stonework this afternoon. Yucca, at least four-feet tall, is straining to open.

2013: In Fairborn this afternoon, I saw red clover, black medic clover and full-blooming hemlock, all of them probably having come into bloom while I was gone to Wisconsin last weekend. Still no privet flowers. Moya has full snow-on-the-mountain blossoms, a fine blue lupine (I haven't seen lupines since our patch died out in the late 1990s.), and a mock orange bush covered with flowers. By the shed, clustered snakeroot is starting to produce pollen.

2014: At the Cascades, only sweet rockets, cressleaf groundsel, one common fleabane, a fading Solomon's plume, and a clump of daisies. All the other markers of spring were gone. At home, I discovered the dying mock orange bush had come into full flower, maybe for the last time, behind the honeysuckles, and the Japanese wisteria was opening on the trellis. On the south hedge, bittersweet nightshade was hanging open from the forsythia.

2015: Robins a little after 4:00 a.m., cardinals at 4:30, doves about 4:45, and then song sparrows and crows by 5:00. A hummingbird finally showed up at the new feeder, a brown female. Maybe she has been around for weeks and I just didn't notice. Downtown, the columbines and blue flag iris are in full flower, the yellowwood tree is done blooming, and the first lamb's ear is coming in. As I loped through the village to Ellis Pond, I was surrounded by the fragrant and heavy cloak of honeysuckle and sweet rockets, and I found cottonwood cotton all about down Stafford Street.

2016: Jill reported cottonwood cotton in her yard from the neighbor's tree. In my north garden, I found a number of ditch lily stalks with buds.

2017: Storms bring down privet flowers to the High Street sidewalk.

2018: The first stella d'oro lily has opened in the east garden, first lily of the year. Over the west end of the pond, a long-bodied orb weaver built a web in the night. Snow-on-the-mountain flowering here and on Dayton Street. The first wild thin-leafed daisy that I brought from the quarry a year ago and that I had thought had died out bloomed today. Osage flowers, shriveled and brown, brought down by the rain, are scattered all across the hosta leaves of the southwest corner of the yard.

2019: Jill's bittersweet vine is flowering. Stella d'oros at home have buds, and the peonies are in full bloom, more abundant than they have been in years. Hackberry fruit noticed. Along Corry Street, the white fringe trees are in full flower. To the Covered Bridge with Ranger, my border collie: The habitat is lush from the rain and heat of the past week. Wide swaths of white-flowered bedstraw (*Galium asprellum*) line the path to the bridge. Wood nettle, thigh high, covers acres along the river. Touch-me-nots are up to my waist. Many grasses fully developed. Angelica is seven feet tall, skunk cabbage leaves still giant and still deep green, and a few watercress flowers hold. Delicate honewort and multiflora roses are in early bloom. Clustered snakeroot has its pollen. A few white violets still keep their petals. Spent petals from a tulip tree found scattered across a stone landing down river. Several black damselflies seen, and two bright green beetles *(Cicindela)* flew away when I approached them. A tiger swallowtail zigzagged along the shore as I came back toward the road. Late this afternoon, I heard harsh "scrawing" sounds in the back trees, the language of the fledglings.

2020: The first peony, creamy white, opened in the night. Jill's spiderwort, and my second spiderwort bloomed, too. Moya's mock orange is lush with blossoms. The azalea in the east garden and the huge snowball viburnum at the north wall have both lost all their petals over the past two days. Many honeysuckle bushes have dropped their flowers, as well. The hackberry is filling in a little, but the locusts and Osage are still pretty bare. One flower on the hemlock at Ellis. This evening, a flock of several dozen geese flew over while Jill and I were sitting on her back porch: a milestone of activity: the pairing for breeding changing.

Like a sound, spring spreads and spreads until it is swallowed up in space. Like the wind, it moves across the map invisible; we see it only in its effects. It appears like the tracks of the breeze on a field of wheat, like shadows of wind-blown clouds, like tossing branches that reveal the presence of the invisible, the passing of the unseen.

Edwin Way Teale

Bill Felker

May 26th
The 146th Day of the Year

The whole leafy forest stands display'd
In full luxuriance.

James Thomson

Sunrise/set: 5:12/7:53
Day's Length: 14 hours 41 minutes
Average High/Low: 76/55
Average Temperature: 65
Record High: 95 – 1911
Record Low: 37 – 1897

Weather

Clouds and rain rule on the 26th of May half the time. Highs in the 50s occur ten percent of the days, rise to the 60s on 20 percent, to the 70s on 40 percent, and to the 80s on 25 percent, 90s on five percent.

Natural Calendar

Haying begins above the Ohio River, then tobacco planting, then cantaloupe and pumpkin seeding, then commercial sunflower seeding. Then come thistle blossoms and the first ripe strawberries and the hatching of the last goslings and ducklings, the heading of winter wheat and the end of soybean planting in dryer years, the spawning of bass in farm ponds, and the completion of the canopy overhead.

Daybook

1982: First robin fledglings seen. Wild iris open in the swamp. Grackles still nesting.

1984: Mulberries about half size. Ash tree outside my window is flowering.

1985: Sunrise at Grinnell, walk up into John Bryan Park: flowers of the yellow poplar all over the path, first yarrow and multiflora rose open, dogbane budding, early bright fire pink, catchweed with burs. Leafcup, wood nettle, coneflowers, nettle, wingstem all three to four feet. First mosquito bite of the year. Great Indian plantain with small bud cluster on a plant that comes up to my chest. Honewort buds. Solomon's plume gone. Most ragwort gone. Catalpas full bloom everywhere and falling. Blackberries and meadow goat's beard in full bloom. The last week of sweet rockets, robin's fleabane, white violets. Hobblebush budding, wild geraniums gone, redbuds have seed pods, some reddish, some green. First dragonfly seen and the first daisy fleabane. Purple vetch full bloom, first nodding thistle, first cinquefoil, yarrow. This afternoon: first chicory in Dayton.

1986: At Cowan Lake, poison ivy has its first flowers, common cinquefoil well along, and blue-eyed grass (Thoreau found it on the 30th, near Concord, 1856). At Antioch School, red spirea has opened.

1988: Down Jacoby Branch for the first time: Blackberries flowering. Northern Spring Field Crickets loud, black raspberry fruit setting, great mullein almost two feet, grasses chest high. Groundhogs plentiful. Time of sweet rockets and corn salad. Bright green six spotted tiger beetles along the maze of deer paths. A young buck seen, antlers maybe a third grown. Thin orange-bodied darners. First leaf hopper, first gold-collared blackfly seen, grasshoppers seen with yellow inner wings, first cinquefoil and yarrow open. Dock in flower, catchweed pulling and tangling around my ankles. Orange blight all over the blackberries. Tight green bud clusters on the poison ivy. Well into the woods, the ruins of a farm, charred timbers, rusted implements overgrown with chickweed and catchweed, locusts surrounded by the block foundation, the old yard a glade of brome grass. Further south along the river, lots of soft-shell turtles, first blue-bodied damselfly. Last of the golden ragwort, watercress still late full in the shade, old and falling over in the sun. Two-foot boneset in the swamp.

1989: Eastern Pennsylvania: Lilacs still bloom at Somerset. In

New Jersey, the countryside is almost two weeks ahead of Yellow Springs. At home mock orange, peonies, iris and locusts in full bloom, heavy sweetness day and night.

1990: Red admiral in the garden.

1991: First two fireflies seen high in the back locust trees. Baby robin in the yard, maybe a week or two old. White waterleaf in the pussy willow garden finally blooms.

1993: Half grown groundhog seen on Grinnell. A dozen deep purple Siberian iris in bloom. End of the lily-of-the-valley and the bridal wreath spirea, snowball viburnum rusting. The wood hyacinths disappeared a week or so ago. Mulberries are about half size, green. Outside my window, the ash tree has golden flower clusters in late bloom. Along the east hedge, wild grapes are in full bloom, delicate inflorescence almost swallowed up by the forsythia. Rhododendron seen completely open along Union Street. Bittersweet nightshade full bloom near North Glen. Pale pink peonies early full in the yard, honeysuckle half done.

1994: The first bright orange geum and the first peony and the first Siberian iris all opened today. Lupines are still full bloom.

1995: First small bowl of strawberries picked from the garden this morning. First pale pink peonies opened in the yard. Blue flags are coming into full bloom, white and violet iris continuing to blossom. Privet buds showing white along High Street. Last of the apple blossoms fell from the late trees this week.

1997: At Irmgard's, there is a bank of bright purple rockets maybe 100 yards long and 50 feet deep. By the side of her driveway, the first roses have come out.

1998: Cedar waxwings spend another day in our locusts and mulberries. Now all the chard has been transplanted, and can be picked for salads. The Bibb lettuce is perfect. Foxglove, sweet Williams, at their peak. In the pond, Jacques, the green frog, started calling again after maybe six weeks of silence. And the tadpoles are getting fewer and fewer, more and more hidden. Is Jacques hunting them?

2000: Into North Glen with Mike this morning: Saw the first gold-collared black fly, found fire pink and colombo (tall spike of greenish, four-petaled flowers, each petal containing a round wart-like bump), white violets, clustered snakeroot, a few last white and blue waterleaf. Late Spring flowers were gone, the canopy complete, and May apple foliage was rusting here and there. In the yard, late iris, poppies and peonies are gone now, along with the mock orange and the horseradish. But the air is still heavy with full blooming privet and Japanese honeysuckle.

2003: First Japanese honeysuckle blooms as the last of the rhododendrons unravel. Privet still not open all the way. Two red admirals seen in the garden today.

2007: White yarrow opening at Moya's. Mateo's dense yellow sedum was in bloom this morning. White-flowered penstemon opening. First lamb's ear flowering. Cedar waxwings still feeding in the mulberry tree. Sparrows, starlings, grackles, cardinals, one blue jay and a nuthatch at the feeder throughout the day. The sweet rockets, sweet Williams, midnight salvia, spiderwort, dead nettle, and the last of the blue flag iris create the first major line of color along the north garden. In the afternoon, young grackles and a parent on the lawn, the babies demanding to be fed. Iris declining in town, peonies still completely full bloom in the countryside on the way to Enon. Hemlock tall and flowering in the swales and pastures. One hardy water lily and three water hyacinths placed in the pond this evening. Pond iris are still in full bloom.

2008: Mock orange and locust blossoms still strong and fragrant. Most of the honeysuckle flowers have turned from white to a gold, and one bush is shedding. Almost all the Dutch iris are open now, and about half a dozen peonies. Pond iris budded, showing color, one opening at dusk. Bridal wreath on High Street has deteriorated. Ash seeds are well formed, about an inch long. Five tiger swallowtails visited the garden today. Huge young grackles in the lawn being fed by their parents. Jeanie cut back half the violet wood hyacinths.

2009: This morning, I watched grackle babies being fed by their parents. Mulberries were well formed at Mateo's tree. First buds noticed on the winterberry vines. The first white achillea opened. Yesterday's ten water iris is down to seven.

2010: Water iris down to four, blue Dutch iris almost gone. Panicled dogwood open in the alley. Rockets in the yard suddenly declining. Mock orange gone.

2011: Oranges ripe on their branches over the streets of Rome, Italy. Some large-flowered magnolias seen in bloom.

2012: Tree of heaven in flower, wild grapes some the size of BBs, others pea size, salvia, late allium and the chives in decline, stella d'oro lilies in early full, along with the Asiatic orange lilies. Wild garlic/onion budded.

2013: Moya reported that a whole ootheca worth of praying mantises emerged after she brought the casing into her house. She had left home for a bike ride, and while she was gone, the insects came out of their nest. "They were all over my ceiling," declared Moya, "and everywhere in my house. It took me two hours to get them outside!"

2014: Honeysuckles have started to drop their flowers. The first damselfly seen near the peonies. Joe Pye weed at three feet, river birch yellowing, losing leaves, peonies full bloom.

2015: Soft showers continuing of locust petals, honeysuckle flowers, cottonwood cotton. First Knockout rose, (thirty years ago, Jeanie's roses were in full bloom in the last week of May.) first gold-collard blackfly, buds on the Japanese pond iris. Throughout the day, "scrawing" by the grackles: the fledglings are out!

2016: The first long-bodied orb weaver spider spun its web across the west end of the pond last night. Constant robin peeping through the afternoon, fledgling guiding. Wild grapes and bittersweet both at the same point of late bloom. The trellis wisteria is losing its violet petals, dusky foliage filling all its vines. This evening, Rick wrote: "Fireflies tonight! Summer's here." And: "Walking home today at 10 p.m., I saw the unmistakable blinking of two or three lightning bug larvae! I don't remember them being out so early, but it's nice and humid and warm!"

2017: Along the bike path: wingstem and touch-me-nots knee to waist high, poison hemlock late full bloom, a small bud on one of the Japanese pond iris (which I had saved from the koi, transplanted by the peonies). Buds on the black raspberry bush on Limestone Street near High.

2018: To Oxford, Ohio, down toward the Ohio River: From the window of the car: catalpas, daisies, fields of yellow sweet clover, tall full hemlock, cattail foliage waist high, the canopy of leaves appearing mostly complete. In town near the university, acorns about the size of a pea, linden bud clusters, black walnut seed catkins on the sidewalks, full catmint and purple perennial salvia, roses, pink spirea, a great blue hosta and the first privet in flower, birch catkins turned to fruit, a few wild onions headed, one red maple with half-inch seed wings. Coming home, I just missed running over a turtle that was crossing the highway near the Great Miami River.

2019: This morning, I sat on the back porch and talked with Neysa, watched the erratic flight of a golden fold-wing skipper. On a drive to Dayton, I saw full blooming wild daisies and yellow sweet clover on the roadsides. Tonight, still no fireflies, but steady chanting of the tree frogs.

2020: Peonies early bloom. One pale yellow sulphur butterfly. From Goshen, Indiana, 200 miles northwest of town, Judy writes: "Our daisies and sweet rocket are finally beginning to bloom, and the Solomon's seal is out, along with carpets of white violets." That's about right for daisies, late for Yellow Springs sweet rockets. From Rick Donahoe: "Had first visit to my knee-high milkweed by a bright and new looking female monarch. You have to wonder how they make it through these heavy rains."

I delight in the everyday Way,
Myself among mist and vine, rock and cave,
Wildlands feeling so boundlessly free,
White clouds companions in idleness.

Han Shan, 8th century, trans. David Hinton

Bill Felker

May 27th
The 147th Day of the Year

Wandering new meadows,
Gathering the roses of passion,
The lilies and violas of love.

Sigebert de Liege

Sunrise/set: 5:11/7:54
Day's Length: 14 hours 43 minutes
Average High/Low: 76/55
Average Temperature: 65
Record High: 99 – 1911
Record Low: 33 – 1961

Weather

As the sixth high pressure system of the month moves off to the east, the likelihood for cold temperatures decreases, and the 27th is one of the nicer days in late May. Although chances of rain are close to 50 percent, the sun shines through the clouds three-fourths of the time. Highs are in the 90s five percent of the days, in the 80s thirty-five percent, in the 70s on 35 percent, in the 60s twenty-five percent, and the possibility for frost is remote.

Natural Calendar

The third and final major wave of songbird migration reaches the Lake Erie shore in the last days of May, dominated by female Canada, magnolia, and bay-breasted warblers, the American redstart, indigo buntings, the vireos and flycatchers. By early June, virtually all migrations are complete, and nesting has begun in the marshes.

Pickle planting is complete throughout the Lower Midwest by now, and farmers are harvesting zucchini and squash. More than half the winter wheat has headed in an average year. South along the Kentucky border, one tobacco bed in four is typically full of plants. Off the beaches of the Southeast, shrimpers fish for shrimp at the peak of the season.

Daybook

1983: First peony noticed on Pleasant Street, first roses seen in town.

1984: Mill Habitat: First grasshopper. Frogs croaking.

1985: First blue-bodied damselfly, and the first fireflies. Yellow sweet clover and parsnips in full bloom dominate the landscape with their June yellow.

1987: Osage flowers fall. Roses are at their best. Most mock orange season is over. Siberian iris holds on. At the river, 7:45 p.m., no crickets heard, fish leaping in the dusk, geese and goslings swimming by. First fireflies seen.

1988: Apples an inch long, three-fourths of an inch wide. First fireflies signaling in the wildflowers along the river after dark.

1993: Geese fly over the house at 5:25 a.m. for the first time in months. At South Glen, long-tailed blackflies mating. The canopy is complete except for the locusts (which are still in full bloom). Sweet Cicely gone to seed, daddy longlegs maybe half grown, bleeding heart and azaleas completely gone.

1994: Ash and locusts in full bloom, tulip tree flowers falling.

1995: Now the sweet rockets are coming to the end of the cycle in the south garden. Tulip trees are in full bloom around town. Lindens have buds and pale yellow seed pods. My green ash has also made its slender pods. The air is fragrant with mock orange and locust, peonies and iris. Along the boulevard of High Street, the garlic mustard has almost all gone to seed, mulberries have formed, and grape vines are in full bloom. In the backyard, the high locusts still have a few flowers left.

1997: First Siberian iris opened today, would have been yesterday except for the cold and rain. White mulberry leaves have suddenly developed to maybe a third size over the past week, after waiting until almost all the other trees had leafed out.

1999: First water iris blooms in the pond. Cottonwood cotton drifting through town today. Lamb's ear tall and flowering. Late peonies hold, late flags. Poppies continue in the south garden, gone most other places. More miniature Turk's cap lilies open. Fleabane late full, water cress holds, arrowhead leaves taking on some width. Wild water iris holds its pollen phallus. Hollyhock and yucca heading up.

2000: Nodding thistles have been blooming west of town for about a week, the earliest ever. Achillea opening in the north garden.

2001: First primrose opens at ten this morning. Tree buds and two flowers on the red water lily. Last of the mock orange, peonies and blue flag. Japanese honeysuckle has replaced the regular honeysuckle.

2002: First water lily opened today. Azaleas, sweet rockets, ranunculus, daisies, spiderwort in full bloom. First red admiral seen.

2003: Robins strong when I got up at 5:30. Doves called at 5:47 a.m., blue jay and a blackbird at about 6:00. No cardinals singing in the neighborhood.

2004: Peonies are tattered. Mock orange is almost all gone. Japanese honeysuckle is in full bloom.

From a correspondent in Fort Lauderdale, Florida: "The tababuias usually bloom for about a month, starting sometime in March or April. Same with the Saraca, except the variety I have is supposed to put out blooms that appear right on the trunk at one time of year and then blossoms on branch-ends at another time. My Saraca needs to grow for another year or so before it blooms at all.

Currently mangos are coming into season and should be ripe in a week or so. Our jacarandas are still in full bloom from over a month ago, their blossoms are bright blue-purple. And this year the fire tree or Royal Poinciana has started blooming early. Today I saw one where the blooms were so plentiful on a 40-foot tree, that no leaves were discernible, definitely a fireworks special! Last year the RPs didn't start blooming until July, but lasted through November."

2005: Into South Glen with Bella: The canopy is almost complete now, and it feels like summer in the woods. Birds were calling throughout the walk; the most insistent were two pileated woodpeckers. I must have been too close to their nest. One called long and hard, flying over me once, leading me away another time. Finches and song sparrows also heard. Geese were honking on the river. Wood nettle was overgrowing the sweet Cicely where the red 17-year cicadas first emerged last year. Ironweed and some touch-me-nots were waist high. Silver olive shrubs were done blooming here, and many honeysuckle flowers have rusted. Sweet rockets lined the paths. The first parsnips were just starting to open. Green-bottle flies, newborns, clustered together on the leaves of a honeysuckle branch. A very young fawn found half eaten by coyotes or dogs. In the yard, the blue flag iris are at their best. The Korean lilac is still fragrant even though its flowers are mostly done.

2006: Most locusts are complete in the countryside, petals falling here also. Along the roadsides, parsnips are in full bloom, hemlock well underway. Korean lilac has been gone several days. Lamb's ear and pale violet swamp iris opened all at once. Multiflora roses are in full flower throughout. A few poppies left, many peonies. Mock orange still full, privet buds getting ready to open. Long-jawed orb-weavers noticed in their webs above the pond this morning.

2007: Ruby-throated hummingbird seen this morning about 9:30 at the salvia and sweet rockets. Cedar waxwings continue to feed through the day in the white mulberry tree. Japanese honeysuckle bloomed yesterday, was heavy and sweet when I walked by the hedge with Bella last night.

2008: Peonies are in full bloom this morning, the most flowers the bushes have ever had. Like the hawthorns burned back by the heavy frost last year, the peonies are reacting like pruned shrubs, sending out even more blossoms than ever before. Privet buds cracked, white showing. On the way to Wilmington, I saw early parsnips and poison hemlock flowering by the side of the road. Along the bike path near the college, full bloom of fringe trees, *Chionanthus virginicus.* Yellow poplar seen in full flower on my walk with Bella tonight.

2009: I was up at 5:00 this morning, and the robin chorus was faint in the distance. The volume grew until cardinals began at 5:35, and then the doves came in at 5:40 and then the blue jay bell call at 5:45. The sky was becoming red and violet then, high alto stratus broken by the sunrise. By the time the grackles woke up at 6:00, the chorus was loud and vital. Squirrels joined the grackles at 6:05, crows at 6:10. When I went to wake Jeanie, the intensity of the calls was still growing. By the time I had finished my shower at 7:20, all the excitement was over. First orange candy lilies opened today. Roadsides lush with hemlock, parsnips, daisies, wild roses, red and white and yellow clovers. Henry Meyers called tonight to say he'd seen the first firefly.

2010: Small black swallowtail butterfly seen on the driveway today. First box elder bug seen, first skipper. Dutch iris bloom has ended.

2012: The first zinnia opened, the first dahlia started losing leaves. In the Southeast, another tropical storm, the second of the year, is moving toward Jekyll Island. Record high temperatures recorded throughout the Midwest. Five starling fledglings together at the pond today, exploring, trying to get a drink.

2013: Inventory in the yard: Knockout roses gathering momentum, first flowers on Jeanie's yellow tea rose, still full sweet rockets and mock orange, peonies, Japanese wisteria, catmint, allium, clematis, spiderwort and weigela. Tall primrose, stella d'oro and other lilies budded (one stella d'oro just opening at the mall). Green-bottle flies noticed in the garden after the rain. At Ellis Pond, tulip trees are in full bloom. Thistles are budded. Black raspberries are getting ready to set fruit. Garlic mustard has all gone to seed. Poison ivy is spreading through the undergrowth. Hemlock, brome grass, orchard grass, fleabane, watercress, cressleaf groundsel, sweet rocket all in bloom, and drifts of corn salad along the stream. Pecan trees are well leafed but still have long flower tendrils. The bur oak and the hickory tree have tiny fruit buds.

2014: Liz's yellow rose in full bloom. Decorative grasses at Annie's are waist high. This evening: steady, rhythmic calling of tree or wood frogs, beautiful robin singsong vespers until just a little after 8:00 p.m.

2015: Poppies holding (and Jeanie's lone poppy in the middle of all the bamboo), privets almost ready to come out, primrose, stella d'oro lily, and ditch lily buds prominent now. Starlings continue their raspy calls. Tonight I went outside to look at the moon and saw fireflies; they must have come out days ago.

2016: The first stella d'oro lily opened in the overgrown east garden overnight. The sidewalks are covered with spent honeysuckle flowers, brown and slimy on the damp walkways. Some tulips and hyacinths cut back. Emily Faubert and her father saw fireflies this evening.

2017: Mateo's weigela is suddenly down. At the quarry, not a single tadpole in the pools, many small azure butterflies along the shaded and wet paths, daisies and yellow sweet clover predominant across the barren rocks, with budding small-flowered (panicled) dogwoods, a patch of dogbane with one flower, several moth mullein plants in early bloom, a clump of common cinquefoil, a few cattails with thin pollen stalks rising, some honeysuckle berries ripening, a number of diminutive plants, sprawling with thin opposite leaves, reddish stems, flowers similar to blue vervain only smaller (probably *Verbena simplex:* narrow-leaved vervain). Red-winged blackbirds were warbling and chasing one another across the wetlands. Coming home, we saw a catalpa in full bloom along Trebein Road.

2018: Mateo's weigelas fades. Decorative grasses by the peony garden is waist high. Cottonwood wisps drift down into the still afternoon. Sparrows continue to chant, fledglings insatiable, from before dawn until almost dark, a fifteen-hour day. Finally after 8:00 p.m., the robins begin their vespers, some mating singsong, some sharp, loud calls. No peeping – perhaps the fledglings have not left the nest yet.

2019: The very first gold-collard blackflies appeared in the peonies (still full flower) this morning. Now the hyacinths are finished for the year, foliage flattening among the chickweed tangles in the circle garden. The primroses under the peach tree are budding. At the bird feeder about 9:00 a.m., a molting Baltimore oriole stopped to feed a while. Tonight, the first tornado in nearby Dayton since I have lived in the area – forty years. But not even tree branches down in Yellow Springs.

2020: Synchronous waves: the end of my red azalea, the lush snowball viburnum, sweet Cicely, garlic mustard, wood hyacinths, honeysuckle blossoms and bridal wreath; the start of peonies, daisies, clovers and spiderwort; the budding of elderberries, ninebark, privet; fledglings begging at the feeders (a young starling pestering its parent this afternoon, scrawing and chasing him/her). Common fleabane, ranunculus and iris strong. The huge buckeye tree on Stafford Street creamy white with blossoms.

Cluster of bugle blue eggs thin
Forms and warms the life within;
And bird and blossom swell
In sod or sheath or shell.

Gerard Manley Hopkins

Bill Felker

May 28th
The 148th Day of the Year

May I not serve, then, in Thy garden
And in Thy fields and farm,
Stirring the soil around the radishes
And pulling rhubarb by the fence?
Layering the Latham stems to make new growth
For warm sweet berries born two seasons hence?
Setting the tendril feet of runnered plantlets
In crumbled, tendered soil within the row?
Pausing to know the lilac's dearness,
The gentle petalled rose upon my lips,
The lemon balm so sweet on fingertips,
And the sharp, wild scent of catnip cornered there.
Or, tractor mounted, turn the vibrant earth
Warm to the sun in overlapping layers
Of joy and productivity.
At star shine,
Crimson clover in stretching, wilting rows,
Cut at first bloom to hold all good within.
Quiet in star glow for tomorrow's turning
To tomorrow's sun.

Janet Stevens

Sunrise/set: 5:11/7:54
Day's Length: 14 hours 43 minutes
Average High/Low: 76/55
Average Temperature: 65
Record High: 98 – 1911
Record Low: 33 – 1907

Weather

Another milestone in the progress of summer: from now through the middle of September, the chances of a day in the 90s are at least ten percent. The remaining temperature distribution for May 28: 80s on 40 percent of the afternoons, 70s on 15 percent,

60s on 30 percent, and 50s on five percent. The arrival of the final high pressure system of the month increases the likelihood for a very slight chance of frost tomorrow morning. The possibility of rain declines from yesterday's 50 percent to 35 percent, but skies are often overcast: four years in ten allow almost no sun to shine through.

Natural Calendar
The Hinge of Early Summer

There's night and day, brother, both sweet things; sun, moon, and stars, brother, all sweet things; there's likewise a wind on the heath. Life is very sweet, brother; who would wish to die?

George Borrow, *Lavengro,* 1851

On the hinge of Early Summer, the balance of time and vegetation wavers and swings each day, inventories on either side holding seasonal tides in opposition, residue in compensation with new sprouts. This is a pivotal time that appears to be all in the favor of summer, but really is a door that opens back to spring, as well, allowing a kind of simultaneous passage to and from, eddies in the solar tides, receding and proceeding.

On one side, the blossoms of Late Spring: the pink sweet rockets, the yellow swamp buttercups, the pale blue waterleaf, the violet wild geraniums, white Solomon's plume, deep purple larkspur and columbine, the golden-pollen clustered snakeroot, the iris, the poppies, the peonies, the catchweed with its sticky stems, the wisteria, the honeysuckles, weigelas, mock orange, the high locust clusters, yellow poplars and the fading privets.

On the other side, the side of Early Summer: parsnips, hemlock, orange day lilies, small, golden stella d'oro lilies, purple coneflowers, daisies, fruit of black raspberries and mulberries and strawberries, the lush catalpas, the blossoming elderberries and panicled dogwoods, multiflora roses, crown vetch, pink spirea, yellow and white sweet clover, Canadian thistles, nodding thistles, chicory and the paling winter wheat.

The two tides may overlap, and a drive south two hundred miles pulls up the tide of Deep Summer; two hundred miles north Early Summer lies well behind the height of Late Spring. None of that matters of course: all the seasons are constellations of Borrow's "sweet things." Whether one observes them or not, the particles of the landscape's transition are particles of human transition. Physiology follows the lengthening day like the face of a sunflower follows the sun.

Daybook

1980: First multiflora roses opened under the apple tree today.

1981: First ripe strawberry. First Siberian iris opens, first multiflora rose.

1982: First dish of strawberries, first bittersweet nightshade seen in bloom. End of the garlic mustard and bleeding heart. Hairy waterleaf still in flower. Small orange damselflies noticed by the river. Cattail leaves waist high.

1983: Jacoby, air heavy with the smell of sweet rockets and mint. Tall buttercups, ragwort, water cress, garlic mustard, sweet Cicely are the dominant flowering plants near the swamp now. The cowslips are gone. Red-winged blackbirds warble and cackle. The swamp iris have still not bloomed (noticed full bloom June 8). Clustered snakeroot is becoming more prominent in the woods. Two dogwoods still have flowers. Sedum old. Catchweed overgrown now by the wood nettle and touch-me-nots. Still a few white spring cress, some great angelica five feet tall, mosquitoes troublesome, a patch of waterleaf with violet flowers, a few white and blue violets, and blue phlox peek out from under the Early Summer foliage. Multiflora roses budding. Common cinquefoil found in bloom. Grass waist high all along the river. Golden Alexanders and swamp parsnips full bloom. May apples are speckled with age, but some still flowering. A few wild geranium. Jack-in-the-pulpit limp and pale, some already fallen over. Up the hill towards Middle Prairie, I surprised an opossum coming around a bend; it climbed a tree and looked down at me.

1984: Lilacs gone, Osage about half leafed, sweet Cicely done, winter cress gone, locusts blooming, wild cherry full, catalpas about a third leafed, Canadian thistle with reddish buds.

1985: The first daylily, the first Canadian thistle, the first Queen Anne's lace.

1986: First fireflies, and daddy longlegs mating. Neysa gets her first mosquito bite. First damselflies seen by the river. First tall, orange daylilies seen. First robin fledgling.

1987: Catalpas noticed with new full blooms along Grinnell Road. Love-in-the-mist and garden sundrops burst into bloom today.

1988: First loud Northern Spring Field Cricket in the yard today.

1990: Poppies late, grapes late bloom, some petals falling from the mock orange, blackberries full, purple yellow nightshade early full at Ellis pond, redbuds have their seed pods now, one cottonwood is shedding, black walnuts and locusts are in full bloom.

1991: Quail seen on a fence west of Clifton. Three half-grown groundhogs playing along Grinnell Road.

1993: John, down from New York Mills, eats the first strawberry of the season. At the Cascades, first black damselfly seen, first gold-collared blackfly, first green tiger beetles. Yellow and blue stargrass found. Blackberries in early flowering. Flurries of locust petals fall in the breeze. Yellow poplar hulls on the path. At South Glen fishing with John (three bullheads, one carp caught in an hour and a half - the first bullheads ever found in the river in all the years I've fished there).

Golden Alexander and meadow parsnips common at first prairie. Pink spirea budding at various locations in Yellow Springs. Every blue flag open in the yard, sweet Williams now about a fifth open. Iris, daisies, peonies still full bloom. Foxglove seen in town. Evergreens with up to six inches new growth now. A strong storm after dark, locust flowers covering the back lawn. The next morning the locust season in full retreat.

1996: The days continue gray and wet and cold. Along Dayton Street, the snow-on-the-mountain has come into early full bloom now. Maybe half the blue flags are out along the north garden, and a few of the sweet Williams that survived last year's neglect have blossomed too. The pale blue hyacinths are almost gone in the south garden; beside them the spiderwort has developed large blue blossoms. This year's one poppy has just fallen apart in the rain. The daisies, buttercups, and pyrethrums are full. In the east garden, the bleeding hearts are just about gone; the azaleas have lost almost all their petals. Columbine still tall and strong, dominating the mood of late May in its small patch. Throughout the village and the Glen, the locust flowers hold on rich and fragrant. Honeysuckles and mock orange and peonies are at their height. Scorpion flies noticed in the garden several days ago. Strawberries still very green.

1998: Locust flowers all gone. The last Siberian iris. More yellow sundrops opening. Daisies full bloom. Crown vetch seen full along the freeway, must have started with the yellow sweet clover. More nodding thistles head up, some in bloom. Canadian thistles open here and there. Astilbe coming in now, pink and white.

1999: Catalpas flowering at the end of locust time, after peonies and flags and honeysuckles.

2000: Tiger lilies open in the garden.

2001: Cottonwood or water willow cotton on the path at South Glen.

2004: First firefly seen at the park tonight.

2005: Korean lilac trimmed back. Bridal wreath spirea finished along High Street. Locust and honeysuckle flowers dwindling quickly. Wood hyacinths fading quickly but still providing color to the apple-tree garden. Lanky "buttercups" done. Some pink bleeding heart is holding on along the north wall. Weigela in front of Mateo's is in full flower.

2007: Ninebark that has been blooming for weeks in the alley has declined quickly in the past several days. Iris disappearing, lilies coming in. Hollyhocks budding in town. Ranunculus patch in the southeast garden is down to maybe half of its blossoms. Sweet rockets declining quickly. Black walnut fruits half an inch across.

2008: Lows in the 40s this morning, some 30s north. Iris, Dutch iris, peonies, mock orange, weigela, sweet rockets, late poppies, chives, horseradish hold at full. The back locust trees are still white with flowers, but locust petal fall has begun about town. Most of the petals from the north viburnum have come down. Wren feeding her babies from the suet in the back yard. Mo, the cat, caught a June bug in the living room today. In the late afternoon, three young grackles were being fed by their parents close to the back porch. Heavy bird activity throughout the day, wrens feeding suet to their young, and grackles flying all over.

2009: Four pond iris in bloom today, down from ten yesterday. Large allium are holding, the smaller ones gone several days ago.

2010: Young sparrow seen begging for food. The first dragonfly of the year, large (maybe three or four inches long) came by as Jeanie and I sat on the back porch. From Madison, Wisconsin, Tat reports that her lilies are starting to come in and that peonies are almost gone, bringing southern Wisconsin virtually in line with the trajectory in Yellow Springs.

2012: The first cardinal heard at 4:50 a.m. Ninebark in bloom along Dayton Street, the first purple coneflower in front of Don's side house. Don's cherry tree loaded with ripe cherries. Panicled dogwood full bloom and butterfly bush fully budded along Limestone Street, starting to bud here at home. Constant robin, cardinal, sparrow calls all morning, mixed with the raspy scrawing of the starlings. On my evening walk with Bella, I found the first orange ditch lilies open.

2013: Parsnips open along the road south to Xenia, some multiflora roses, too. Kousa dogwoods hold their petals at the south end of town. Large allium hold. Black swallowtail passed quickly through the yard in the afternoon.

2014: Black walnut flower clusters on the sidewalk this morning. A moth similar to an *Anticarsla gemmatalis* moth, pale tan with a reddish line across its wings, was perched on the wall by the front porch light. First Canadian thistles and parsnips noticed in bloom near the mall. Grackles active in the yard this morning, and two fledglings begging near the suet feeder. Robins sang constantly, peeping and chortling, as I planted zinnias. The red-bellied woodpecker called occasionally through the day. A small black swallowtail flew by me as I walked to the shed.

2015: 8:00 a.m., sun, mild: Potpourri: Weigela at Mateo's house is losing petals. Our weigela half done. Peonies still look good, and four of the tall allium and three of the Japanese wisteria blossoms still violet, white waterleaf flowers by the pond, wild onion heading up in the alley, bittersweet flowers to seed there, tiny buds on the euonymus, nine-bark starting to rust just a little, pink spirea prominent in some yard plantings, garlic mustard all to seed, pie and sweet cherries faintly blushing, constant raspy calls of the starlings (and feeding heavily, along with the grackles), cardinals and doves singing, one stella d'oro lily at the Lawson's next door, eight of the deep purple pond iris are ready to break out, and overnight, June arrived with a great patch of the sundrops opening, so bright yellow. Like last year, however, only an occasional butterfly during the past week: one red admiral and one cabbage white.

2016: The Japanese water iris has a few thin, inconspicuous buds now, and many stella d'oros and ditch lilies are extending their stalks. Most of the pink peonies along the south border of the yard are open, and the penstemon by the peach tree finally is starting to flower. In the daisies and mint, the small orange bugs *(Poecilocapsus lineatus)* continue to damage the leaves. The arrow wood vibunum *(Viburnum dentatum)* that I planted to fill a hole in the south honeysuckle hedge has delicate white umbels in bloom. In the north garden, the one surviving red Knockout rose is becoming a bright marker between the rich purples of the spiderworts at their best. Throughout the village, roses are taking their stage.

2017: Judy writes from Goshen, Indiana: "Is it frog mating season? Our ponds are reverberating with what sounds like cosmic burps!" Here at home, the heliopsis is budding, and the white-flowered waterleaf is blooming by the pond. Almost every peony has melted from age and the rain. Osage flowers have fallen to the hosta near the shed, and red mulberries are darkening the sidewalk on Davis Street and the south end of Jill's driveway.

2018: Two stella d'oros blooming this morning. Tropical storm Alberto comes ashore on the Alabama – Florida coast. Temperatures in the upper 90s across the Midwest.

2019: Storms and heavy rains continue across the Midwest. First ditch lily bud noticed. Don's ninebark is in full flower. Yellow poplar blossoms seen at Ellis. The spindly viburnum I transplanted to near the dooryard garden is finally blooming after four years. When we returned from a movie this evening, I found a June bug waiting near the front door.

2020: Don's ninebark flowered today. Privets already to open. Blackberries in full bloom at the corner of Davis and High. Buds have formed on the stella d'oro lilies in the east garden. Black walnut catkins are down in the alley, and the front path is slippery with spent honeysuckle blossoms. Thin buds have formed on the Japanese water iris planting. Mateo's weigela still holds. The second tropical storm of the season came ashore on the Carolina coast.

Although we are accustomed to separate nature and human perception into two realms they are, in fact, indivisible. Before it can ever be a repose for the senses, landscape is the work of the mind. Its scenery is built up as much from strata of memory as from layers of rock. Environment then is as much the mental as it is the physical.

Simon Schama

May 29th
The 149th Day of the Year

It's time to make love, douse the glim;
The fireflies twinkle and dim;
The stars lean together
Like birds of a feather,
And the loin lies down with the limb.

Conrad Aiken

Sunrise/set: 5:10/7:56
Day's Length: 14 hours 46 minutes
Average High/Low: 77/56
Average Temperature: 66
Record High: 94 – 1895
Record Low: 35 – 1906

Weather

Rain falls more on this date than on any other May day in my history: 70 percent of May 29ths bring precipitation. Skies are often overcast as well, with nearly half of the days bringing very little or no sun at all. Chances of 90s: ten percent, of 80s: thirty-five percent, of 70s: thirty-five percent; of 60s: fifteen percent; of 50s five percent. Lows in the 30s are possible tonight well into the Lower Midwest as the seventh cold front of the month moves through. In the Caribbean, hurricane time is beginning.

Natural Calendar

Containing four or five fronts (at least one of them followed by the first heat wave of the year), the season of Early Summer extends from the final week of May through the final week of June. Strawberries, cherries, mulberries and wild black raspberries ripen in Early Summer. And Early Summer days are the longest days of the year, the sun remaining above the horizon 15 out of each 24 hours.

Daybook

1982: Catalpas seen flowering.

1987: First 17-year cicadas (they came out almost a week ago) begin to sing at South Glen. First chicory blooms at Wilberforce. Bird's foot trefoil full bloom.

1986: First moneywort blooms at South Glen in the middle of butterflies: a silver-spotted skipper, a monarch, a tiger swallowtail, an Eastern black swallowtail, a tortoise shell and others.

1988: Ground covered with withering honeysuckle flowers. Summer cricket song increasing. Mock orange petals starting to fall now by the rabbit cage in the back yard. Poppies late bloom.

1989: Back from New Jersey to find first strawberries ripe, snowball viburnum fading, mock orange all the way open, golden Alexander, poppies, hemlock full, watercress and ragwort tall, well into Early Summer.

1991: First cricket heard. Poppies gone. Yarrow early full bloom, Japanese honeysuckle early full, follows the mock orange. Winter wheat turning quickly in the warm afternoons. First Canadian thistles open. Panicled dogwood full, catalpas at least half fallen. Linden seeds completely formed at Wilberforce.

1992: Swamp iris full bloom across from the Covered Bridge. At home, full bloom of the Siberian iris, peonies, mock orange, daisy and pyrethrum. Sweet rocket, geum, and ranunculus waning but strong. Sweet William has opened completely. To Chicago: Trefoil is blossoming, and a field of yellow sweet clover is in bloom halfway to Fairborn. Hemlock early full, foxtail grass is out, wild cherry late bloom. Some locust in bloom, many fading. Along the freeway, large patches of orange dock, yellow rape and sweet clover. All corn about three inches from Yellow Springs to northern Illinois, wheat tall, waving, and turning pale green. At Crown Point, Indiana, the locusts are in full bloom, entire wood lots of them.

1993: First bowl of strawberries for breakfast. First rose opened, yellow-pink; first achillea, pastel pink. First fleabane in the garden suddenly decays. Mornings definitely quieter. Catbirds, doves, grackles still call, but the cardinals are less obvious, and blue jays seem to be gone. May apple fruit the size of a cherry pit at North Glen. Silver olives and black walnuts noticed in bloom.

1995: New growth on the spruce trees at the park has reached two to three inches on most of the branches and darkens a little now.

1998: The tadpoles are almost all gone from the pond, and the green frog barks and bongs day and night. Privet opening and fragrant now. Japanese honeysuckles full bloom and sweet. Common fleabane season ends, the first daisy fleabane opens.

2000: To Goshen: Full parsnips, yellow sweet clover, crown vetch, nodding thistles, blueweed, blackberries, coreopsis, Canadian thistles, daisies and hemlock. Cottonwood cotton drifting. Redwings still nesting. Corn three inches. Grasses and wheat turning. Turtle seen near St. Mary's. Peonies in Van Wert. In Goshen: pink rhododendrons, red clover.

2002: Very first pink spirea opened in Washington Court House. First deep purple Japanese iris bloomed in the pond. Two water lily flowers open so far.

2003: At Charleston, South Carolina, elderberries and catalpas full bloom. At Santee, wheat is dark brown, corn waist high. On the reservoir, ospreys are nesting, flying back and forth with small fish to feed their young.

2004: Yellow swallowtail and black swallowtail seen today, the first group of five cabbage butterflies, and a large hatching of green-bottle flies. First linden flowers open in the park.

2005: The mountain maple at Antioch School has seeds about a fourth of an inch long. In our yard, blue flags, daisies, catmint, peonies, mock orange, cressleaf groundsel, sweet rockets and swamp iris are in full bloom. Sweet Williams and spiderwort are in early bloom. Tat called this afternoon from Madison, Wisconsin, her peonies and iris only a little behind those in Yellow Springs.

2006: Several hot days in a row now have brought the spinach and lettuce to full height, have given the tomatoes a growth spurt, have pushed the rhubarb into a decline, have brought red and pink roses to the garden, ended the honeysuckle, opened a few privets, pink spireas, some white achillea, pulled a fourth of the petals from the mock orange and the peonies. Rockets are aging but still dominant in the north gardens, punctuated by sweet Williams and cressleaf groundsel. The purple rhododendron along Elm Street is magnificent; the lone surviving rhododendron at home is bravely in full bloom.

At the park by the church, one yellow poplar tree is loaded with blossoms. A few red oak trees have acorns a fourth of an inch in diameter. Along Limestone Street, the linden is flowering. The cherries on the pie cherry tree on Dayton Street are almost half size. The ash tree in front of the house has all its green seeds, a little more than an inch long. Peaches on Neysa's tree are blushing, an inch and a half long, an inch wide. One volunteer redbud transplanted today, one pansy redbud planted along the south central edge of the yard underneath the honeysuckle and the hackberry.

At about 3:30 this afternoon, we heard droning in the back yard and saw that a swarm of Italian bees was moving into the old locust along the west border. By 5:00, they had settled in for the night. Over the last several days, two small camel crickets found in the sink, the first of the new brood to explore outside their crawl space.

2007: Cedar waxwings were feeding in the white mulberry tree this morning at 8:30; then they moved on by midmorning.

2008: No red-bellied woodpeckers calling this morning, nor for several mornings. Some robins clucking, but the alley was rather quiet. In the back yard, though, grackles, the blue jay, the wren and sparrows were flying all over the feeders. One hummingbird seen. Yellow and red sweet clover found blooming by the side of the road, more parsnips and hemlock. Lamb's ear and the tall, blue, five-petaled flower with the bristly stem I haven't identified yet opened overnight. Locusts still full throughout the countryside. The new wisteria is in full bloom. Red wiener-like mushrooms still appearing like they have for the past two or three weeks. Don's pie cherries about half size. One yellow swallowtail flew across the yard. Two grackle babies begging from their parents.

2009: Grackles have been so loud all day, mating and feeding their young. Jeanie saw a father cardinal feeding its baby. Daisies, yellow sweet clover, nodding thistles, red and white clover, white hemlock, yellow parsnips have taken over the countryside. First daisy fleabane open in the north garden. Sweet rockets are holding at about a third to a half, cressleaf groundsel still full. Peonies are almost done, and only four pond iris remained today, a few last mock orange flowers, a few honeysuckle, a few locusts. Now Japanese honeysuckle fills in for the lost fragrance of middle May. Two cabbage whites were tucked into a peach leaf, mating quietly as I walked by this morning.

2010: Evening primrose opened overnight. Five swamp iris blooming in the pond. Tails have formed on the lizard's tail. Constant morning clucking of grackles and the rasping whining of young starlings. Small green bee fly on the porch, narrow winged alypia-like brown moth on the back screen, single markings on each wing.

2012: A new hatch of cabbage whites in the past day or so. A sulfur and a polygonia this afternoon. The yard loud all day with sparrow and robin, grackle, wrens, and starling calls, steady, insistent. Occasionally I glimpse a fledgling being fed. The great blue hosta is starting to bud along the west garden. Evening primrose at peak of full bloom. Near Fairborn, winter wheat pale golden with a hint of green, some corn knee-high.

2014: First pink spirea noticed at the church this morning. Honeysuckle flowers falling more intensely now. The circle garden of spent hyacinths is a mess, foliage collapsed everywhere, some browning. Only one or two cabbage whites seen in the yard all spring. Casey says he has a lot of male tiger swallowtails out at his place along Nash Road.

2015: As I was getting ready to leave for Wisconsin, I found the first deep purple Japanese water iris had opened during the night, just like on this day in 2002.

2016: Cloudy and very mild 65 degrees. Walk to listen for birds with Emily: Clucking in the bushes probably by an anxious robin at 3:35 a.m., first cardinal at 3:56, robin chorus beginning faintly at 4:05 and gathering momentum for the next hour, song sparrows and chipping sparrows, Carolina wrens joining in, blue jays and crows and house sparrows around 5:00, a red-bellied woodpecker at 5:20. Emily heard warblers, but wasn't able to tell which kind. We didn't hear cedar waxwings, but Emily said she had heard one yesterday and that she and her father had seen a firefly on the 27th. A male tiger swallowtail flew by me as I transplanted zinnias this afternoon. Hard rain this evening collapses peonies and spiderwort.

2017: Jill saw the first firefly tonight, then more appeared as we walked. Jill also said she and Dimi had found numerous very small toads during one of their walks yesterday. Throughout town, coreopsis and lamb's ear are in full bloom – I missed their early flowering, must have been over a week ago. At the Brukner center honewort blossoming, mosquitoes thick.

At the Lockington preserve, poison ivy almost in bloom, Virginia creeper budded, another full flowered catalpa seen, a nodding thistle blossoming, a red admiral butterfly, a male tiger swallowtail. A first golden day lily just open at Dimi's, two of her stella d'oros starting, her baptisia almost gone, a dogwood nearby still full flowered but aging.. Bright yellow primroses coming in throughout the neighborhood.

2018: Buds have formed on the Japanese pond iris, a little later than the day lily buds.

2019: Storms and rain continue. At 4:30 this morning, robins and cardinals loud and clear. Buds appeared on the milkweed overnight. I saw the first green bottle fly in the bee balm and a red admiral butterfly at the hummingbird feeder. Pink spirea full bloom about town, some tea roses, yellow and red, seen on Dayton Street. Chicory stalks grown tall in the field past Ellis. Still no fireflies in the yard tonight.

2020: Privets opening. Two scorpion flies seen in the ditch lily bed, the first of the year. Rain and cool throughout the day.

The spring is fresh and fearless
And every leaf is new,
The world is brimmed with moonlight,
The lilac brimmed with dew.

Sara Teasdale

Bill Felker

May 30th
The 150th Day of the Year

All our living is regulated by the revolving seasons. They determine what we do, what we think and talk about, what we eat, the pattern of each day. Our house adjusts to the seasons, opening in the summer and closing against the winter's cold.

Harlan Hubbard

Sunrise/set: 5:09/7:56
Day's Length: 14 hours 45 minutes
Average High/Lo: 77/56
Average Temperature: 66
Record High: 95 – 1895
Record Low: 37 – 1947

Weather

The likelihood of rain (a full 70 percent yesterday) falls to just 35 percent today. The sun shows through the clouds 80 percent of the time instead of just 55 percent. The temperature distribution is even a little better: chances of 90s: ten percent; of 80s: thirty-five percent; of 70s: thirty-five percent; of 60s: twenty percent. Although frost does not usually occur on this date, the seventh high pressure system of the month can drop lows into the upper 30s.

Natural Calendar

After locust trees are done flowering, then snow-on-the-mountain blossoms and sweet Williams, clematis, and spiderwort open. White-spotted skippers and red admiral butterflies visit the garden. Gold-collared black flies swarm in the pastures. Leafhoppers look for corn.

Bright green six-spotted tiger beetles race along the deer paths of the woods. Grasshoppers flutter across the fields. Northern Spring Field Crickets, the first crickets of the year to sing, are singing. Robin fledglings are out of the nest. The antlers of white-tailed bucks are almost half grown. Reckless adolescent groundhogs wander the roadsides.

Multiflora roses, pink spirea, yellow sweet clover, Canadian thistles, privet, and yellow poplars are budding and blooming. Evergreens have four to six inches of new growth. Sycamore and ginkgo leaves are almost full size, and the rest of the maples are filling in. Rhododendrons follow the azaleas, joined by the raspberries and blackberries. Wild strawberries climb, bright yellow, through the purple ivy and the sticky catchweed. Blue-eyed grass is open. Grasses along the riverbanks are waist-high and more.

Daybook
1983: Yellow poplar noticed in bloom at Antioch.

1984: South Glen along the railroad tracks: Grapes, common cinquefoil, sulfur cinquefoil, red clover, first poison hemlock, angelica, ragwort, raspberries, meadow goat's beard, sweet rocket, fire pink, wild geranium, henbit, columbine, white campion, parsnips, fleabane, golden Alexanders, tall buttercups, honeysuckle, corn salad, cow parsnip, black medic, Miami mist, smooth-leafed dock, Virginia spiderwort, Solomon's plume, field parsnip, clustered snakeroot, daisies, waterleaf, sedum, tall white violets in bloom. Catchweed, garlic mustard, sweet Cicely going to seed.

Last days of the winter cress, field peppergrass, purple deadnettle, and spring phlox, larkspur, Jack-in-the-pulpit, toad trillium. May apples formed. Last petals of a dogwood lying on the needle floor of the Pine Forest. Indian hemp lanky at three feet, budding. Poison ivy and blackberry bushes budding. Wild petunia and pokeweed foliage a foot tall. Coneflower foliage knee high. Yarrow and meadow rue budding. Buckeyes have half-inch burrs, yellow poplar flowers falling to the ground. Sycamore leaves only half developed.

A cluster of thin black caterpillars eating nettle. Leafhoppers are out, and small box elder bugs. Two geese with three fat goslings. Four deer seen, two with foot-long antlers covered with velvet. Solar eclipse at noon, I watched it in a rain puddle.

1985: Privet in bloom.

1986: Mill Habitat: Crickets loud about five in the afternoon. Long black cricket hunter seen on the seeding parsnips. Round seed heads of the goat's beard are common. Fire pink full bloom. First avens of the year in bloom. First enchanter's nightshade. First moth mullein seen. First timothy has emerged from its sheath. Daisy fleabane and water willow blooming. Rockets almost gone. At Wilberforce, first chicory blossoms, and lesser stitchwort discovered open. Another baby robin seen today and a tortoise shell butterfly.

1987: Fields of red and yellow clover. First Canadian thistles flowering. Privet full bloom. Dogbane high and flowering. Catalpas are out everywhere. More chicory seen.

1988: Crickets in the yard start to chant in the early morning. Cedar waxwings feed in the locust flowers, the flower petals falling with the light breeze into the seeding grass. Squirrels seen half grown. Peonies full still, and mock orange. Still a few last garlic mustard. First tropical depression of the season begins to form 250 miles southwest of Havana.

1989: Osage is flowering today. Locust finally seen in bloom, full along Corry Street.

1990: Buttercups almost gone at home, forget-me-nots gone, sweet rockets disappearing quickly. In the country, rockets holding better. Many poppies gone, iris fading to maybe a third, with a few buds left to open.

1993: Tat calls from Chicago: heavy rain and hail there. After dark, a tornado touches down 30 miles south of Yellow Springs.

1995: July's coneflowers are a foot tall now. Phlox are almost at their summer height. Roses are just starting to open. All the purple Siberian iris are blooming, all of the daisies, the pyrethrum, maybe three fourths of the sweet Williams. The new multicolored Siberian iris have just started to open. Asiatic lilies are budding. Daisy fleabane by the bird feeder is almost five feet tall.

1998: Catalpas in full bloom on Allen Street. Privets early bloom everywhere. Very last bleeding heart and mock orange. Purple coneflowers have headed up, along with the heliopsis. The water iris are just past their peak. Roses lush. Poppies continue in the south garden, but past their prime. Red pyrethrums ready to cut back, early daisies full. Green frog calling. The toads have disappeared completely. First long black cricket hunter seen by the pond. First pale chicory seen along the freeways, and birdsfoot trefoil full, some moth mullein. Great mullein heading quickly. Motherwort early in the yard.

1999: Full catalpas, locust canopy closing quickly, wheat rich gray green. Mock orange collapses and peonies melt, pond iris all disappear by the end of the day.

2001: First hurricane of the year forms off Baja California.

2002: First poppy in the yard unravels, first yellow sundrop primrose (*Oenothera fruticosa*). End of rhododendron bloom along the south garden. In the woods, garlic mustard season is over.
    The basic sequence of bird calls: 4:17 a.m. full chorus of robins, 4:40 a.m. first titmouse, 4:46 a.m. first doves, 4:48 a.m. first cardinals, 5:00 a.m. squirrels active, robins mating, 5:10 a.m. grackles, 5:14 a.m., first crows, 5:15 a.m. first carpenter bee out of the woodwork.

2003: At Santee Cooper in South Carolina, early rose of Sharon is blooming at the cabin, clearly marking a four-week difference between central Carolina and Yellow Springs.

2004: The first chicory seen blooming along the freeway in Kettering. Catalpas full throughout, have been open at least a week. Only the late pink peonies hold. Japanese honeysuckles and the yellow sundrop primrose patch have been in full bloom about three or four days. Water willow was flowering in the pond today, Japanese pond iris late full, lizard's tail completely formed, four water lilies blossoming. Two patches of small golden lilies are in full bloom. Another orange lily, a taller one came in this morning. Tufts of cottonwood cotton float by on the wind.

2005: The first poppy in the yard opened fully overnight in the cool rain. The frog is still here, calling just before the showers intensify. The parakeets Jeanie brought home from school yesterday started singing at 5:45 a.m. EST. Mock orange and peonies are still completely full.

2006: First yellow sundrop in the east garden unravels. The pond iris are blossoming beside it. Japanese honeysuckles are starting to flower throughout the forsythia hedge. First nodding thistle noticed open along the freeway on the way in to Dayton. Hemlock and yellow sweet clover full bloom. Sweet gum seed clusters are a third of their mature size. Kousa dogwoods hold on in the park.

2007: First bright yellow evening primrose has opened in the north garden. More orange and yellow lilies in bloom. More rose blossoms, yellow and pink. Lettuce and radishes ready for salad. Cedar waxwings still in the white mulberry for a little while. A row of old amaryllis bulbs planted in the garden, and a handful of hardy gladioli. On the way home from Dayton this evening, I saw parsnips and catalpa trees in full bloom.

2009: First yellow evening primrose. Full yellow tea roses. Nine candy lilies in bloom. Foxglove full bloom in town.

2010: Yellow swallowtail in the garden, one skipper in the fading circle garden. White achillea blooming at Moya's, oakleaf hydrangea and hobblebush coming in along the western border of our yard, maple leaf waterleaf in bloom, birdsfoot trefoil bright yellow along the road to Fairborn. Jeni, visiting from Portland, reports a whole field of fireflies at the edge of town.

2011: Italy: From the train windows: corn was at least a foot tall throughout Umbria, and wheat had turned gold. Jasmine found in full bloom on our return to Spoleto from Rome.

2013: Umbria, Italy: Corn is only three to six inches tall, the rivers full, reflecting the cold wet spring. Jasmine in full bloom, yellow ginestra blossoms bright and common throughout the countryside, orange poppies in bloom, pink spirea open at the Trabalza house, in Campello Alto, figs green and full size, will be ripe in two to three months. The canopy closing, flowering thistles, sage, roses, yellow sweet clover, white clover, yucca, purple vetch, black medic, and small headed hawkweed, and especially the wide open mock orange, all put the season at about the same as in Yellow Springs.

2014: I walk in the morning an hour before sunrise, and the robins are in full mating song, and their chorus has spread throughout the neighborhood, equally boisterous from block to block. Robins race across the street in front of me, zoom above me, whinnying, swerving around tree branches, erratic as bats in the twilight.

Yesterday, I found a robin fledgling sitting on the trellis; the first brood has left the nest, but the flock still exults in the first days of Early Summer, breeds and breeds, loud and reckless. They must be happy, I say to myself. They must be living in such intensity, consumed first with lust and then with nurture and then with guidance (never leaving their fledglings out of the sound of their steady calls), and then with restless retreat and grouping for migration or winter survival in the local honeysuckles.

I walk the garden to check the cosmos and zinnia seeds that I have planted. I take inventory of the progress of the lilies. The deer have not eaten the buds yet; maybe they will eat lilies elsewhere. I see that moles have pushed up the dirt in the middle of the yard, the first moles here since we moved to High Street in 1978.

The peonies are so lush and heavy they are falling into the grass that has grown too long. Petals from the locust trees fall at my feet. By the shed, the last flowers of the mock orange are still sweet. In the circle garden, all the hyacinths have collapsed, leaving a tangle of decay in place of the rich, violet blossoms of three weeks ago. Jeanie always cut away the leaves and stalks to make a place for poppies and penstemon. I haven't gotten to that yet.

The first damselfly comes to visit the pond. A pale female hummingbird visits the feeder Ruby gave us years ago. There are no butterflies this year, and I wonder if the bitter winter took its toll or if the Sixth Extinction is really at hand. I look up trying to find the cedar waxwings that always used to sing high in our white mulberry tree this week of the year, but I see only two starlings. Against absences, the robins chatter and chirp in the honeysuckles that surround and protect the yard. The birds are modest in the daylight, perhaps exhausted from so much riotous venery, maybe simply babysitting, watching and teaching.

2016: A bright and wet dawn after an evening of thunderstorms: A black damselfly circled the water garden. Robins peeping continually in the honeysuckles, grackles clucking. The air is heavy with the scent of Japanese honeysuckle. A green-bodied damselfly came by in the afternoon. I cut back the hyacinths in the circle garden and replaced the foliage with zinnia sprouts. Cottonwood cotton floated down on the lawn, spreading a seed-laden coverlet on the roadsides Privets are just starting to open along High Street. On the way to Ellis Pond, I saw the earliest hosta with white flowers. Catalpas are budding by the pond. The Kousa dogwood at the triangle park has a few final petals, the last dogwood petals of the year there. Along the bike path: blackberry flowers and multiflora roses. Some corn along Polecat Road is almost knee high.

2017: A gold-bodied green-bottle fly seen in the heliopsis foliage. At the North Glen: white violets, late waterleaf and a clump of fire pinks in full bloom (another clump seen a few days ago along the bike path). Two black damselflies near the creek. I saw a family picking pie cherries from a tree near the bike path.

2018: The pond was speckled with foam this morning, the heat and sun of the past week changing the chemistry of the water – or possibly the grackles have been dropping fecal sacks into the water. Yesterday afternoon, the fish were active, even jumping, perhaps less happy than uncomfortable. First buds on the milkweed, six stella d'oro lily blossoms, Annabelle hydrangea and hobblebush hydrangea well budded along the north property line, quickweed blooming among the zinnia sprouts, peonies and mock orange almost complete, the weigela holding well past many others in the neighborhood. When I went for a bike ride yesterday, faded peonies and a few mock orange bushes seen in bloom. Walking downtown this evening along Elm Street with Jill: we saw coreopsis in full bloom, two orange Oriental lilies – the first of the season, an oakleaf hydrangea just starting to flower, an elderberry bush with bud clusters and a yucca plant with five-foot stalks.

2019: Continued rainy and mild through the day, catalpa flowers falling along Polecat Road. Stormy in the evening.

2020: Cool and sunny, the May 29 high-pressure system arriving exactly on time. Yellow poplar flower petals found on the ground at Ellis.

The summer winds is sniffin' round the bloomin' locus' trees;
And the clover in the pasture is a big day fer the bees,
And they been a-swiggin' honey, above board and on the sly,
Tel they stutter in theyr buzzin' and stagger as they fly.

James Whitcomb Riley

May 31st
The 151st Day of the Year

One has only to sit down in the woods or fields or by the shore of the river or lake, and nearly everything of interest will come round. The change of the seasons is like the passage of strange and new countries; the zones of the earth, with all their beauties and marvels, pass one's door.

John Burroughs

Sunrise/set: 5:09/7:57
Day's Length: 14 hours 48 minutes
Average High/Low: 77/56
Average Temperature: 66
Record High: 97 – 1895
Record Low: 36 – 1897

Weather

Chances of rain are near 40 percent today, but the sun shines seven days out of ten, and the temperature distribution covers the range between mild to hot. Highs in the 90s come ten percent of the time, 80s forty percent, 70s and 60s twenty-five percent each.

Natural Calendar

Spring pasture now reaches its brightest green of the year, and haying moves towards the Canadian border at the rate of about one hundred miles a week, will be taking place almost everywhere in the United States by the middle of June. Spring wheat is just about all planted in the North, and all the oats are in the ground between Denver and New York. Potatoes and commercial tomatoes and pickles have all been set out along the Great Lakes. Winter wheat is turning a pale gold below the Mason-Dixon Line. Blueberries are setting fruit in the Northeast. In Southern gardens, squash bugs and Japanese beetles are out in force.

Iris and peonies bloom at elevations near 4,000 feet in southern Idaho. Aspen leaves are the size of a thumbnail, and the raspberry plants are just getting their leaves in Yellowstone.

Blackberries are in full bloom in the Northwest, and dogwood trees are open around Sequoia National Park in California at the same time that the canola and winter wheat crops are about ready to be harvested in the Midwest. In the Southwest, blackberries have set fruit, and wildflowers such as chicory, salsify, moth mullein, great mullein, and milkweed are open, marking the full bloom of the sunflower crop in southern California. North of Sacramento, the wheat is darkening, just like it is in Indiana.

Daybook

1983: First multiflora roses on the bush under the apple tree. Some peonies past their prime. To Ellis Pond: Saw white campion, the first wild parsnips in bloom, milkweed three feet high, arrowhead beginning to emerge from the water, old but strong water and winter cress, full bloom of the sweet rockets, tall locust trees flowering, some Canadian thistles budding, blackbirds singing and swooping, swallows sailing up and down the stream bed looking for food.

1986: White yarrow along the freeway, some nodding thistles full bloom, a few catalpa flowers seen. First cherry in the yard half red.

1987: First nodding thistle blooms, moth mullein with several flowers open, yuccas sending up their stalks. Elderberries are completely open, locusts almost gone. Very last bleeding heart disappears today. South Glen, late evening: Carp swimming lazily in the river do not take my bait, even in the quiet pools. Fireflies more numerous: four days ago, only an occasional blinking across the yard. Now, maybe ten or fifteen different lights counted in the space of a minute.

1990: The wheat has turned pale green now, the heads, emerged, are paler than the stalks and leaves. First daylily seen along Grinnell today. At the freeway, yellow sweet clover and hemlock are in full bloom. Now the field grasses wave like the wheat, tall and also turning, but darker. No fireflies tonight. One or two bleeding hearts left.

1991: First chicory, first tiger lily, first cherries turning. First broccoli bolts in the heat wave. Locusts completely gone.

1993: Iris beginning to decline now, honeysuckle petals falling heavily to the sidewalk with the locust petals. Cherries half size. Peonies hold in the cool.

1994: Tall yellow cressleaf groundsel still in full bloom throughout the pastures. Water iris open in the swamp across from the Covered Bridge.

1997: North 100 miles or so to Canton: We drove back almost a week in time, from the full bloom of blackberries up into last week's azalea bloom. Dogwoods were out in Zoar, but had fallen days ago in Yellow Springs. Although the canopy is almost full here at home, it is definitely thinner and brighter there. Honeysuckle flowers starting to weather here, full there. Spitbugs found on the thistles at a rest stop.

1998: A large formation of geese flew north across town this morning at 7:00. Morning birdsong still loud these days. First orange tiger lily opened in the north garden. Mulberries, black and white are falling to the street, the same time that Osage orange blossoms fall along the west border of the yard. Pink and white astilbe suddenly early full. Yucca stalks are up to my chin and full of buds.

1999: Camel cricket seen in the house at 4:30 a.m. The first mulberries were ripe in the alley west of High Street yesterday. Privet bushes are in full bloom along our north hedge and all over town. Catalpas also full, some brand new flowers already falling.

2000: First sundrop primrose opened against the south wall today. Motherwort noticed blooming, probably started a few days ago. Roses full early bloom. White rhododendrons stay. Catalpas early bloom throughout town.

2001: First tiger lily opening in the yard. Moneywort open at the Mill.

2004: Wild multiflora roses have disappeared. Tiger lilies seen by the side of the road on the way to Fairborn. Dark mulberries falling to the sidewalk along Dayton Street. Small camel cricket found in a coffee cup in our cupboard. Cressleaf groundsel is going to seed, but still provides color to the garden. Some Canadian thistles going to seed along the highway. First achillea flowering. Peach-leafed bellflower late. Sparrows and cardinals still building nests in the back yard. Peaches are the size of large acorns. Allium seed heads fully formed. Sweet rockets almost completely gone, cut back.

2006: In the back yard, the Dutch iris and the violet standard iris are almost gone, the mock orange is losing all its petals, the Osage flowers fall, the sweet rockets decay quickly. The alley has changed so much since spring. Of course there would be changes. Why do I expect it to provide more stability than the garden? Why do I miss the flock of winter starlings in the black walnut tree at the corner? The lilacs, the magnolias and bridal wreath spirea are gone. Mateo's weigela is down to about a third of its petals. The bed of aconites has disappeared, leaves yellowing a month ago.

The alley was a private passageway, common to all, but mine at those few minutes every morning when I walked through it. Did I confuse privacy with constancy? Or is it something else like the quietness of the houses, the cutting down of the great euonymus vine, the solitude of certain neighbors, the dying maple in Lil's old back yard that produces a mild melancholy that I confuse with the end of spring and other closures, the vague emotions mixing and blending?

2007: The first two Japanese iris bloomed dark purple in the pond today, and the pale violet pond iris continue late full (and one in the redbud garden as well). White clovers have recovered from the mowing after dandelion bloom, fill the lawn again. Cressleaf groundsel has been going to seed this past week. Daisy fleabane flowered yesterday near the variegated Japanese knotweed. Ranunculus has dwindled to maybe a tenth of its most extravagant bloom. More yellow coneflowers have sprouted and developed over the past week, so slow to form. The transplanted stella d'oros have buds. Other ever-blooming lilies have been out quite a while now in the area. This evening about 7:30, a hummingbird visited the feeder near the pond.

2009: A hummingbird came to the penstemon this morning before sunrise, and the red-bellied woodpecker called at 6:00. In the garden, the first stella d'oro lily opened overnight. The tails of the lizard's tail have started to form. Don's pie cherries are turning red, and the black raspberries in the alley have formed small, green fruit. The grackles and cardinals continue to feed their babies in the yard. The fragrance of Japanese honeysuckles and privets have replaced the fragrance of peonies, iris, mock orange and Korean lilacs. Yucca stalks are three or four feet tall.

2010: Very strong cardinals and robins at 4:30 – 5:00 a.m. Another huge yellow swallowtail today. Chicory and elderberries all over along the freeway to Dayton. Blanket flowers and some coreopsis seen along Dayton-Yellow Springs Road. A few strawberries red in the garden. Very thin blue darner laying eggs in the pond.

2011: In Spoleto, Italy: All the locust flowers and the azaleas of early May are gone, and buckeye blossoms have turned to spiny green fruit. Mock orange in late bloom. Linden buds ready to open.

2012: Inventory: First raspberries red at Peggy's, ours almost red. Full bloom of oak leaf, hobble bush, Annabelle hydrangeas, first orange achillea open, first two zinnias in bloom, the second dahlia opening, Knockout roses full, spiderwort full, deadnettle lamium still full, sweet William still full, perennial salvia at the top of their stems, golden stella d'oro lilies and bright yellow primroses and clematis full in the yard, the yellow reblooming lilies open, the great blue hosta budded, the last peony collapsing. Yucca five feet and buds extended. Astilbe is in bloom now. Liz's and our allium to green seeds, her prairie false indigo done for the year. Lace vine totally full bloom, pink spirea full, a new brood of cabbage whites yesterday, seven on the clustered bellflowers. Yellow-orange sulfurs yesterday and today. Gooseneck coming in. Last pink weigela flowers. Butterfly bush budded at home (early blooms on the bush at High and Davis Streets), heliopsis with two new flower this morning, purple cones budded (Don with one cone open). Cherries still plentiful and red on Don's tree. White mulberries turning pink, Sage flowers very late, penstemon still full, chives about gone. Birdsong continues intense from doves, cardinals, robins and grackles. The family of five grackle fledglings was back at the pond today. They have stayed together like the brood of cabbage whites. Ninebark flowering along Dayton-Yellow Springs Road, early bloom. Kousa dogwood continues in full bloom along Limestone Street. Above the porch, Chinese wisteria almost completely gone. Winter wheat turning golden green, some haying seen. Peonies declining quickly in the yard.

2014: To Oxford, Ohio about 80 miles southwest of Yellow Springs: Yellow primroses, pink spirea, roses and sow thistles full bloom. Privet bushes starting. Linden flowers had turned to small berries, the flower sheaths fallen to the sidewalk, catalpa just starting.

2015: Madison, Wisconsin, about 500 miles northwest of Yellow Springs: Late geum; many Dutch iris budding, many flowering; peonies throughout; cottonwood down; most locusts still seem fresh, but occasional trees are shedding. Lilacs and Korean lilacs late but still prominent in many yards, astilbe well budded, sweet rockets everywhere, garlic mustard gone, violet waterleaf, daisies, iris, peonies, wild spiderwort, celandine, baptisia full bloom, raspberries fruited, several golden lilies open, the color of stella d'oros but a different daylily variety. The cornfields had sprouted throughout the region, height of sprouts seeming only to vary because of planting dates.

2016: Jeanie's two ancient tea roses, one yellow and one pink, opened overnight. Mateo's weigela suddenly down, mine more than half. Maple waterleaf around the yard has started to bloom, the white and the violet. Around town, full blooming primroses (mine still budding) and bright yellow yarrow. Some meadow goat's beard along the road to the pond, hemlock all in bloom. The hackberry trees at the north end of the pond park were losing foliage, showers of yellowing leaves. Some losses noted in town, as well.

2017: Jeanie's tea roses are finally gone now. One Knockout rose still has a flower or two, but it will also be gone soon. The first two of my primroses bloomed overnight. I opened up the garden gate to the street this morning, the primroses adding just enough to the areas of violet spiderwort to draw the eye in. Walking at John Bryan Park, very few flowers in bloom, but leafcup was getting tall, to four feet. The pond iris bud shows purple petals still wound tightly. Looking back at this date over the past thirty years, I see consistency and stability for plants in the yard and the region. The only concern I have is about insects. Fireflies have appeared on time; mosquitoes and the striped beetles are certainly healthy, but I see fewer butterflies, bees, flies.

2018: Sparrows raucous, helter-skelter back and forth, fledglings lining up on honeysuckle branches to be fed. The frenzy is much like their winter flocking and descending on the food and then, when startled, to exploding up into the trees together. In last night's storm, new privet flowers stripped from their branches, more honeysuckle blossoms down, first pokeweed buds – the stalks about six feet, Japanese honeysuckle seen open, Strawberry Rains throughout the Midwest. In the pond, yesterday's mysterious foam has disappeared, the water tests normal and the fish are even more active than before. This morning, a spring field cricket heard near Jill's property. Four stella d'oro flowers in the east garden. The bright yellow primroses started over night: two blossoms. And the Japanese water iris: one bud revealing the purple core of petals.

The average temperature for this May was 70.3, the warmest since I began records in the early 1980s.

2019: Osage flower stems fell overnight on the path to the studio. The rain brought down a few privet flowers, too. A few buds on the Japanese water iris now, the peonies past their prime, shedding, collapsing. Don's pie cherries and our sweet cherries are blushing just a little.

2020: It seems like it has been a cold, wet May, but the average temperature was just a degree below normal (60.7), and rainfall only a little more than an inch above normal (5.78"). I looked for the primroses to open, but a deer had eaten them off in the night.

Vivir es ver volver: To live is to see each thing return.

Azorin

Bill Felker has been writing nature columns and almanacs for newspapers and magazines since 1984, and he has published annual almanacs since 2003. The radio version of his column is broadcast weekly on NPR station WYSO and is available on podcast at **www.wyso.org.** His two collections of short almanac pieces, *Home is the Prime Meridian: Essays in Search of Time and Place and Spirit* and *Deep Time Is in the Garden: New Essays in Search of Time and Place and Spirit,* as well as the entire twelve volumes of *A Daybook for the Year in Yellow Springs, Ohio,* are available on the internet.

For more information, visit Bill Felker's website at **www.poorwillsalmanack.com**

Bill Felker

Made in the USA
Columbia, SC
15 May 2021